You Don't Have To Be Blind To See

Jim Stovall

OLIVER
NELSON

THOMAS NELSON PUBLISHERS
Nashville • Atlanta • London • Vancouver

Published in Nashville, Tennessee, by Thomas Nelson, Inc., Publishers, and distributed in Canada by Word Communications, Ltd., Richmond, British Columbia.

Library of Congress Cataloging-in-Publication Data

Stovall, Jim.
   You don't have to be blind to see : how to find and fulfill your destiny regardless of your circumstances / Jim Stovall.
      p. cm.
   ISBN 0-7852-7737-4
   1. Stovall, Jim. 2. Blind—United States—Biography. 3. Television broadcasting—United States—Employees—Biography. 4. Self-realization—United States—Case studies.
I. Title.
HV1792.S76A3 1996
362.4'1'092—dc20
[B]   95-26216
                                                                                                CIP

Printed in the United States of America.

1 2 3 4 5 6 — 01 00 99 98 97 96

TO

My wife, Crystal,
who is the true writer in our family,
Kathy Harper and our entire NTN family
for making dreams come true, and everyone at Nostalgia Television
for helping the dream to grow.

CONTENTS

FOREWORD

GAINING A VISION
FOR YOUR FUTURE

by Dr. Denis Waitley

I was spellbound the first time I saw and heard Jim Stovall speak to an audience in person. After Jim was introduced to the group, he walked to the podium confidently and with a strong stride, took the microphone from its stand, and proceeded to walk about the stage unassisted as he spoke, occasionally coming right to the edge of the platform to peer into the faces of those who sat before him. Then Jim walked down the steps from the stage to speak directly to the people in the first few rows of seats. He remembered not only what each person said to him as he questioned first one and then another, but also where each person sat, so that he might continue to have a personalized and individual dialogue with several of the audience members.

There was no indication at any time that Jim was the least bit intimidated by the large audience he was addressing. There was certainly no indication that Jim was, and is, *blind*.

Jim lost his eyesight completely when he was twenty-nine years old, after years of a degenerative eye disease that left him only partially sighted most of his teenage and young adult life. He has not, however, lost his *vision*. Not even a little.

Watching Jim speak, I realized very quickly from my years of personal experience in speaking before countless audiences that Jim's style was no gimmick. He wasn't trying to con his audience. The exact opposite was true. Jim was prepared. He had rehearsed what he intended to say and how he intended to say it. But even more important, Jim had something genuine to say. He spoke what he *knew* to be true in his life. He sincerely sought to convey to those before him the truths he had learned through losing his sight and gaining a vision for his life. He genuinely sought to encourage his audience to discover and pursue a personal destiny of greatness.

I count Jim Stovall as one of my most valued friends today. The more I have come to know him, the more I admire him—not only for his amazing mobility and motivational skills, but for the inner qualities of his life. Jim is the person he wants to be. He bears the marks of a man who intends to be at the top of his field and who intends to live his life on a daily basis as a man of integrity and quality.

Jim has an Emmy Award for his innovative work in helping visually impaired people to "see" television in a new way. He has been named among the Ten Outstanding Young Americans by the Jaycees. He is the founder of the Narrative Television Network, which has a broadcast base of more than one thousand cable systems and broadcast affiliates, reaching more than twenty-five million homes. He consults with many international corporations in the areas of marketing and motivation. He travels and speaks extensively. Few people have achieved what Jim has achieved. Few are as qualified as Jim to motivate others to seek and pursue their own definition of success.

I encourage you not only to read Jim's story but also to adopt Jim's message as your own: *You can envision a bigger and more personally fulfilling destiny for your life. And what you begin to see, you can begin to have.*

ACKNOWLEDGMENTS

I would like to acknowledge the contribution of Victor Oliver and everyone at Oliver-Nelson for believing in me and this project.

I would like to thank Dr. Denis Waitley for gracing this book with his foreword and for gracing my life with much of the inspiration contained in these pages.

And I would like to thank the thousands of people around the world who think enough of my work on television, video- or audiotape, the speaking platform, and now this book to write me and let me know about the positive changes they are making in their lives. They are the everyday heroes who make the world go around.

1

SEEING WITH NEW EYES

I wasn't always blind—
but I didn't always see!

I wish I could read this book that you are holding in your hands today. But with even greater desire I wish I had read this book at the time when I was just leaving my parents' home and starting to live my life. If I had read this book then, I'd be even farther along the road to realizing my dreams and goals—my full potential—than I am today!

How can I make such a bold statement?

Because I know that what I am sharing with you in this book is true. It works. I've lived this story, and I know that the principles I'm about to share with you are real. If these concepts could work in my life, they certainly can work in your life.

The fact is, however, that when I could read books, I didn't. Oh, occasionally I'd pick up a book and thumb through it, but I wasn't an avid reader. I didn't see much value in reading.

The fact is, also, that I am blind today and can no longer read a book with my eyes.

Now before you think about feeling sorry for me, you need to face several more facts.

One fact is that you are blind, too.

Everybody is blind in some way. Each one of us has blind spots—things we don't see, or don't see accurately, about ourselves, about others, about life as a whole. You may have the full capacity of physical vision, but that doesn't mean you always perceive what lies before you or perceive what is useful, appropriate, accurate, or worthy. Even if you have the capacity for *looking*, you may not have the capability of *seeing*.

> **Everybody is blind in some way. Even if you have the capacity for** looking, **you may not have the capability of** seeing.

There's a big difference. One involves a physical ability. The other requires inner vision and creativity.

I Lost My Sight but Gained a Greater Vision

When I awoke one morning and discovered that I couldn't see anything—not even unfocused light—I faced the stunning, numbing, brutal fact of physical blindness. There were things I needed to learn, and relearn, so I might function. I also needed to overcome the psychological blow of losing my sight.

But in the process, I discovered that there's a second kind of blindness that everybody has, and it has nothing to do with physical eyes. It has to do with your ability to make sense of your life and then to make the most of your life. It has to do with your true potential—the full scope of your ability as a person to feel, respond, and transform your life and, ultimately, to become the person you truly were created to be.

I may have lost my sight, but in the aftermath, I gained a greater vision than I had ever had before.

Do you have a vision for your life?

The fact is, most people don't. Most people don't have an inner ability to see themselves fully or to see themselves as they want to be.

Are you among them?

The fact is, if you are among them, you don't need to be. You can make a new decision, exercise a new option, choose a new path.

You can have a new beginning in your life. You can acquire a vision for your personal destiny. You don't need to wait for a tragedy to give you a wake-up call about your priorities and your dreams. If you can grasp this concept, the person you are when you finish reading this book will be very different from the person you are as you begin reading this book.

> *I may have lost my sight, but I gained a greater vision than I had before. Do you have a vision for your life?*

You don't have to be blind to see!

Create a Vision for Yourself

One thing that sets us human beings apart from all other animals is that we have the capacity to learn from generation to generation. We can receive knowledge, add to it, and pass it on. My great hope in this book is that you can learn some of the things I've learned without going through as much of the adversity that I've experienced. The ultimate ideal for me would be to know what I know at my present age without having lost my sight. But that wasn't and isn't the way life unfolded for me. I *am* blind. And much of what I learned, I learned because I faced the knowledge that I was going blind and the reality that I am blind.

Even so, if I had to give up everything I have become, done, and received in exchange for my sight, I can honestly say that I wouldn't make the trade. I would rather be the person I am today and be blind than be the person I once was and have my eyesight.

I am convinced to the core of my being, however, that you don't have to be blind to see the truths presented in this book. You can learn from my experience. And I hope that you will.

The fact is—yes, my promise to you is—that if you will acquire an enlarged and greater vision for your life, your life will never be the same. Are you willing to consider that possibility?

If you are, then read on. If not, do something else with your day. This book is for the person who may not have hope but who would at least like to have hope.

Hope Is Everything

A recent psychological study revealed that the number one fear that most people have about disease or disability is the fear of going blind. People fear blindness even above dying.

I feared blindness, too. But more than I fear blindness today, I fear not living. I fear not being my best. I fear not maximizing my potential and not doing everything I can do to achieve what I want to achieve, be who I want to be, and have what I want to have. I fear not trying. I fear not hoping.

Being blind isn't the worst thing that can happen to people. Living without hope is the worst thing.

> *Being blind isn't the worst thing that can happen to people. Living without hope is the worst thing.*

So today I'm asking you to have a little hope—not great hope—just a little hope that maybe, just *maybe*, things can change for you.

Do you have a feeling of despair, perhaps a feeling of gloom about one particular area of your life? Do you have a sinking feeling that the future may not be any better than the present? Do you have a gut-level dread about tomorrow?

I'm here to tell you, you've got a chance for something more, something better. I'm not going to promise you the sun, moon, and stars. I'm not going to promise you a sweet by-and-by. When I sat in a room in total blindness, I wouldn't have believed anyone who told me that I could have *anything* I wanted. And I certainly won't be the one to tell you that.

But what I did hear, and what I did begin to believe after I experienced complete blindness, was this: "*Maybe* you've got a chance, Stovall."

Maybe I could get back into life's game and win a few rounds. *Maybe* there was more for me. *Maybe* my chair in my room didn't need to be my universe.

You may not be able to embrace the concept of a great, fabulous, wonderful success in your life. But will you at least accept this possibility, "Maybe—just *maybe*—there's a chance you can have a better tomorrow. Maybe—just *maybe*—there's a shot you can take, a decision you can make, an option you can exercise, a choice you can act on that will make a difference. Maybe—just *maybe*—tomorrow can be better than today"?

I'm not asking you to hope for a blissful, no-worry forever. I'm asking you only to hope for a little something more.

Starting now.

2

COMING OUT
OF THE DARKNESS

*So what are you going
to do with the rest
of your life?*

I awoke one morning, and it was dark. I knew I was no longer sleeping. I knew I had opened my eyelids. But it was still dark.

I blinked. Nothing changed. I rushed to the bathroom to stand as close to a light as I could. But nothing changed. Panic raced through me. *It's happened. It's happened.* The total darkness I had feared for years was a reality.

Experiencing total and sudden blindness is a feeling few people can understand. You wake up. You know you're awake. You open your eyes. You know they're open. And yet everything is just as dark as it was when you were asleep.

Up to that moment, I had had at least some sense of light. I might have had to stand staring at a lightbulb from just a few feet away, but still, there was a sense of light. And with a sense of light, there comes a sense of shadow and of forms. Suddenly, everything was dark, and with the darkness came a new degree of disorientation I had never known.

I was blind.

As devastating as the realization was, my blindness was expected. I had lived in dread of that day most of my life.

A Losing Struggle to Be Like Other Kids

My parents had lost two children—one, a son, before I was born. Then a few years later, my older sister, Nancy, died of a form of leukemia when she was four years old. Nancy is one of my earliest memories, but mostly I remember she wasn't there. Her death affected my parents greatly, and I felt the impact of her death more through their response than through my own understanding. When I was five years old, my brother Bob was born. I am very proud of him and his success. He is a great brother and a great friend.

Understandably, early on I felt a great responsibility to my parents not only to be a typical kid but to make their lives happy.

When it became apparent at a fairly early age that I was going to have serious visual problems, and that I wasn't going to have normal sight, I felt great sadness for myself and for my parents.

The first time I noticed that I couldn't see well was when I was about seven years old and I was playing Little League baseball. My father, as a teenager, had considered a career in professional baseball. He played for a semipro team in Springfield, Missouri, and they scheduled a practice game with a visiting team that featured Mickey Mantle. Dad truly loved the sport of baseball, although he admitted that when he saw Mantle, he realized he had better get "honest work" of some type because, in Mantle, he had seen a level of play that he hadn't known existed.

As a little boy hearing my father's stories about playing baseball, I decided that I wanted to be a baseball player, too—more for my dad's sake than my own.

When I first started playing ball, I was given the number 14. I didn't know a major-league star who had that number, but eventually, I discovered that 14 was Pete Rose's number. At that time, which was in the late 1960s, Pete Rose wasn't well known, but anybody who talked about Pete Rose always commented on how hard he worked as a player. So I decided that he was my guy. Everybody else on the team was trying to be like Stan Musial, but I decided to be like Pete Rose and work hard.

In those days, we played our games in the early evenings after school. The coach began to ride me for what he perceived to be my lack of effort during the last few innings of each game. He told my father one time, "If we only counted the first three or four innings of each game, Jim would be leading the league in batting. But in the last three or four innings, Jim doesn't even get a hit. He starts out with a bang, and then he begins to loaf. He's just not giving us any effort."

I didn't think I was loafing. I thought I was trying. I didn't know why I couldn't seem to hit or catch the ball during the last few innings of a game. Finally, it dawned on me that as it started to get dark, I couldn't see the baseball. During the first few innings, the sun was still bright enough for me to see clearly, but as twilight set in, I couldn't distinguish the ball from other things in my surroundings. In talking this over with my father, we both realized my baseball playing days were over. We didn't talk about it much, but we both knew it to be true.

Many Saturdays my father would go to the office in the morning, and then in the afternoon, we would go fishing. Saturday afternoon was the real quality time I could count on spending with my father. Our fishing expedition was the prime time for our communication. When I began to lose my sight, we still went fishing. But my loss of sight wasn't something we talked about. *Blind* became the *B* word that we didn't use. We might not have had baseball to share, but we had fishing.

■ *Someday I would lose all of my sight and there was nothing the doctor could do about it.*

The real diagnosis of my eye problems came when I was seventeen. I went to the doctor for what I thought was a fairly routine examination—actually, it was a physical exam required for college admission—and the doctor noticed something during the exam that caused him alarm. I was sent to a specialist and then to other specialists. The bottom-line result of many tests and trips was that a specialist finally took me aside in a hallway and told me that he wasn't sure why, and he didn't know when, but he did know beyond a shadow of a doubt that someday I would lose all of my sight and there was nothing he could do about it.

The condition I had is called juvenile macular degeneration. The macula lutea is the center part of the retina, the "screen" on which images form. Mine, for an unknown reason, didn't regenerate so that as I got older, it started slowly falling apart. It would be like showing a movie on a screen that slowly begins to form holes and fall apart until one day the entire screen has disintegrated and there's nothing left.

Macular degeneration is common among people in their eighties. Physicians usually tell their older patients, "You've got an eye condition that's going to continue to deteriorate over the next eight to ten years, but it's really no big crisis." The fact is, they will probably die before they go completely blind.

But juvenile macular degeneration means this process happens to a young person. And when you are told at age seventeen that over the next eight to ten years you will completely lose your sight and there's nothing anybody can do about it, it *is* a big deal!

Some people have the luxury during their teenage years and early twenties of floating through college and never quite facing up to what they are going to do with their lives. At age seventeen, I had to begin seriously to consider, What am I going to do in and with my life?

What *Can't* I Do? That Was My Question!

The foremost question looming in my mind wasn't a positive one: What will I do with my life?—but a more negative one: What am I *not* going to be able to do?

I quickly realized that I wasn't going to be able to drive. That's a devastating idea to a teenager.

It's pretty amazing that I even had a driver's license at the time. Like all sixteen-year-olds, I had to take the regular tests to get a driver's license. I passed the written portion of the test without any problems. And then I had to take an eye test. I knew that even with my glasses, I couldn't see the chart on the far wall, but I have a better-than-average memory. So I listened closely to the person in front of me as he was given the eye exam, and I memorized his answers. When the time came for the woman to give me the eye test, she followed the same pattern of asking me to identify particular letters. I repeated verbatim what the person in front of me had said.

When the test was over, the woman said, "This is truly amazing. I've been working here seventeen years, and I've never had two people in a row miss the exact same letters." Fortunately for me, the person in front of me passed the eye exam, and therefore, so did I!

I managed to make it through the driving portion of the test because I had rehearsed it so many times that I had turns and stops timed to the second. And so it was that I was issued a driver's license. In my home state, if you have a clean driving record and you pay the appropriate fee, you have no difficulty automatically renewing your driver's license every four years without any further tests. So, even though I am completely blind, I *still* have a valid driver's license! You don't need to worry, however. I value my life, and yours, far too much to use that license for its intended purpose.

Back at age seventeen, I had been driving for about a year, but I was kidding myself even then that driving was a safe thing for me to do. I didn't drive very far and then only on streets that I had thoroughly memorized.

My father and mother had serious qualms about my driving, but I kept insisting that I could see what I was doing, even though I couldn't see much at all. In retrospect, I'm grateful that I didn't kill somebody. The worst damage I had caused was hitting a few bushes.

My father called me from work one day to pick him up. He worked in a large building near a major convention center, and they were having an event at the center that day. The area was very busy, and to top it all off, Dad's building was at the top of a hill with an intersection on the hill. I said, "Dad, I don't have time to get you."

He said, "No, come on. Pick me up." He finally backed me into a corner where I had to admit, "I don't feel comfortable driving in that area." He replied, "If you don't feel comfortable driving out here, you shouldn't drive anywhere." He was right. Even though Dad's office was in a location that was difficult for me to negotiate, it was a location with well-marked streets in a generally suburban part of town.

A few days after that incident, while driving only two blocks from my house on an otherwise deserted street, I ran into the back of a parked police car. The police officer had responded to a home alarm that had gone off accidentally, and while he was checking out the house, I plowed into the back of his vehicle. That was the last day I drove a car. When you hit a parked police car on an otherwise empty street, you're obviously not seeing well enough to drive.

I grew up in an upper-middle-class neighborhood, although my family wasn't wealthy. Most of my friends had cars that their parents had purchased for them. In my case, I had worked all summer to buy the car I was driving, and I had had it only a few weeks when I ran it into the back of the police car and totaled it. I was only slightly hurt. But the worst part of the accident was having to call my parents to come to the scene and take me home.

My father and mother were having dinner with a person who was very important in their lives, and I had to call my dad out of his dinner meeting and say, "I'm sitting here with a police officer. I totaled my car and his car. I'm not hurt and I didn't kill anybody, but I need for you to pick me up."

My father showed very little emotion about the incident at the time, but I know it probably hurt him more than it hurt me. One night some time later he sat down on the edge of my bed and we both cried together about the fact that I could no longer drive, but we never talked about it. We just cried together.

And I've never driven a car since that day.

Today I'm not bothered at all that I don't drive. I have a limousine and Michael Brooks, my associate, picks me up every morning. On my way to work, I either relax or start my workday. My limo is equipped with a television, a VCR, a tape deck, and a telephone. It's beyond any car I could have imagined as a seventeen-year-old.

That isn't to say that I don't miss having the ability to move about on my own. I do miss that. I told my wife not too long ago that at times I feel as if I'm a football and everybody just passes me along. "Who's got him now?" "I've got Jim. I'll take him from here to there, and then I'll pass him off to the next person." It's been more than eight years now since I went from Point A to Point B totally on my own, with very rare exceptions—outside my house and neighborhood, outside my office building. And I do miss being able to self-determine exactly where I go and how to get there. But I don't miss driving a car. At age seventeen, that was something I could *not* have imagined. It was at the top of my list of things I knew I could no longer do as a blind person.

No More Books—but a Desire to Read

I also faced the fact at age seventeen that I wasn't going to be able to read much longer. I wasn't that much into reading in the first place, but once you realize that you can't read, books take on more importance. At first, I had a reader—a person who read aloud to me the college textbooks and related materials that I needed to know.

Now I listen to books on tape. I have a high-speed tape player, and I can listen to books faster than most people read. I "read" about five books a week, which is more than 250 books a year. I probably hadn't read five complete books in my life before I faced the fact that I would be blind.

Reading isn't something I force myself to do or psych myself up to do. Once I understood the wealth of information in books, I couldn't stay away from them. It's like having a private gold mine, always available. Just think! I can listen to the wisdom of Winston Churchill and Alexander the Great and Abraham Lincoln and Harry Truman and whomever else I may have brought home from the library, right in the privacy of my home or car. That's an amazing luxury we have in this generation. And it's a luxury available to all of us.

No More Football, No More Scholarship

For related but slightly different reasons, I also realized about that time that I wasn't going to have a career in football. After my earlier failure in baseball, I had turned to football as my sport of choice. I was big and strong, and as a blocker, I didn't need to be able to see the ball—only the guy who had it and the guys who wanted it. They were a lot bigger than a baseball, and I had no trouble hitting them!

I had a good career as a high school football player—at least for a couple of years.

An incident during my sophomore year was something of an omen of things to come. Only one other guy and I made the varsity team as sophomores. Our opening game was at Skelly Stadium, the largest football stadium in Tulsa, with forty thousand seats and AstroTurf. We were scheduled to play a night game, which was an especially difficult time for me to play ball. I was just starting to lose my sight in a significantly measurable way, and I had little ability to see the contrast in the colors of jerseys or the contrast between the ball and oncoming players.

To that point, I had never told anybody on the team, much less my football coach, that I had a vision problem. I would rather have had them think I was stupid or wasn't paying attention than to have them think I couldn't see. In retrospect, I'm not sure why that was the case, but it was.

The coach sent me to the backfield in punt situations so that I could block for a kid who was a very fast runner and a good punt returner. His job was to catch the ball, and my job was to block any opponent I could once he had it. I didn't need to see the ball in that situation. I needed only to see him and which way he was running, and then to block the guys running toward us.

As we were preparing for the first punt, we were standing in the backfield, both of us scared to death. It was the "big time" as far as we were concerned as high school sophomores. We were in a major stadium playing before a big crowd, and it was our first varsity game of the year. We were having our own little backfield huddle when my teammate shocked me by saying, "I have a serious problem. I lost a contact lens in that last series of downs, and I can't find it in my eye. I'll be able to see the ball when it gets close, but you're going to have to get me under the punt. Tell me left, right, back, forward, and I'll move whichever way you tell me."

I said, "We've got a problem a lot more serious than you thought we had! I'm not going to get anybody under a punt. Our deal has been that you tell me which way you're going to run with the ball and I move that way, and that's about all I can do. I've got eye problems that contact lenses can't fix."

A referee was standing near us, and I asked, "Can we get a time-out?" He said, "No, they're lined up. This is live." So the ball was punted, and during the next three or four seconds I prayed harder than I had in years, hoping that the ball would come somewhere close to us so that one of us could see it. It bounced right between the two of us. He saw it, caught it on a bounce, and we were off.

Because we made it successfully through that game, I never needed to admit to anyone else that I had a vision problem. My fellow player probably figured that if it hadn't mattered in that situation, it probably wasn't as great a problem as I had thought. So I continued to play without incident. I was good in the tenth grade, I was very, very good in the eleventh grade, and I was really psyched up for a great senior year. I had been selected for several preseason all-American teams, and the college recruiters were sniffing around. A scholarship offer seemed a sure deal.

Then in the first game of my senior season, I was coming back on a pass block, and in a freak accident, my leg snapped and broke completely through. In a matter of seconds, my football career was over for the season. I didn't play again until the last game at the state play-offs. Even so, about thirty major universities sent recruiters, most of whom were completely oblivious to my failing eyesight and my almost-failing grades.

Shortly after I broke my leg, I went to the state fair. Two things happened there that affected me personally in a profound way. One was that I saw an exhibition by the national Olympic weight-lifting team, which was on tour at the time. The other was that I went to a concert in the fairgrounds stadium. I came away from the state fair thinking, *There are at least two things I could do as a blind guy. I could lift weights, and I could play music.* I began to pursue both activities with new interest and enthusiasm.

Since I also had suffered a knee injury in playing football, my doctor advised me as the college football recruiters continued to pursue me, "Lift weights instead if that's interesting to you. If you lose your sight, you can still lift weights, but if you lose your sight, you can't play football."

It was a good move. I didn't need to give up being an athlete. I didn't need to give up my competitive drive. I think subconsciously I figured, *I may go blind, but I'm never going to be weak. I'm going to be the strongest blind man people have ever seen.*

I also began to place greater and greater emphasis on music. Eventually, I did some studio work and helped make a few records. For a while, I seriously considered pursuing a career in music. Music is something I have always enjoyed. I bought a guitar and taught myself to play it. I also bought a keyboard. I became pretty good at playing both instruments. A few years ago I worked with a group for six weeks in producing an album, and then it was time for the group to hit the road for concerts. But I decided that riding in a van with six guys and a female singer was not what I wanted to do with my life. I decided that I'd like to enjoy music for the rest of my days as a hobby and recreational pursuit, but not as a career. I still write songs occasionally and do various gigs with friends, but I have no desire to make my living in the music industry. That was an alternative I considered, and to which I said no.

As a high school senior, however, lifting weights and playing music formed a bridge for me. Thinking about these two activities and pursuing them took me from thinking about what I *couldn't* do as a blind person to thinking about what I *could* do.

That's a significant transition for any person to make.

Planting My Seed Ideas

Another important thing happened to me shortly after I received the diagnosis of my eye condition and the prognosis that I would one day be blind. A large positive-thinking rally was scheduled in Tulsa. The speakers at that time had grouped themselves together and had gone on tour, renting large arenas, and one of the sites they chose was just a few miles from my home. The speakers included Zig Ziglar, Ira Hayes, Dr. Robert Schuller, Art Linkletter, Dr. Norman Vincent Peale, Paul Harvey, and Dr. Denis Waitley.

Even though I was given a ticket to the event, I almost didn't go. I didn't think much of those people—I thought they were a bit strange. But since the ticket was free and I didn't have anything else to do that day, I went. What I heard amazed me and awakened me. The speakers were fun and interesting. When lunchtime came, my friends said, "Do you want to go out to lunch with us or stay and hear the speaker they've scheduled?" I astounded myself by saying, "I think I'll stay and hear the speaker." I'll always be grateful that I stayed. That was the first time I heard Denis Waitley speak, and on that particular day, he spoke about visualization.

I realized that the ideas flashing in my mind that I could be a first-class weight lifter or a top-notch musician were the beginnings of visualizations—and that if I would just build on those dreams, I could turn them into reality.

I left the conference that day thinking, *I'm not weird and these guys aren't weird. All of these ideas that I've been thinking about are just like seeds. And if I will just water them a little and fertilize them a little and cultivate them, they'll grow. What I'm thinking about can become a reality in my life!*

> *Everybody has seed ideas. Recognize your ideas as seeds and cultivate them.*

Everybody has seed ideas. It's part of our ingenuity and capacity as human beings to imagine and think and dream about things that aren't yet real. Having seed ideas isn't unique. But recognizing your ideas as seeds and then cultivating them—that's a concept that many people haven't tapped into yet.

After that rally, I began listening to inspirational and motivational tape recordings of seminars and books.

As I lost more and more of my sight, I spent more and more time in my room at home. I think it's probably true for most people that as they lose their sight, they desire to stay in places familiar to them. After I became totally blind, I thought I would never leave my house again.

Being blind carries with it a feeling that is difficult to describe to people who can see. It's a feeling of being in the middle of nowhere. You know that things are out there—somewhere—but you have no sense of how far away things are or exactly what is out there. It's a much different feeling from what you have when you close your eyes.

When I first heard the prognosis of my blindness, I used to try to "practice" being blind by closing my eyes. I would think, *Well, this isn't so bad.* But it's much different when you are in a situation where you can't open your eyes, get your bearings, and reorient yourself.

In the early days after the diagnosis, I had what I now call a magic bedspread. I would lie on the bedspread, and there, alone in my room, I would think, dream, imagine. Everything became possible for me! I didn't realize at the time that many of the things I'm doing now were beginning to take shape. I simply knew that in the realm of my dreams, there were no limitations. When I would open my eyes and step out of my room, I was back into reality, but alone on my bedspread in my room, I could do anything, be anything, and go anywhere.

That bedspread had some tearstains, to be sure. I did my share of mourning the loss of my sight—before I lost all my sight and after—but in many ways, my tears watered the seed ideas that I thought about as I lay on the magic bedspread.

Much of what I thought about related to the speakers I had heard at the rally or to the tapes I had heard since the rally. I came to a conclusion. If the guys I had heard were wrong, I didn't have much of a chance. But if the guys I had heard were right, I could do anything I wanted to do in spite of blindness. I didn't know with certainty at the time if they were right or wrong, but I knew that I had to believe one thing or the other. I had to believe that what they said was valid, or I had to believe that what they said was a lie. I chose to believe they were speaking truth to me.

I readily recognize that anybody reading this book has the same choice. You can believe the principles I share with you in this book, or you can choose not to believe them. That's your choice.

In many ways, my impending blindness forced me to come to grips with my future. Many people are never forced to do that. They roll through life without giving too much thought to what they can and cannot do.

I knew that I had to make choices and face the fact that there were some things I could realistically do and other things I could not realistically do. But when it came to my desires, dreams, and goals, there had to be a way for me to become what I wanted to become, do what I wanted to do, have what I wanted to have, and fulfill my destiny in life *regardless of any circumstances,* which in my case included blindness.

Above all other conclusions, I came to the realization that . . .

Your Dream Must Be *Your* Dream

We all have dreams about what our lives might be like. In many ways, our dreams fuel us. They motivate us to get up in the morning and make something of a day.

The important thing about dreams, however, is not how big they are or how achievable they might be. The important thing is this: Do you own the dream? Is it *your* dream? Or have you adopted somebody else's dream?

Lots of things might have captured my imagination at age seventeen. Lifting weights and making music were the two things that intrigued me and excited me. They were *my* dreams. I owned them.

If you are trying to fulfill another person's dream for your life, you'll always feel hindered in some way. And when a crisis comes—an adversity, a problem you can't readily solve, a point of termination—you will likely abandon the dream that isn't yours and feel a great sense of failure in the process.

Many people I meet are going through life without a dream, or they are trying to fulfill a dream that doesn't belong to them. Both are surefire setups for failure. Make sure the dreams you are pursuing are ones that flow out of your desires.

As I mentioned, I spent part of my childhood trying to fulfill my father's dream of a baseball career. It wasn't something my father laid on me as much as something I thought I should do for his sake. When I realized that I wasn't cut out to be a baseball player, I faced the prospect of finding out what pleased me. I had to face my life and forge my dream. I had to take ownership of my desires for my life. Ultimately, that approach pleased everyone else I was hoping to please in the first place because I had a much greater likelihood of success.

> **Take ownership of your life. You are where you are because of decisions you have made in the past.**

In trying to be a first-rate baseball player, which was my father's dream, I was setting myself up for failure. I didn't want failure for myself, and my father certainly didn't want that for me.

In pursuing my dream to be a world-class weight lifter, I set myself up for success. Success was not something I alone wanted. My father wanted success for me, too, and he took as much delight in my success as a weight lifter as he ever would have taken if I had achieved success as a baseball player.

Accept the Responsibility for Making Your Choice!

You must take ownership of your life. It's *your* life. You are where you are because of decisions you have made in the past. Granted, you may have had some tough things happen to you in the past, but the past doesn't need to dictate your future. Your life is still your life, and if you don't like the life you're living, you can do something to change it.

Nothing will significantly improve unless you first take responsibility for your life and say to yourself, "I am where I am today because of decisions I have made in the past."

> *You have the right to choose! Don't give it away to anybody else.*

Once when I was flying, I sat next to a guy who would probably win a medal if they ever decided to have an Olympic event for most negative human being. When the flight attendant came by to ask me what I wanted to eat, chicken or beef, I said, "I'll take the chicken." She then turned to this man and asked, "Sir, what would you like?"

He said, "It doesn't matter. Bring me either one."

A few moments later, she placed a chicken dinner in front of me, and she handed this man a beef dinner.

For the next twenty minutes, I listened to this man moan and groan about how bad his beef dinner tasted. He didn't remotely see that his bad meal was his fault. In his thinking, the flight attendant had given him the beef dinner. In reality, he had chosen that meal for himself by failing to make a choice.

Are you blaming somebody else for your lot in life? Very likely, the reality is that you're blaming the wrong person. Look in the mirror. The chances are that *you* made the decision that has put you in the situation you are facing today—either you made the decision directly, or you made it indirectly by giving someone else control over your life.

Some people make right choices and decisions. A few people make wrong choices and decisions. But I've concluded that most people don't know they have a choice, or they let others do the choosing for them. And most people don't like the choices they feel are foisted on them.

Don't be among that sad majority.

Recognize that most of the time, you can make a choice. Be bold in making your decision. Don't let someone else decide for you the extent to which you will be a failure or success. Don't let someone else forge your career.

If you do, you are likely to feel stuck with something you don't like or stuck with the leftovers of somebody else's success. Face up to the fact that you get what you choose, most of the time.

I certainly didn't choose to be blind. But when I look at my life as a whole, I realize that blindness is one of very few choices I didn't get to make. I have had control over countless choices about what to do and how to live now that I am blind. Blindness didn't eliminate my right to make choices about my life.

And I believe the same for you. No matter how restricted you may be as the result of an unforeseen or unfortunate circumstance, accident, or event, you have the privilege to make choices about how you will respond to that event and what you will do in its wake.

You have the right to choose! Don't give it away to anybody else.

Self-Direction Isn't a Bad Thing

All this emphasis on having *your* dreams—and pursuing what *you* want out of life—may sound self-centered to you. Most of us have been raised from childhood not to be selfish or self-centered. The fact of life, however, is that we are self-centered creatures. All that we do begins with an awareness of ourselves.

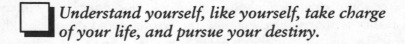 *Understand yourself, like yourself, take charge of your life, and pursue your destiny.*

It's important that you understand yourself. Otherwise, you probably won't understand your motives or your behavior, and thus, you won't understand much about your relationships or about other people.

It's important that you like yourself. Liking yourself means accepting yourself. That doesn't mean you can't change some things you may not like. It does mean that you must accept things you can't change. If you don't accept your foibles, differences, uniqueness, and personality, chances are, you won't truly be able to accept the unique traits in another person.

Ultimately, it's important that you love yourself. That means treating yourself well, doing the right things to nurture your body, mind, emotions, and spirit. If you don't love yourself, you probably aren't going to be capable of loving anybody else or of giving to another person, helping that person to become all he or she can be physically, mentally, emotionally, and spiritually.

And only when you decide to take charge of your life and pursue your destiny can you truly bring about a change in your life for the better.

Facing a diagnosis that I was going to be blind could very well have marked the end of my life. I could have let blindness squelch my ambition, my goal setting, my pursuit of a personal destiny. Instead, I chose to face that diagnosis with the deep-seated, rock-bottom conviction that blindness would not be the end of my life.

What appears to be the ending can be the point of a new beginning!

No matter what situation or circumstance you are facing, you have the option of making that same decision about your life. What appears to be the ending need not be. It can be the point of a new beginning!

3

CATCHING
A GLIMPSE

You are only one quality decision
away from a new beginning.

Most of us would like for a positive change in our lives to come instantly.

It can!

Most people won't tell you that. They'll tell you that change is a slow, long process and that you shouldn't expect too much change at any one time. I disagree on the basis of this statement: You change your life by changing your mind.

And you can change your mind in an instant. When you change your mind, you change the direction of your life. Not only do your decisions ultimately determine what you do with your life, but they determine who you become as a person.

> **You can change your life by changing your mind.**

A change in your mind may mean a change in your priorities, goals, focus, or methodology. That change results, over time, in practical, visible, physical, mental, and material changes. You may not be able to change your entire life in an instant, but you start the change of your entire life in a moment's time. Simply change your thinking.

If you change your mind while you are reading this book, I'll be thrilled to hear about it! If that happens, it means that when you close this book and get up out of the chair where you've been sitting, something about you is different. If something about you is different, things around you are going to be different.

Think about the best things that have ever happened to you. Think for a moment specifically about the things that are better in your life today than they were five years ago. Then think about how the changes occurred. The great likelihood is that you made a quality decision someplace along the line that things were going to be different in your life and they were going to be better.

Most of us have made and need to continue to make "this I will do" statements of resolution—statements that go far beyond New Year's resolutions to become life-changing landmark decisions.

I stay in a lot of hotels as I travel, and each time I do, I am aware that somebody made a quality decision about building a hotel in a particular location. That decision maker came to a point in time in which he or she said, "This I will do." The hotel would not have sprung up on its own without that decision. The decision was the first day of the hotel's actual existence. Up to that point, it was only an idea. From that point on, the hotel began to be a reality.

This is true for every real thing in our lives, whether it's something we own or something we do, including the relationship with a spouse, the relationship with our children, or business associations that are long-standing and permanent. Our possessions, our activities, our relationships—all are the result of our decisions.

Moving Beyond Your Comfort Zone

I don't know what your comfort zone is—a comfort zone differs from person to person. But I do know this: Your basic tendency is to stay within your comfort zone. By contrast, success demands that you get out of your comfort zone and take a risk. It's one of the laws related to success. You cannot remain comfortable and hold the status quo for your life, and move forward and upward at the same time. You are going to have to fight comfort virtually every day of your life if you are going to experience your full destiny.

For some people, a comfort zone involves routine. They do the same things every day, almost to the hour and minute, and if their routine is interrupted, they fall apart.

> **Success demands that you get out of your comfort zone and take a risk.**

For thousands, perhaps even millions, of people in our nation, a comfort zone involves the pattern of going to school for X number of years, graduating, and getting a job in which they work forty hours a week and have the weekends off and two weeks of paid vacation. That's the cookie-cutter model for our culture. It's our national comfort zone. Some may conclude their schooling at high school and others at the college level. Some may work fifty hours instead of forty. Some may have four weeks of vacation. But overall, that's the pattern we've defined for ourselves.

The very idea that people might break that mold—and succeed without going through the "right" number of years of schooling or succeed by working for themselves and having a very different schedule—almost seems avant garde. But for many successful people, breaking the mold was the beginning of their success. Their success began the day they decided to crash their built-up system and start over, walking their own path to the beat of their own drummer to their own destination in life. Success begins by feeling uncomfortable.

Moving Forward with What-Ifs

A technique that seems to help people move beyond their comfort zones is asking what-ifs. Asking these questions causes the imagination to soar.

You may find these key questions useful to you as you focus on what you really, *really*, REALLY want to do in and with your life.

Question #1: What would my life be like if money were no object?
What if money were not a consideration? What a great question! It removes most of the barriers people have to unlocking their true personal dreams and goals. I recently read a research report that said the average American hasn't made a decision in twenty years that

wasn't based on money. If you make all of your decisions in life based on money, you'll short-circuit your potential because you'll *never* have all the money that you think you need to accomplish anything that you really want to do—at least at the outset.

If you can make decisions solely on the basis of what is right or wrong, good or bad, yes or no—all in relationship to what you want to be, do, and have in life—your decisions are going to be more focused, and in the end, you'll find that you have enough money, even if you have virtually no money initially.

- What kind of vehicle would you drive if money were no object?
- What kind of house would you live in if money were no object?
- How would you spend your days if money were no object?
- What would you want to do with your talent and ability if money were no object?
- What could you do, and would you do, for other people if money were no object?

Millions of people literally work and fret, and then slave and worry over the same five hundred dollars every month, because that's about how much they have remaining in expenses each month after they've run out of money.

> **If there's change in doing nothing, it's likely to be for the worse.**

If I could take you aside for one week and let you live as you secretly believe you ought to be living or as you secretly desire to be living—if I could give you a taste of what your life could be like when you are truly living in full accord with your personal destiny—you'd never settle for the way you are living today. You'd never go back fully to the way things used to be for you.

Question #2: How will my life change if I continue to do exactly what I am doing right now?

What if I don't make any changes? What happens to a person's dreams when that question is asked? Most people I know will have to answer, "Nothing will change. I won't reach my dreams." If there's any change anticipated in doing nothing, it's likely to be for the worse rather than for the better.

Most people are on a track of mediocrity. Things could be worse for them; things could be better. But rather than risk anything to make things better, they choose not to risk the possibility of making things worse. They'll continue to be who they are, do what they do, and have what they have pretty much for the rest of their lives, at least until retirement, and then depending on how much they are setting aside on a routine basis, they'll probably feel diminished, do less, and have less than at present.

Do You Have the Peanut, or Does the Peanut Have You?

An interesting animal to me is the spider monkey. The spider monkey is a tiny animal that lives in South and Central America. It's very hard to capture. People for years tried to shoot spider monkeys with tranquilizer guns or capture them with nets, but they're so fast that they're hard to capture either way. Then somebody found the best method is to take a clear glass narrow-mouth bottle, put one peanut inside the bottle, and wait. The spider monkey will come up to the bottle, reach inside to get the peanut, and once he has hold of the peanut, he's yours!

You see, the spider monkey can't get his hand out of the bottle as long as his hand is clenched into a fist around the peanut. The bottle is so heavy in proportion to his size that he can't drag it with him. And the spider monkey is too persistent—or perhaps too stupid—to let go of that peanut he has grasped. You could dump a whole load of peanuts or bananas around him, but he won't let go of that one peanut in his grasp!

Sometimes what you must do to pursue your ultimate destiny is to let go of the one peanut to which you are clinging. It isn't a matter of risk as much as it's a matter of being willing to change habits, willing to be flexible, willing to try a new method, willing to give up something you are clinging to with all your strength.

Ask yourself,

- Is what I'm holding on to better than anything I might be holding on to in the future?

- What will I lose by letting go of this one thing? What might I gain?
- Am I being slowed down by the thing that I'm clinging to as if it's the only "peanut" in the world?

I don't know what the peanut in the bottle may be for you. It may be a job you've had for years and years. It may be the neighborhood in which you live. It may be a physical condition that you've never really sought to remedy. People find comfort in all kinds of negative situations that hold them back from having the full vitality, energy, creativity, and enthusiasm for living that one needs to truly live a full, balanced, and fulfilling life.

Take stock of your situation. Is one peanut in the bottle worth the freedom of soaring to greatness?

Do you have control of your life, or does your life have control of you?

Question #3: *What am I likely to regret* not *doing or trying in my life?*

What if today was the last day of your life? A sobering thought. What would you wish you had done, been, or tried?

My father currently is the chief executive officer of a retirement center, which includes a full-care nursing facility. A couple of times a month I visit the people in his center. At one time, seventeen people who were older than one hundred lived in the center, and many of them were as lucid as you or I.

I've asked these people on various occasions, "What do you regret about your life?"

They've all said to me that they regret *not* having tried something or *not* having pursued something. Not one person has ever said to me, "I regret having tried that because I failed," or "I regret pursuing that because I made a few mistakes or hit a few snags in the process." No. People regret what they *didn't* try, not what they did try.

Nearly all people have something that they wish they had done or tried or experienced or pursued. As far as I'm concerned, *if only I had* are four of the most haunting and pitiful words a person can utter.

If you get stuck in analyzing your sense of destiny, revisit the dreams you had for your life when you were a child or a teenager or a college student. What did you want to do? Do you still wish you had done that? It very likely isn't too late!

One Quality Decision Away from Your Desire

Most people are only one quality decision away from a thing they want. And for most people that decision boils down to asserting, "I'm going to go for it!"

> ◼ *Nothing on this planet is more powerful than a person who has made a decision to achieve something.*

As far as I'm concerned, nothing on this planet is more powerful than a person who has made a decision to gain or achieve something. You need to know a couple of things, however, as you make this decision.

First, never get the how *of achieving your decision mixed up with the* what *of your dream.*

Your first decision should be very narrow in its focus. Decide *what* you want. What do you want to be, do, have, eliminate, pursue, or gain?

You should be able to state your decision in a simple sentence: "I want to _____." Fill in the blank with virtually anything you want as long as it is *your* desire.

In many ways, this is a little like being a kid turned loose in a candy shop with a ten-dollar bill and Mom's permission to choose anything you want! Have fun filling in the blank. Don't put any limits on yourself. The only thing you need to be certain about is this: Do you *really* want it? Is it something that you want with urgency, persistency, deep desire? Strip away all the inhibitions and the constraints you may have placed on your dreams in the past and say boldly and directly, "Yes, with all my heart, I want to _____."

Second, don't second-guess your dream.

Once you have focused on the thing that you really want to be or attain, shut the door on everything you have said, done, and accomplished prior to that decision. Burn the bridge behind you. From now on, it's just you and your new decision. There's no turning back! View this decision as if you have just crossed a deep ravine on a swinging vine, and now you have no way to get back across the gorge. You're on the other side, and you are faced with figuring out *how* you are going to accomplish what you want.

If you get the *how* mixed up with the *what*, you'll never grow. The *how* will always defeat you and stifle the *what*, and you'll never attempt anything beyond where you are right now.

If you begin to second-guess your dream, you'll never pursue it with the energy needed to attain it.

Many people get caught up in waiting for all the lights to be green before they leave the house. That type of thinking will ensure that they never leave the house!

The Great Power in Making a Decision

I once served on the board of a church I was attending. The big issue in the church was, Are we going to stay in this building, or are we going to move into another building? As long as I had been on the board, that had been the question. Various members of the board would come to a meeting and say, "I saw a building we should consider," and then we'd all rush over to take a look at it and talk about it, but we never did anything beyond that.

At one meeting, a man I'll call Tom stood up and said, "One of two things is going to happen today. Either we're going to resolve this question, or I'm going to leave this board. We can either stay or move, but we're going to have to decide. If we make a decision to stay, we're staying. If we decide to move, let's pack up and find a place to move. But if we make a decision to stay in this building, I don't care if the Astrodome is for sale for a hundred dollars and we can move it free of charge to a downtown location on free property, we are staying put. And if we make a decision to move, we act."

Tom called that board to action. I don't think it really mattered to him one way or the other what the board decided. He didn't see it as a great spiritual matter of faith. Tom was a businessman, and he knew that ultimately, reaching a decision mattered most. Otherwise we were destined to wallow around forever in our so-called searching. Wallowing around is a waste of time and energy for all involved. Deciding and acting are far more efficient, even if you make a wrong decision and have to make a new and better one. Stop to think about it. You could probably have made several decisions and acted on them, achieving at least some forward and upward motion in your life, during the time it took you finally to make your last major decision.

There's great power in making a decision. It sets you on a course. It puts you on a track. It gives you an agenda.

"But what if I don't like my choice?" you may ask. "What if I find that I really didn't want what I thought I wanted?"

Then make a new decision!

Force Yourself to Voice a Decision

Voice your decision. Speak it aloud. You may be the only person in the room, along the bike path, or on the ledge overlooking the canyon below, but give voice to your dream and to your decision to pursue it.

Make it a declaration. That's the best way I know to come to a decision—one that you can use as a reference point for all your future decisions.

You can think about what you really want out of your life all day and night and then all the next day and night and then all the next days and nights for the rest of your life.

Decide.

When I approach someone with an offer of an opportunity I think is right for that person—perhaps a product to sell or perhaps myself to sell—I do so in a straightforward manner. I say, "I'd like forty-five minutes of your time to share with you what I believe is a great opportunity. I'm going to tell you about it, give you a sample of the product to try, answer your questions, and then ask you to make a decision. If your answer is yes, then we're in business together. If it's no, then you'll never hear from me again about this. We can still be friends, but I won't bring this up again."

I recommend this approach to you if you are involved in selling, which most people are at some point in their lives. (In virtually every serious encounter you have on your staircase to success, you are going to be asking various people to purchase things from you, hire you, give things to you, or be involved with you in some way.)

Tell people what you want from them. Tell them what you are going to do.

Give them a sample of what's going to be in it for them.

Answer their questions as best you can.

And then ask them to make a decision. If they are for you, great. If they aren't, you at least know that and can move on.

Don't leave them in the dark about your intentions. Don't promise them a sample you can't deliver or provide. Don't hedge in answering their questions; answer them in a straightforward, honest manner. And don't let the decision dangle. Force the decision. Yes or no. Bring closure to the possibility that you have placed between the two of you.

1. State your intentions.
2. Make your claims.
3. Give a sample.
4. Answer questions.
5. Get a decision.

That's the five-point Stovall method for doing business!

If you can get another person to decide, there's a good probability he or she will decide in your favor, buy what you are selling, or give you what you need. At the very least, some of the people you approach are going to decide in your favor, and if you ask enough people, you are going to get enough "yes" answers to win the day.

Don't settle for a maybe. That isn't a close. A close is a decision, and maybe is only a delaying tactic. Insist on a decision, even if it isn't in your favor.

I've told you all that to say this.

I want you to do the same in your life *about your life* today. What do you intend to do with your life? Think it over a bit. Weigh the pros and cons of your dreams.

Imagine a few scenarios.

Ask yourself a few questions about how much you really want this and why.

Evaluate your desire for this over time. Is it something you just thought about, or have you had this thought periodically throughout your life?

And then decide.

What are you personally destined to accomplish? Who are you destined to be? What are you going to leave behind as your mark in this world?

Make a decision!

Choice Requires Personal Courage

Many people are reluctant to make the one quality decision that will change their lives because they don't really believe they have a choice. I'm here to tell you that you do have a choice. You can make a decision today that will affect mightily everything that you say, do, and think from this day forward.

Don't be afraid to lasso a dream.

Other people seem afraid to lasso a dream. They don't think they are "worthy" of achieving what they dream of achieving. I'm here to tell you that you are worthy of your dream. Not only are you worthy of it, but you have been given that dream so that you will pursue it and attain it.

I heard someone say once that hell isn't going to be fire and brimstone. Rather, hell is going to be standing before your Maker and looking at a picture of what you *could* have been, done, and had if only you had enough courage to be, do, and work for what was destined to be yours.

Every time a person has a thought such as, *I ought to do this,* or *Wouldn't it be great if I could do that?* or *The ultimate as far as I'm concerned would be to . . . ,* that person isn't just having a little thought or a daydream. That person is facing a choice. Each of these things, by virtue of the fact that it has passed through the mind and the being, is possible for the person. I don't believe we are allowed to have thoughts that are not within the realm of possibility for us. I don't believe our Creator would allow us to think or dream or conceive of things that are outside our reach.

Whenever we dream about something we'd like to be, do, or have, we are, in essence, confronted with that thing as a menu item. We can select it if we choose to, and we can have it if we are willing to do what it takes to get it.

> *Dreams are doable. They come true when we make them come true.*

Dreams are doable. They are achievable. They are within the realm of possibility—perhaps not today or tomorrow, but certainly someday. Dreams come true when we *make* them come true.

I learned that in a major way when I tackled college as a visually impaired student. Nobody handed me my destiny on a silver platter. Oh, not even close.

4

LOOKING AROUND
TO SEE WHO'S THERE
Somebody believes in your success
as much as you do.

───────────

You may think you are the only person in the world who truly believes that you can become a success or that you can achieve the personal destiny you have envisioned.

I'm here to tell you otherwise.

At least one other person somewhere believes in your success as much as you do. I don't know who that person is. You may not know yet, either. I don't know when or under what circumstances you'll meet that person. But I believe that person is there for you.

I've never met someone who was pursuing a life dream—a sense of personal destiny or purpose—and failed to encounter such a person. That person is there for you, just waiting for you to take the appropriate steps to put yourself into that person's sphere of influence and activity.

I encountered several such people when I was pursuing a college degree.

Nothing About College Was Given to Me

College was tough for me, but not solely for the reasons you might think.

In the first place, I went to a university founded on a healing ministry—Oral Roberts University. My father worked for the Oral Roberts Ministry most of his life, and I grew up very well acquainted with Oral Roberts personally and with his ministry. I have a great deal of respect, admiration, and affection for Oral Roberts.

Even so, if you are going blind, and you are in a college founded on a healing ministry, there's a great expectation that you should be healed of your blindness. It's very easy to say, and even easier to imply, "If you just had enough faith, you'd get healed."

In going to college I faced this matter of faith and healing.

One professor insisted that I take a test reading it like everyone else. It took an administrative move to get him to let me take an oral test. He hated every minute of giving it to me. As for me, I decided that if it killed me, I'd score the highest grade in his class. I didn't care whether anybody knew it other than the two of us, but I was determined to earn the highest grade he gave, and I did.

I could never understand the people who took the approach this man took. Perhaps he felt that he was being compromised as a teacher. No doubt some of the people at Oral Roberts University felt that accommodating my blindness was something less than a genuine act of faith on their part. After all, the place was founded on taking God's healing power to this generation. They had given their lives to turn that call of God into a reality, and they no doubt felt they had failed in some way if they couldn't take God's healing power to one blind student.

It's Not Where You Are but Where You Are Going

I don't believe for a second that God made me blind. Frankly, I don't think it's important to dwell on who or what caused my blindness. The important issue is what I do with my life. Blindness is just one aspect, one circumstance, one situation I have encountered. It isn't the sum and substance of who I am. It certainly isn't the determiner of my whole life. Although my blindness influences certain decisions I make on a daily practical basis, blindness does not frame my entire perspective on life or on the future.

Dennis Byrd has become a good friend of mine. He was paralyzed in an accident in the NFL, and his story is chronicled in the book

Rise and Walk. Dennis and I have been through some of the same struggles. I don't believe for a second that God planned for Dennis Byrd to break his neck. If anybody gets hit that hard in just that way, his neck is going to be broken. Things happen in life. Certain genetic codes get scrambled; accidents happen; certain combinations produce unexpected or unwanted results. Life is life. Far more important than what happens to us is what we do in the wake of the experiences.

The things Dennis has learned since his accident, and the things he has discovered in learning how to walk again, are amazing to me. And I have no doubt at all that God is with Dennis in his struggle to regain his physical capabilities, just as I have no doubt that God has been with me in my struggles to live and achieve and become all that I can be.

God is there with us in times of tragedy. God is there with us as we struggle through our troubles and problems and as we strive to overcome any obstacles that land in our paths. Of that I have no doubt.

At the time I started at ORU, the university had had virtually no students with disabilities—at least none who fully completed the course and graduated with a degree. Students were injured from time to time playing intramural sports, so you saw an occasional student on crutches, but no students who were permanently disabled were enrolled at the time I attended. I know of only one blind girl who had attended ORU several years before me, and I believe she was there for only a semester.

Then I showed up. I could see just enough to read a little bit, but not much, and that ability was going fast. I started attending classes, and I had to stay up until three or four o'clock in the morning just to wade through the basic text materials. I couldn't do it. I lasted ten days as a freshman and quit.

I moved out of the dorm and back home, unsure about what to do next. I had been psyched to attend college. The beginning of a school year is always an exciting time—new people to meet, new routines, a new place to live. Ten days later, it was over for me.

I had a terrible feeling of failure as my dad and I moved my stuff out of the dorm. We never talked about it. The issue was too big. The pain was too great.

Before I left, I went to talk to Dr. Harold Paul and to tell him that I was leaving ORU.

Dr. Paul was a professor of humanities at Oral Roberts University for many years. He was, and is, an amazing man. He has been a professor emeritus for years now, and he still makes regular visits to the university to assist in various areas. On the wall of his office were photos of him with several presidents of the United States. He was an educator for more than forty years, and as far as I'm concerned, he was the greatest teacher I have ever had.

Dr. Paul has an incredible love of life and also a great love of other people, including college freshmen. He had a practice of greeting every freshman student at the door of his classroom. He told you how glad he was that you were there, and he did it in a way that you truly believed he meant what he said.

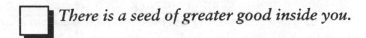 *There is a seed of greater good inside you.*

I had attended only two class sessions with Dr. Paul, but I felt I owed it to him to tell him I was dropping out of school. He responded by saying that there was a "seed of greater good inside me" and that someday, we'd both look back and know that to be true.

Today's Defeat Is the Seed of Tomorrow's Victory

One summer job I had when I was in high school was that of a construction worker. Because I was big and strong and put in a full day's work, I got paid more than some of the other laborers. That was rewarding to me. I was only a day laborer, but I saw a way to become a very good and well-paid day laborer. I shoveled concrete. The more concrete I shoveled, and the faster I shoveled it, the more I earned. I decided that being a big, strong concrete shoveler was something I could do. So . . .

When I left college, I began shoveling concrete again. I wasn't sure how much longer I would be able to do that because I could see very little at the time, but it was just about the only thing I knew to do. During my lunch hours, I'd sit around with the older construction workers—since all of the young guys had gone back to school after the summer—and to my great surprise, Dr. Paul started showing up at lunchtime. I was working for a contractor who was doing some work for ORU, and I happened to be assigned to the project he had going at the university. The project, by the way, was the baseball stadium, which is one of the finest college stadiums in the Midwest. Given my father's interest in baseball, I find that something of an ironic twist in my life.

Dr. Paul didn't say anything about my returning to school when he came to see me at lunchtime. He'd just come out in his suit and pull up an overturned bucket and sit there with me and some of the dirtiest construction workers in Tulsa and eat lunch. I worked the rest of the fall semester while many other people my age were walking to and from classes all around me.

A turning point came early one morning in January. It was seven o'clock on a Monday morning, and I was in a ditch we had dug the previous Friday. It was about twenty degrees, the wind was blowing, and since it had rained over the weekend, the ditch had about six inches of freezing water in it. I was down there in the ditch with a bucket scooping out this water so that as soon as the sun came up, we could pour concrete into the ditch. I was wet, cold, and pretty miserable.

I didn't complain about this being my lot in life. I was the only grunt laborer those guys had after all the other college guys went back to school, and I was in great shape physically. It was my job to do just what I was doing, but still, I resented that the other guys were drinking coffee over in the construction shack and waiting for the concrete trucks to roll up. They all knew what I'd gone through. They'd been there when Dr. Paul came out to see me and have lunch with me. Just as I was thinking, *Scooping freezing water out of this ditch is all these guys think of me*, the door to the shack opened and all of the guys inside came out and started toward me.

One man, obviously the designated leader of the group, came over to me and said, "We've been talking and we'd like for you to leave."

I said, "Why? I've been working hard, and I carry more than my weight. All of you guys know it. I work harder than anybody here!"

He said, "Yeah, that's right."

"What's the problem then?" I demanded.

"We're here because we're stuck here, Jim," he said. "We can't go anywhere else or do anything else. This is what we do. And if you don't get out of here, you're going to be like us someday, old guys with nowhere else to go and nothing else to do. We'd like to see you do something with your life. This isn't where you should end up."

They really got to me.

So I called Dr. Paul and said, "I'm coming to school next fall." He didn't say anything other than, "That'll be fine, Jim. *You* are what's important to me. Whatever you want to do is fine with me."

I returned to school the following fall, and I enrolled in two classes. I worked hard, and Dr. Paul waded through a mountain of red tape for me and was able to hire a reader to help me. One of my first readers was Crystal, who is now my wife.

At the end of the first semester, I got a call from Dr. Paul. He said, "I need to see you in my office right away." I knew grades were coming out the next day so I immediately thought, *This is it. I didn't make it.* I walked across the campus and sat down in his office. There he sat with tears in his eyes. He said, "Jim, I've been a teacher for forty years, and I think this is one of the most significant educational accomplishments I've ever seen. You earned a B and a C in your two classes."

My mind was spinning. I thought, *This guy is the professor of the year at this university and he just told me I got a B and a C in two freshman courses that don't count for much, and he's telling me that I'm a significant educational accomplishment?* I had no doubt that Dr. Paul was genuinely pleased by my progress, but I couldn't understand *why*.

Dr. Paul went on: "This is only the beginning, Jim. I think you can be an outstanding student at this university. Now it's time for you to do even better. There are going to be students with disabilities following in your footsteps someday, and they deserve to have the best role model they can have. I think you can do better. I think *you* know you can do better. And I want to see you become the very best you can be."

What Dr. Paul said lit a fire in me. And I responded to his challenge, determined to prove him right about my potential and ability. I was determined to give it my all.

And I did. I graduated from ORU with a combination degree in psychology and sociology, summa cum laude—with highest honors. I never earned anything but A's from that semester onward.

Success Doesn't Impact Only You

About ten years after I graduated, an official at ORU called me and said, "Jim, we'd like for you to speak at a function we're having."

I said, "Frankly, I'd rather not. I speak all over the world. I'm tired. I'm busy."

The person responded, "Well, please consider it. We're honoring Dr. Harold Paul and all the honor students with a banquet." I didn't think about it another second. I said, "I'll be there."

Michael drove me out to the campus and told me what I needed to know about walking into the auditorium. Usually when we're in a parking lot, Michael will tell me where the curb is, but this time he said, "We'll just go up this wheelchair ramp." I stopped in my tracks. A wheelchair ramp? I was amazed. Not only had I come a long way since my college days, but ORU had.

> *You don't have a right to be anything less than your absolute best.*

In that moment standing on that wheelchair ramp, I suddenly remembered what Dr. Paul had said to me: "Jim, you need to do your very best, not only for yourself, but for the students who are going to come after you. Many students with disabilities are going to come through this university in the years ahead, and they are going to be judged in part on what you do and how you succeed here. You don't have a right to be any less than your very best for their sake."

What he said stuck with me, and I believe it's a valuable principle for everyone.

You really don't have a right to be anything less than your absolute best. Not only for your sake. But for those who will come after you. The people who follow you may be your children. They may be people you mentor, teach, or influence in some other way. They may be people who receive from your generosity. They may be people who observe your example from afar. They may be people who never know your name or know anything about you but who benefit from what you do while you are on this earth. You need to be, to give, and to do your very best for people you can affect in a positive way and for people who will live in the years to come beyond your lifetime.

That's an obligation we all have and all face daily, but few of us have that bigger picture—that bigger responsibility—in mind when we make choices about our lives.

When I was given an award from the Jaycees as one of the Ten Outstanding Young Americans, Dr. Paul phoned me. He was upset that his health wouldn't allow him to attend the ceremony, but he wanted me to know that he considered my success one of the greatest events of his life. He then said, "Jim, the best is yet to come for you."

> *Mentors lead you by their example and nudge you to become all you can be.*

Even now, Dr. Paul is a mentor—a man who encourages me, speaks truth to me, and won't let me get by with second best or a slack effort. He couples applause with accountability and responsibility. I hope you have someone like him in your life. And if you don't, I hope you'll seek out such a person. Such people are called *mentors*—they lead you by their example and nudge you to become all you can be. One or more mentors are out there for you.

Look for them.

Learn from them.

Do what they challenge you to do!

Mentors and Motivators

Every successful person I know has had at least one mentor or teacher, and the successful person openly acknowledges that individual in his or her life.

Nobody in this day and age has either the time or the need to learn everything from scratch. We don't need to reinvent what has already been invented and works well.

I consider that every person I meet is my superior in that I can learn something from him or her that I don't already know. It may be a skill, a tidbit of information, or a major principle. I'm always on the lookout for a learning experience.

I've discovered, however, that many people aren't looking for teachers or mentors. They're looking only for people who will tell them what they want to hear, to encourage them, or to build up their egos. They don't really want someone to hold them accountable or to take them to task in any way.

A number of mentors encourage me, and they are encouraging to me by their very lives and examples, but more than anything else, they require better from me and hold me accountable for pursuing the very best I can become.

The old saying tells us that carrots motivate donkeys better than sticks do. That may be true, but in the end, *both* carrots and sticks are important if we are to end up at the place called excellence. You can motivate a donkey right off the edge of a cliff with a carrot. The "sticks" in life usually guide our direction rather than compel us to move. We need both—motivation to move forward and a good direction in which to aim.

Don't cheat yourself by surrounding yourself only with colleagues or helpers, or even friends, who will expect very little of you and tell you only what you want to hear. Associate with people who will speak the truth to you.

Cheerleaders and Referees

In many ways a mentor is like a coach—somebody who will teach you some of the rules of life's game and then show you some of the best plays to make, always expecting you to give your best effort and to win the game.

I believe two other types of people will affect your destiny, but they will wear different hats. They are people I liken to cheerleaders and referees.

Just as in the case of your mentors, your cheerleaders and referees are out there. You'll find them as you begin to pursue your sense of personal destiny. Take advantage of what they have to give you!

In my life, neither my first cheerleader nor my first referee was at Oral Roberts University, but I met both during my college years.

Shoelaces and Mortarboards

Shortly after I returned to college, I began to do volunteer work at a school for blind children in Tulsa. When I reflect on that experience now, more than fifteen years after the fact, I'm not sure what my real motivations were at the time. They were probably mixed. One part of me was probably trying to learn a little more about what it meant to be completely blind. I've never spent much time around blind people or been part of an institution for people who are blind, so there's a lot I don't know about blind people, generally speaking. One part of me was probably seeking to be a teacher, perhaps to mask the fact that I really was a learner in the situation. Another part of me may have been trying to make some kind of deal with God—one of those quid pro quo deals we try to make with our Creator, saying, "I'll do this for You if You'll do this for me." These types of deals never really work, by the way, because ultimately, we all are in a position only to say yes or no to God's way of doing things, not to barter or bargain.

Whatever my motives, I volunteered, hoping to make a difference in the life of at least one child.

I was taking only two courses at ORU, so I had time to spend a couple of hours a day at the school for blind children. I said to the school officials, "I don't have any background experience or teaching credentials in this area, but I'm here to help in any way I can." They assigned me to Christopher.

Christopher was four years old, and they wanted me to work with him one-on-one. They said, "Christopher had a cerebral hemorrhage, and he isn't able to learn very much, so we aren't expecting you to be a teacher. He has balance and coordination problems. There are only two things we ask of you. Keep his shoes tied so he won't trip on his shoelaces, and keep him away from the stairs so he won't fall down them. Other than that, we ask only that you play with him to keep him quiet and to keep him from disturbing the other children as they learn."

I said to Christopher the first day I met him, "Young man, before I leave here you'll be able to tie both of your shoelaces, and you'll be able to climb those stairs without falling." He said to me, "No, I won't."

I said, "Yes, you will." He said again, "No, I won't." If you have ever spent any time with four-year-olds, you know they can argue back and forth like that all day.

We had a repeat of that conversation for about a day and a half, and then Christopher relaxed a little and we began to work together. We walked. We tied shoes. We climbed the stairs with me holding his hands. I'd watch what the other teachers were doing with their students, and I tried teaching various skills to Christopher.

Meanwhile I was having my own difficulties. I was back in college for the second start, and it was just as tough the second time as it was the first time. Once you've had a failure and embraced it, as I had the year before, it's easier to opt for a failure the second time. The pressure is off somehow. You once failed, you bailed, and you survived, so it's easier to accept failure and bail again. Success breeds success, but failure also breeds failure. A tolerance for failure sets in.

After a few weeks of classes, the thoughts began to come, *I can't do this. I'm not getting any help. I can't cut it.* I was preparing myself mentally to drop out again.

I went to talk to the principal of the school for blind children, and I told her, "This is probably my last day here. I can't make it in college, and I'm going to have to drop out, so I won't be able to volunteer anymore because I'll need to get a full-time job."

The principal didn't care what I did one way or the other. She was a little sorry to see me go, but she didn't try to talk me out of my decision. She accepted what I was telling her.

Christopher, however, did not.

Christopher's parents had dropped him off at the school a little earlier than usual that day, and while I was telling the principal that I would be quitting, Christopher was standing outside the open door listening to every word.

For weeks I'd been telling Christopher, "Yes, you can, yes, you can," every time he told me he couldn't do something.

I turned away from that principal to see Christopher standing in front of me, and he said to me with a very firm little voice, "Yes, you can."

I said, "No, Christopher, I can't make it in college." He said, "Yes, you can."

I said, "Christopher, this isn't like tying your shoes. This is serious grown-up stuff."

He said, "Yes, you can." And it hit me just as hard as if I'd run into a wall at full steam: *Stovall, quit lying to this kid, and tell him the truth that he can't tie his shoes or climb those stairs. Or prove to this kid with your own life that a person* can *overcome obstacles and make it through tough times.*

Either way, I had to give the truth to Christopher. I had to exemplify the "yes, you can" truth, or I had to admit to him that I was lying all along and that the truth was that he couldn't make it any better than I.

Christopher was seven years old when I graduated from the university with my A average and my combination degree in psychology and sociology. But Christopher also had a graduation day of sorts. I was still able to see well enough at that time to watch him tie both shoes and to climb three flights of stairs and stand proudly on the top step with a "yes, I did it" look in his eyes.

Later that same summer, after we both had "graduated," Christopher had another cerebral hemorrhage and died.

At the funeral, a teacher from the school said to me, "Isn't it a shame we will never know what he could have done had he lived a full life?"

I said, "Wait a minute. Hold the phone. He has made his contribution because anything I do from this day forward I owe to him."

To date, I have shared Christopher's story with more than a quarter of a million people in public speaking events, and a good number of them have told me that Christopher's story marked a turning point in their lives.

Christopher taught me that there is no such thing as an insignificant person. Christopher directly changed my life, and indirectly, he has changed the lives of thousands of people around the world.

He also taught me that there is no such thing as an insignificant relationship. All of them are important. There's no such thing as an insignificant day. All are precious. And when we are living our lives the way we are supposed to live them, there's no such thing as an insignificant moment because each moment holds within it the seed of our ability to change our lives by changing our minds.

■ *Sometimes you find the strength within yourself simply because someone else believes you can do it.*

Christopher was a major cheerleader in my life at the point when I desperately needed one. He was the first person who taught me, by example, that you change your life when you change your mind. He also taught me that you sometimes find the strength within yourself to do what you want to do simply because somebody else believes you can do it.

Never discount what a cheerleader says to you—a cheerleader who is genuine, who truly cares about what happens to you, and who truly wants what is best for you. That cheerleader is there to give you a boost when you need one. Take what that person has to give, and be grateful for it.

Referees See—and Call—Your Fouls

The third type of person you will find valuable in your life is a referee. Most of us don't think we need this person—and most of us don't like what this person has to say to us much of the time. But in retrospect, we all know that the person who was the toughest on us, demanded the most from us, and required the best we had to give has been influential in making us who we are.

I studied psychology in college, and psychologists often use a "best-worst" exercise in which the psychologist asks a person to identify "the best experience I ever had" and then to identify "the worst experience I ever had." The list can be expanded to include the best teacher, worst teacher; best relationship, worst relationship; best life lesson, worst life lesson; and so on. People who take this test often conclude that the best and worst instances in their lives are the same. What at the time may have seemed difficult or bad may very well turn out to be the very thing that caused the most good in their lives.

Educators know this, too, from researching students who take exams. Students tend to learn more from the mistakes they make and the questions they miss than from the right answers they give.

Referees aren't necessarily mean-spirited. They call it as they see it in life as a whole and in your life in particular. They don't let you get away with what you may think are no-harm, no-foul experiences.

Lee Braxton was a referee for me. I treasure the hours I spent with him. But some of them were very difficult hours at the time.

During my senior year in college, the recruiters started to show up on campus to hire students for their corporations. I saw some of my fellow students being hired for top jobs, and I knew I had better grades than they did and I worked harder than they did. I don't mind telling you I was a little upset, a little disappointed, a little angry—not at anyone in particular, but at life in general.

Out of that experience, however, I made a quality decision. I went over to my dad's office and said, "Dad, I've made a decision. When I get out of school, I'm going to go into business for myself. I don't know much about being in business for myself, but at least I'll always have a job. Nobody can fire me! Nobody can find an excuse to let me go because I'm blind."

He said, "Great! Come back tomorrow and I'll see what I can give you to help you get started."

I was excited. My father wasn't, and isn't, wealthy, but he had always managed money well and he had saved quite a bit of money through the years. I thought maybe he'd give me $50,000 or $100,000 to help me get started.

When I went to see him the next day, however, I was in for a big surprise. He said, "I'm going to give you the best thing I know to give you: knowledge. The first piece of that knowledge is this: You will have what you *earn* in this life."

To be honest, I was a little disappointed. But then my dad went on: "I don't know how to be an entrepreneur or start a business. I've never done that. I've always had a job and worked for somebody else. But I know a man who has been in business for himself, and I'm going to introduce you to him. I've already talked to him about this, and he's willing to work with you and teach you how to be in business for yourself."

A few days later Dad introduced me to Lee Braxton, a man who was a true entrepreneur and one of the most successful people I've ever met—both in his financial dealings and in his personal life. Over the next several months, I spent quite a bit of time with Mr. Braxton. He taught me more than I could ever have imagined.

Mr. Braxton called me boy and I called him sir. He said to me one day, "Boy, I've been watching you for a lot longer than you've been coming to see me. You are the biggest waste of human potential I've ever seen in my life. I'm too old to wait around on your potential, and you're too young to understand what I'm saying, so we've got to do this fast. I'm going to teach you a lot of things that you're not going to begin to understand, but someday you'll remember what I told you, so I'll just tell it to you and you force yourself to remember it. Later on, it'll dawn on you that what I've told you is true."

And that's pretty much the way it was and has been!

Lee Braxton had only a third-grade education, but he became a self-made millionaire during the days of the Great Depression. He counted among his personal friends such people as Dale Carnegie, Henry Ford, and Charles Lindbergh. He led an amazing life. And I feel privileged that he shared his time and wisdom with me.

One of the first things Lee Braxton taught me was accountability. Each time I went to visit Mr. Braxton, he'd give me a book or a tape, and then he'd say, "Come back when you've read that or listened to that."

A few times I'd get so excited about what I was reading or hearing that I'd rush over to the Braxtons' house, eager to hear what Mr. Braxton had to say about the matter. He'd let me in, and I'd sit there in his living room with him and he'd ask, "Boy, did you read that *whole* book?"

I'd admit, "Well, not the whole book, but I have this question. . . ."

Once he heard that I hadn't read the *whole* book, he'd refuse to talk with me. He'd turn to his wife, Norma, and say, "Miss Norma, Jim will come back when he's read that whole book," and then he'd get up and leave the room.

I'd protest, "But I don't want to talk about the whole book. I just want to talk about this one part. I've read that part completely." My protestations always fell on deaf ears.

I learned from Lee Braxton that there's a price to pay in having a teacher. I learned that there's value to learning all that another person is saying—whether in a book, in an article, or on a tape—before drawing preliminary conclusions. And in the end, I learned a great deal about what it means to be an entrepreneur.

Be on the Alert for Your Helpers

As I said earlier in this chapter, I don't know who your mentors are going to be. I can't tell you where to look for cheerleaders or how to go about finding a fair and helpful referee.

But I do know this: You need each of these people in your life. Each is there to help you reach your destiny and to fulfill the purpose you envision for your life. In their respective ways and manners, they will be people who believe in what you are doing and in who you are becoming.

Take the help they have to give you. Don't reject it. Don't dismiss it as trivial or negative. Treasure their words and their deeds. And learn from them.

5

SHARPENING
THE MIND'S EYE

To claim the gold medal
of your destiny,
you first must see it.

I've probably been through at least fifteen hundred biographical and autobiographical books on tape about the greatest people who have ever lived, and I've come to a conclusion about these people. They had a sense of their own destiny.

They believed that there was something bigger and better and more powerful than themselves, and that they had been sent on a "mission to earth" to accomplish something. They also felt compelled to complete that mission, to make it happen, whatever the cost.

You might say they were mastered by their destiny—molded and made and ruled by it. But they also became masters of their destiny. What they felt they should be and do with their lives, they were and did. They forged greatness in the process.

We call them heroes and heroines. They did what they felt destined to do.

While I was a college student, I made an appointment to visit with Dr. James Buskirk, who was the dean of the university's school of theology at the time. Dr. Buskirk had experienced visual problems somewhat similar to mine. Our conversation about eyesight quickly turned to the importance of a person's vision, specifically the need for a person to have an inner vision about his or her destiny.

Dr. Buskirk shared with me that very early in his life, he had been able to "see" himself standing in a pulpit, giving a positive message that could make a difference in the lives of the people gathered.

"When I actually stood in a pulpit and gave my first sermon," he told me, "I felt almost as if I had been there before. It was like putting my foot into my own shoe. Preaching was a perfect fit for me." Indeed, Dr. Buskirk is one of the finest preachers I've ever heard.

He also said, "As much as I enjoy academia, I have a deep need to be in a pulpit as often as possible."

Dr. Buskirk is now the senior pastor of one of the largest and most respected United Methodist churches in the nation. Preaching is still his passion, and although he certainly must engage in a great deal of administration on a daily basis, I suspect standing in the pulpit is still the place where Dr. Buskirk feels his greatest sense of destiny and personal fulfillment.

Seeing Your Destiny

I am firmly convinced that nothing happens in a strong, positive, successful way in your life until you first see it happen in your mind's eye. You may discover buried treasure in your backyard today, or you may receive an unexpected inheritance. But even in that one-in-tens-of-millions situation, you probably aren't going to be able to make the most of being a treasure finder or an inheritance recipient. In other words, you aren't going to be able to live that life successfully unless you are first able to visualize yourself living at that level.

Visualization directly relates to turning your desires into something that can be pursued.

Visualization directly relates to turning your desires into something that can be pursued. Desires tend to be vague. They become more focused when you turn them into specific dreams. They become even more focused when you turn them into goals and plans. It's only when you tightly focus your desires that you can put the full force of your energy and effort toward accomplishing them. Desires, therefore, are the first step toward visualizing your life in its future reality.

The key question to ask yourself as you visualize is this: What is my desired life like? Visualize that life as fully as possible. You don't have to be able to see with your eyes to do this. You'll probably be able to visualize your desired life better with your eyes closed. A little blindness can be to your advantage in visualizing what isn't yet, but what you believe can be!

This is the time to take off all the shackles that have been tied to your soul. Eliminate all of the "but I could never" thoughts. Wipe out all of the "but that isn't ever going to happen" thoughts. Don't allow yourself to think any "impossible" thoughts!

Don't get any *hows* mixed in with *whats* at this point. Just imagine a new world.

For example, let's assume that you desire to live a simplified life, perhaps out in the wilderness where the air is clean and the scenery is stunning, and that you desire to write books, take photographs, and hike a lot. These are desires. They probably stem from basic beliefs you have about life, about the environment, and about your destiny to be a writer and photographer.

Now how do you visualize that life? Where do you see yourself living? How are your days ordered? Let's say that you visualize living on the top of a mountain somewhere, hosting friends and clients for photographic backpacking excursions and cross-country ski trips, and writing novels in between the outings.

Can you really see yourself in that setting? What do you wear? What does your house look like? What type of vehicle are you driving, or do you have a vehicle? What type of gear do you have and need? How do you communicate with the world?

Visualize a typical day. What time do you get up? Where do you go? What do you do? When, where, how, and what do you eat? Who are you with?

Do you like what you visualize? Does it seem comfortable and easy to you? That is, do you fit in this environment, and do this environment and this lifestyle truly suit you? Is this something you can imagine yourself doing for a vacation, or can you visualize living this way for week after week, month after month?

It's in our ability to visualize that we truly test our desires and form them into dreams. We weed out desire from desire until we come to the visualized life about which we say, "Aha! That's the life I want. That's the life that suits me, fits me, is right for *me*. That's the way I truly want to live the coming years of my life."

> **It's in our ability to visualize that we truly test our desires and form them into dreams.**

However, we need to be realistic and very vivid in our visualization process. Otherwise we will dream only pipe dreams. You may need to do some research in visualizing your future life, especially if it is a life you've never been around.

Some people like to visualize life as a movie star. They visualize only the glamour—the glitzy lights, the fancy clothes on Oscar night, the limousines, the big homes. That's not a full visualization of the life of an actor. It's only one tiny slice of the life of most of the working actors I've met.

Movie stars have a waiting-game life for the most part. They often have worked for years upon years in bit parts or minor roles before they are "discovered" and catapulted into fame, usually related to one movie, one show, one play, or one performance.

Actors work long, hard hours in doing a particular show or film—often their workdays are twelve to fourteen hours long, and much of that time is spent waiting for scenes to be set up, in rehearsal, or in take after take after take of a scene.

Actors often go without work for weeks, months, and sometimes years between jobs, or before another truly great role comes along.

They also ride the waves of public opinion. Sometimes they are hounded by people with cameras who want interviews and photos to the point that they have very little personal privacy. And yet at other times in their lives they can hardly get a publicist to knock on the door or write a good word about them.

Meanwhile, they have to pay the bills associated with their cars, homes, and other material possessions. They have to make decisions about investing the money they've earned. If they are involved in the creative aspects or the business aspects of a project, they have almost daily concerns about budgets, creative control, and who holds the power of a project.

The glamour is only a small part of this life. And even as you visualize the glamour, visualize the need for greater personal security, the fact that you might be approached by people you don't like or don't want to talk to, and the fact that an actor's schedule is often not of his or her own making.

The point is, visualize the life you want to live as fully as possible. Consider what happens in sickness as well as in health. (You may not want to be living on the top of a mountain if you have a chronic health problem!) Consider what happens if the work you produce falls by the wayside. (What happens if your novel or your photographs don't sell well?) Consider what happens to your current relationships that you consider to be valuable. (You may not want to live that far away from family or friends.)

This isn't at all to discount the importance or worthiness of your dreams, or to diminish your desires. Rather, it is to say, visualize your dreams as a reality as fully as you can, and make sure that your dreams truly match up with the desires of your heart. Do you really want that particular lifestyle? Are you willing to invest yourself fully into it?

An essential question to ask about your visualized ideal life is this: How much am I willing to risk to make this happen? What are you willing to give up to attain the goals you have set for yourself? What are you willing to risk? What are you willing to do without for a while?

People who set out to make positive, self-fulfilling, destiny-seeking changes in their lives have to give up something, do without something, or risk something. That something may be sleep. It may be hours spent watching television. It may be personal luxuries. It may be a savings account.

In a true life's destiny dream, a person is nearly always willing to risk virtually everything to make the dream come true. Nothing is more challenging, fulfilling, or worthy of time and effort. Nothing promises more return or greater reward.

Why Is Visualization So Important?

Why is it important to visualize so thoroughly? Because the vividness of your visualization is directly related to whether you will pursue this life. If what you visualize is completely enjoyable and satisfying and fulfilling to you, if there's no cost that seems too great to pay to see this dream become a reality, there's a much greater likelihood that you will turn that dream into a goal or plan, and put the energy and effort necessary into accomplishing it. If your visualization is weak, you are going to be much less likely to make changes in your life or to sustain the effort you need to turn that dream into a reality.

If your dream is false—not rooted in facts or in a sound understanding of what a particular life is like—your dream is going to burst like a bubble. You'll feel disillusioned and unsatisfied. You'll quickly bail out of your efforts to reach your dream life, or you'll find the dream life, once accomplished, to be empty and unsatisfying.

Visualize thoroughly. And visualize concretely. Think in terms of these questions:

- How would I live?
- With whom would I live and associate?
- Where would I live?
- What possessions would I have?
- What would a day be like?
- How would I interact with others?
- In what activities would I engage, and with whom?

The more vivid and exciting and realistic your visualizations, or your dreams, the more likely you are to set goals and make plans for reaching the dreams.

A Lesson Learned from Yashimoto

When I turned from football to weight lifting, I did so with all my heart and strength. I was determined to be a champion weight lifter, and I trained and developed my body and mind with a highly focused amount of energy toward accomplishing that goal. I won a few events, and before I knew it, I was competing on an international level. During that time, I became friends with a Japanese boy named Yashimoto Ishigan. He taught me a great lesson.

When you come into an arena to lift, this is the procedure. You walk up to the bar that has been adjusted for the weight you are hoping to lift, and then you have three minutes from the time the last competitor completed his lift to the time that you attempt your lift. If you don't attempt a lift during that time period, you are disqualified from that round. This keeps the competition moving. No competitor can take unlimited time to get himself psyched up or pumped to take a lift. You need to come to the bar prepared and ready to lift—both physically and mentally—as much as possible.

During one competition, I noticed that Yashimoto usually stood over the bar until just a few seconds before the time expired before he attempted his lift. And sometimes he was disqualified from a round because he didn't attempt a lift in time.

While we were in the workout room backstage, I asked him, "What's the problem? I don't make every lift I attempt, but at least I make an attempt."

He said, "I never touch the bar until I have seen myself in my mind successfully completing the lift. We learn in the Eastern countries that the part of your mind that releases your physical or emotional strength doesn't know the difference between something that is vividly imagined, dreamed, or visualized and something that actually is happening. I know that if I can visualize myself completing the lift, I can complete the lift. If I can't visualize it, I can't do it, so why attempt it?"

His words hit home with me. I thought immediately of the many times I had seen this principle at work in athletics. A team suddenly gains momentum, and the result may be a dramatic shift in a score. What causes that momentum shift? Very often it is a play, a word from a coach, a roar from the crowd, or something else that triggers within the players a belief that they can win. They have caught a glimpse of "it's possible." They put out extra energy and strength and effort when they truly believe victory is in sight. That victory hasn't been accomplished yet. But the team member or entire team begins to think and respond as if it has been! Team members play as if they are already winners. They play as if they *can't* lose.

You show me a team in which the members have caught a vision of themselves winning—a vision they hold with the full strength of their conviction that this is their moment, their hour, their trophy, and that they can't lose—and I'll show you a team that has a much greater likelihood of pulling off a victory, despite incredible odds.

Visualization Is Not Just Wishful Thinking

Visualization is far more than an idle whim or wishful thinking. Visualization is mental rehearsal for what will happen in a given circumstance or situation.

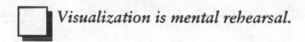 *Visualization is mental rehearsal.*

Part of the process is purely chemical in the brain. The part of your brain that releases your physical, emotional, and mental capacity to accomplish a task is deep within your subconscious, and that part of your brain doesn't know the difference between something vividly imagined and something real. It doesn't know whether you did something or not. If you can visualize that activity or event with enough clarity and detail, your subconscious will interpret that event as something that has happened in your life and that is subsequently a part of your capacity or your capability.

You can sit in a horror movie, or visit a virtual reality chamber, and experience a rise in your blood pressure, an increased pulse rate, and a change in your respiration pattern—even knowing in your intellect that what you are experiencing isn't real.

You can also visualize something positive in such real terms that your body and mind and intellect start to see the world from that perspective and begin to function—literally and physically, not only psychologically—as if you already are living that life you are imagining.

I once sat through an IMAX movie with my wife. IMAX is the large-film format that projects onto huge screens. People who are sighted tell me that it's the most real visual image they have ever experienced, in part because of the high resolution of the film and in part because of the size of the screen. Viewers apparently feel as if they are in the picture because the picture is so clear and it so completely fills the field of vision.

We went to see a movie about astronauts and the training they go through to prepare for weightlessness, reentry and takeoff G forces, and motion sickness. Those chosen to be astronauts apparently are among those with extremely high tolerance for motion. The people in the theater around me were not. A number of them became sick. I wasn't fazed, of course, because I couldn't see what they were seeing. A movie—which they knew intellectually wasn't real—had the capacity to cause them to become nauseous, even though, in reality, they were sitting in stationary, well-cushioned chairs in a dark theater.

A Hidden Source of Very Real Strength

Take into consideration for a moment that you have a child and you and your child are walking along the street. Suddenly, you are involved in an automobile accident. Somehow your child is trapped under the car. In numerous instances this has happened, and without thinking, the parent became immediately and completely focused on lifting that car off the child. Nothing else in the world mattered at that precise moment.

The parent didn't stop to think, *I can't lift this weight.* The parent didn't ponder the possibility, *I've never lifted anything this heavy before. I wonder if I can lift this car off my child.* No! The parent moved into action with a deep inner, subconscious belief that he or she *could* move that car. In fact, the parent *had* to move that car off the child. There were no other options. It was something that *had* to be made to happen.

Those people moved weights they had never moved before and most likely never will have to move again. But for a few seconds they had the strength they needed. They accomplished their goal!

That's the force that moves into the subconscious and completely takes over once you have snagged onto your real dream and goal for your life. That's the real power that emerges when you visualize fully and completely the dream life that you desire deeply to have for your destiny to be fulfilled.

Not only have scientists recorded great feats related to a person's ability to believe and to visualize a previously unseen reality, but they know that these visualized images tend to remain in a person's mind.

The images we visualize tend to be imprinted indelibly in our minds, especially if they are tied to strong psychological or emotional reactions. Most people can recall precisely where they were and what they were doing when they heard the news that President John F. Kennedy had been shot in Dallas. They can also tell you how they *felt* when they heard that news.

The same is true for the *Challenger* space shuttle that blew up shortly after launch.

The same is true for the time when you heard the news about the death of a loved one, the birth of a baby you had long anticipated, or the time when the one you love finally proposed marriage to you (or finally agreed to accept your proposal).

Strong emotions seal visualizations into our minds. They become memories, and they affect the way we think from that time forward.

Something changed in all of us who were alive at the time of the Kennedy assassination. We may not have been in Dallas. We may not have known President Kennedy personally. But we all visualized what happened. We felt strongly about it. And we mourned, as individuals and as a nation. That event altered the way millions of people lived their lives from that moment on.

The same thing happened in a little different way as we visualized the Vietnam War. We saw that war nightly on our television sets. The images of the war imprinted themselves on our minds. They affected the way we have thought and responded as a nation ever since.

This principle will hold true in your life as you visualize the life you fully expect to lead in fulfilling your personal destiny on this earth. The clear, vivid, highly detailed, emotion-laden images that you hold in your mind actually affect the way you think and respond from that moment on.

See yourself functioning as if you've already achieved your goal.

See yourself in the role you will be playing.

Feel what it is like to be you in that setting.

Visualize Yourself in a Setting Subjectively

Visualize the world as if you are looking at it through your eyes. For example, if you have a goal of being a public speaker, don't visualize yourself standing up on a stage. Rather, visualize an audience seated before you. In your mind's eye see the lectern in front of you. Imagine holding a microphone or perhaps walking freely about the stage with a cordless microphone. Imagine others who may be on the platform with you. Feel their presence. Look into the faces of audience members as they listen to you talk. How do they respond to you? What looks do you see on their faces?

The more you begin to see yourself in this role—not objectively, but subjectively—the more comfortable you will be with your new identity as a public speaker.

Do you want to be on television in some capacity—perhaps as a news anchor or an actor? Don't visualize yourself as if you are sitting in your living room and watching yourself on your TV set. Rather, visualize yourself being on a set and looking into the lens of a camera. See the director giving you directions to move from camera to camera. Respond to the others who are on the set with you.

Whatever you begin to visualize in this way, work to bring your visualization into clear focus with as many details as possible. Imagine not only the way things look to you, if you can see, but also the way things sound, feel, smell, and even taste. Internalize these sensations. Become comfortable with them. Your subconscious will begin to want to perform at that level and in those situations, and will send motivating signals to your conscious mind.

My Desire for a Gold Medal

Weight lifting was not something I considered an end unto itself. My real goal was to be strong and, in being strong, to be a winner. Being strong and winning were goals I had had for some time, even before my diagnosis of juvenile macular degeneration.

A short time after I began lifting seriously, I met a former AAU national weight-lifting champion, and he started training me a little. As I discussed in a previous chapter, a mentor will come your way as you move toward your dream. I didn't seek this man out, but our paths crossed, and I took advantage of everything he could teach me.

At the time I didn't realize fully how many people were taking me under their wings. I was pretty naive at seventeen, and it never occurred to me to question how things were paid or why certain things were happening to me. I went to an athletic club for years and never paid anything, and it never occurred to me once during that time that somebody else was paying my bill. I never paid this coach anything, and it never occurred to me at the time that somebody else had. Eventually, I put the pieces together and realized that much of my way during those years was paid for by a man who had been very successful in the oil business. He had been a neighbor of ours, and I had known him for years. He worked out at this particular club, and he was the one who first invited me to go with him to the club.

There was a separate section in the club where competitive weight lifters worked out, and this man took me into that section and introduced me. After I could no longer drive and getting to the club became a major problem for me, this man invited me to come over and work out at his house. He had converted his garage into a gym and had bought thousands of dollars' worth of world-class equipment to outfit his private gym. He traveled quite a bit, and he said to me, "I don't use this equipment very much. Why don't you take this key and let yourself in whenever you want to lift?" So I worked out in his home for two years. It never dawned on me at the time that this man rarely was there when I showed up to lift weights every other day. I rarely saw him use all the expensive equipment he had purchased.

Later, when I went to various weight-lifting meets across the nation, and eventually competed for the national championship, this man was often in the audience. He always said that he had some business in the area and that he had just dropped in to watch. It wasn't until years later that I realized all he had done for me!

He was one of the original oil guys, a hard-core wildcatter. He wasn't the kind of man who gave anything to anybody, and I don't think he would ever admit to me, or perhaps even to himself, that he had done so much for me or that he had gone out of his way to encourage me at competitions. But so be it. *I* recognize now that he did more for me than I would ever have asked for or could have imagined.

The first time I went to the national AAU championships, I came in third. Up to that point, I had won every meet in which I had competed. Suddenly, I was third best. I was beaten even before I went out to lift.

Don't Be Defeated in the Warm-Up Room!

In the warm-up room, I watched the two guys who eventually beat me as they worked out. They had been lifting weights for ten years. They were great. They had access to the finest equipment and coaches and training programs. Both of them were shorter than I am—probably more like five ten or five eleven. When you pack 242 pounds into a smaller frame, you have more power. The muscles are shorter and bulkier. Plus, you don't have to lift the bar as far from the floor to the overhead position as you do when you are six four. Just their physical size and shape and presence were awesome to me. They intimidated me. I was convinced they'd beat me before I ever walked out into the competition area.

Oh, I visualized all right. I visualized them being numbers one and two. And sure enough, they were. My visualization was accurate!

The next year, I went back to the competitions with the full belief and visualization that this time, the gold medal was mine. Two months before the meet, I just *knew* that medal belonged to me. I visualized the lifts I was going to do to win it. I visualized that medal hanging around my neck. I didn't know what weight those guys were going to lift, but it really didn't make any difference to me. Whatever they lifted, I was going to lift more.

As far as I was concerned, I was going to Kansas City to lift a few bars and pick up my gold medal. I didn't give one thought to what kind of equipment my competitors had, how many coaches they had, how much experience they had, or what kind of training program they had been on. The gold medal belonged to *me*!

Being firmly convinced that the gold medal was mine didn't make me lax in any way. In truth, I probably worked a little harder because that's what I visualized a champion would do. I expected the best from myself because I was going to wear the gold medal that said I was the best.

When you catch a glimpse of where you're going and how life is going to be once you've arrived there, getting there doesn't seem nearly as difficult a challenge as when you are struggling and working hard and have no idea where you're going or why.

I once heard a man talk about a football game. He was a big Dallas Cowboys fan, and a friend came over to his house at his invitation to watch a Cowboys game with him. The Cowboys were on the two-yard line with only thirteen seconds to go, and they needed to score to win the game.

This man's friend said, "I don't get it. You're the biggest Cowboys fan I know and yet here you sit, unemotional and totally calm. You aren't screaming at the TV set. You don't seem the least bit upset that your team might lose if they don't make this touchdown in the last few seconds of the game!"

The man said, "Oh, this game isn't live. I taped this game earlier. I'm watching the replay. I know they're going to score and they're going to win."

That's the way I felt in competing for the national championship the second time. I knew I was going to win, so I didn't get real emotional or uptight about the competition. I didn't worry or sweat about what to do to be a champion. I acted like the champion I already saw myself as being. I went into that championship in the best shape I've ever been in, physically and psychologically.

I was hard as a rock, a world-class athlete. At that moment in my life, I was probably one of the ten strongest guys in the entire world. I was competing in the weight range of guys 220 to 242—the heavyweight class—and at 242 pounds I was the heaviest you could be and not be in the "unlimited" or superheavyweight class. That's the ideal condition to be in!

But then . . .

Just a couple of weeks before the meet, I broke three fingers. When you lift and you pop the bar over, it rests on the palm of your hand. But if the bar pops over too far, it comes to rest against your fingers, and that isn't good. When you are lifting weights greater than four hundred pounds, the four hundred pounds can literally snap your finger bones. That's what happened to me.

Almost immediately, my vision of wearing a gold medal took a serious hit. My chances of winning didn't look good at all. And still

I hung on to my visualization. I knew that was my gold medal, broken fingers or not.

The day finally came for me to pick up my medal. My broken fingers were taped together, and off I went to the competition.

When you lift weights in competition, the person who is doing the lifting decides what weight he wants to lift. You have three chances to lift that weight. If you don't do it, you're finished. If you do lift the weight you've called out, you can say you want to lift again at a higher weight.

The weights always go up. So, for example, if you say you want to lift at 400 and you lift that weight, and then I come up to the bar, I need to say that I'm going to lift at 401 or 410 or 420. If I succeed, the guy after me is going to have to lift at an even greater weight than I lifted. And so it goes.

My coach said, "Listen, let's ensure ourselves of a top ten finish. I think your fingers will hold together, so let's name a high weight and you lift it and then that will be that."

I said, "No, that's my gold medal hanging over there. I know I don't have many lifts in my hand today, and yet I am going to have to lift more weight than anybody else here to get my medal. What I want to do is wait until everybody else is finished lifting, and then I'll name a higher weight and go out and have three shots at it."

I knew that lifting at any lower weights, and then having to lift again, would only sap my strength and hurt my hand even more.

So I sat there and waited and waited and waited. Finally, everybody was finished. It was my turn to announce the weight I wanted to lift.

When you come out to compete, you face three judges. Each judge watches your lift to make sure that your form is proper and that you lock your arms totally in the lift position. Once a judge has determined that the lift has been completed in proper form, he gives you the signal of a white light. If the judge determines that something is improper about your lift, he gives you a red light. Once all three of the lights come on, you can drop the bar. You need two of the three lights to be white in order to have the lift count.

Well, by that time, my eyesight had degenerated to the point that I couldn't see the lights, so my coach would call to me when the time was appropriate for me to drop the bar.

The first lift I made, I got the bar up, but because my three fingers were taped, I couldn't get my left arm extended fast enough. I got three red lights. My coach called for me to let go of the bar. He came over and said, "No lift, Jim. You've got two more shots." The second lift, I had two red lights and one white one. Again, no lift. My fingers were hurting, and they were starting to swell.

I had three minutes to make a third attempt. I remember thinking, *This must be the time I get it right because that's my gold medal and I've got only one try left.*

I lifted the third time. And I got two white lights! Sure enough, that gold medal was mine!

Afterward, I went backstage into the warm-up room, and there were the two guys who had beaten me the year before. I watched them a while and came to the conclusion that they really were better than I was. They were better than I probably would ever be. Except for that one day. I wore the gold medal, and they didn't.

Visualize Your Award Ceremony

I don't know what you want to be and do in your life. It's your decision. It's your dream. It's your destiny. It's your life.

But whatever you want to be and do, visualize yourself being and doing that at the very peak level of performance. Visualize your award ceremony in whatever field you may be in. See yourself being handed the trophy, picking up the plaque, having the title placed next to your name. Envision yourself as being the best at whatever you choose to do.

If there is no formal award ceremony for the dream you have, imagine one.

Let the winning of that award compel you to greater effort, greater skill, and greater involvement with life than you have imagined to this point. To win the top honor, you're going to have to be in top form. To be in top form, you're going to have to live a disciplined, focused life.

It's possible.

Because whatever you see as your future reality, you can have. It's within your grasp if you'll only reach for it with all you've got.

6

FOCUSING

*Define your success
in terms of what you really
want to be, do, and have.*

How do I define success? I don't. At least not for anybody other than myself. Success to you is whatever *you* say it is.

Never, never, never let somebody else define your success for you. Only you can determine what you want to be, do, and have. Only you can determine what will truly bring you satisfaction and a sense of fulfillment in life.

The closest I can come to defining success is to describe it for you as your destiny. Destiny is what you believe you were put on this earth to be and do, and as a part of your being and doing, what you are destined to have, receive, win, own, or accomplish. Your sense of destiny is directly linked to your set of beliefs and what you value in life.

The key question to ask yourself is this: Why do I believe I'm here on the earth? The answer to that question is going to come as you take a look at what you believe about God, yourself, and other people. It's related to what you believe to be true. It's directly related to what you perceive as being your unique talents, abilities, skills, personality traits, and aptitudes. What you value is always an expression of what you love and what you believe is most worthy of love.

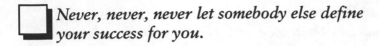
Never, never, never let somebody else define your success for you.

I can't and won't tell you what to believe.

Or what to love.

Or what to hold as truth.

I know in my life what I believe, love, and hold to be true. You must do the same for your life. If you don't come to these conclusions on your own, and as part of your process of self-discovery, what you believe, love, and hold to be true is not going to motivate you.

Neither am I going to tell you who you are. I can tell you that you are unique, a one-of-a-kind person, a distinctive and purposeful creation. Nobody else has what you have, can do what you can do, sees the world from your vantage point, has your contacts and relationships, or has your particular set of personality traits and background. The point is, only you truly have a good bead on *you*. Others may be helpful to you as you discover more of your potential and abilities, but in the end, you must define yourself and know yourself. No other person can know you fully. Only God knows you better than you know yourself, and as far as I'm concerned, it's only as you and God talk that over that you can draw conclusions about what He knows that you don't.

Ultimately, then, your destiny is *your* destiny. It's your purpose for living. It's distinctive and unique. It's an unfolding glorious and exciting mystery, and one you are challenged to pursue to the end with all your energy, strength, and ability—in other words, with all your heart, mind, and soul!

Consider Your Reason for Being

The people I've met who have achieved great success in their lives have had an inner sense of destiny. They all hold this in common: They believe that they are on this earth for a reason, and their reason for living is to do the thing that they are doing. Thus, they feel worthy of the rewards that come with their having done what they were created to do.

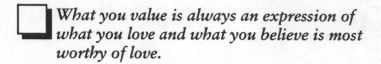

What you value is always an expression of what you love and what you believe is most worthy of love.

What do you believe you were placed on this earth to do? If you don't have an answer to that question, search for an answer. Explore your ability and aptitudes. Study your heart. Think about what causes you to be filled with enthusiasm. How would you like to see the world changed, and why?

Your destiny may very well flow from your answer to one or more of these questions:

1. What are you *gifted* to do?
2. What do you *want* to do?
3. What can you hardly *wait* to do?
4. What do you firmly believe *needs* to be done?

You can start with an answer to any one of these questions, but as you develop your unique sense of destiny, you'll likely discover that you will be able to answer all four of them with the one destiny dream that's right for you.

Before you can truly become a success—from the inside out, and not just in your bank account or investment portfolio—you have to discover what you believe is important in life and, very personally, what is important in and for your life.

I meet many people who seem to be treading water in their lives.

Every swimmer needs to learn this skill. It can be a means of survival. Certainly, it's important if you are required to swim a long distance and need to be able to stop periodically to rest and to regain your bearings. But treading water is a pretty stationary activity. In essence, you are standing still in the water. And many people are like that, in the water and moving their arms and legs, but not going anywhere. They're waiting for their ships to come into port from a faraway land, laden with exotic riches, even though they've never sent out a rowboat.

Making a Concrete Set of Desires and Dreams

How do you go about defining your personal destiny? You begin by getting to the core of your dreams—by coming to that secret place in your heart—about something you want. Actually, *want* is too weak a word. You've got to *desire* it. And you have to desire it a lot. As a friend of mine has said, "You've got to want it R-E-A-L bad."

That something you have stuck in the deep crevice of your soul is uniquely yours, but everybody has something in that place in the heart. That something is the essence of the destiny for your life. The difficulty for most people is that they've never fully explored what they want to get out of life, accomplish in life, or do with their lives. And because they've never come to the point of saying, "This is who I am destined to be and this is what I am destined to do," they eventually give up exploring what their destiny might be.

> *Ultimately your destiny is your destiny. It's your purpose for living.*

Have you ever gone window-shopping when you had no money? That can be a very frustrating experience. But it's only frustrating if you believe that the things you are looking at and desiring are beyond the realm of possibility for you. If you believe that you can own the things someday, window-shopping can be fun. You'll probably have a blast because you'll be looking with the attitude that you are engaging in solid consumer research so that when you have the means, you'll know where to go for the best quality at the best price.

I see people who are window-shopping with their lives. They observe various levels of success, and they are frustrated that they aren't experiencing that kind of success. Why? Because they don't truly believe they can have such success. People who believe that they are on their way to a high level of success are rarely envious of others with success. Rather, they regard those people as role models or as sources of inspiration that someday they, too, will be walking in similar shoes.

Ask yourself, How do I feel about really successful people? The answer will give you a clue about your expectations for your life. Ask yourself, too, How do I define a really successful person? You'll have a big clue about what you truly want to be and how you truly want to live.

To one person, the truly successful person might be a missionary living a meager but spiritually full life on the outskirts of nowhere, smuggling Bibles into places they aren't legally supposed to go.

To another person, the truly successful person might be someone who has amassed a fortune that has been turned into a foundation to help people in need.

To yet another person, the truly successful person might be a parent or a teacher or a physician or a cancer researcher or an inventor.

Success is how you define it. The successful person is the one you hold to be successful. Success is living out your destiny.

Let me suggest to you a way to get started on this quest for something that you truly want to do in and with your life. Take a sheet of paper and make three columns labeled "Be," "Do," and "Have." Then write as quickly as you can everything that you have ever thought in your life that you'd like to be, do, or have. List at least fifty things in each category. That may sound like a lot to you, but most people can get to one hundred easily and quickly.

Consider these examples:

- I'd like to be able to run five miles.
- I'd like to write a novel.
- I'd like to meet the president of the United States.
- I'd like to be president of my own company.
- I'd like to be a husband (or wife).
- I'd like to own a Rolls Royce.
- I'd like to be able to give away $1 million to charity.

You can probably make this list in an hour or two. They could be the most valuable hours you have spent in a long time, perhaps in your entire life. Let your imagination soar. Remember your childhood dreams. Remember your goals and dreams as you headed off to college or as you started your first job. Think big. Don't put any limits on yourself. The only stipulation is this: You've got to want this, and it has to be a personal dream—not something that you think other people want you to do or what other people might want to do in their lives.

And then take a look at that list with some cold, hard objectivity. You may want to set your list aside for a day and come back to it the next evening, or perhaps make your list one weekend and then come back to it the next. I'm not that patient, but you may be. Some people can become objective about their lists very quickly. For others, it takes a little time and distance.

As you take a second look at your list, keep in mind these three phrases: "most important to you," "most challenging," and "in line with your values."

Most Important to You

When you take this second look at your list, focus on at least one thing that seems to be the most important item in each category. You may want to define *important* as most significant, most meaningful, most inspiring, most rewarding, most fulfilling, or most satisfying.

This is the point where your values, your personality, and your innate traits really come into play. If you put two people's lists next to each other, you are likely to find a few similarities. But if you can put your list next to the list of another person and find that they are virtually identical, and you both highlight the same thing in each category as being the most important, one of you isn't being honest.

No two people have precisely the same set of dreams and goals for themselves. Why? Because no two people are alike.

The ultimate point I'm making here is this: The definition of *important* must be your definition. What is important to you?

I could put "find a cure for multiple sclerosis" on my list of things I'd like to do in my life, but that wouldn't be an honest answer for me. I think finding a cure for multiple sclerosis would be a very noble thing for a person to do. This disease needs to be eradicated from our world. But working in a research lab isn't my forte. As a businessman, I'm not geared in any particular way toward wanting to invest money toward that particular cure. And again, not because I don't think it's a worthy cause. It isn't in my area of interest, expertise, experience, or desire.

If you talk about finding a cure for juvenile macular degeneration, I can get interested. Not as a scientist, but as a potential funder.

And if you talk about finding a means of restoring sight to a person who has lost sight, I'm even *more* interested.

You may say, "Well, Stovall, that sounds very self-centered."

Yes. It is.

And that's the way life is. As much as we may want to sound completely unselfish or other-centered in our lives, we aren't. We can never be. And frankly, I don't think we were designed to be. You were born in a particular circumstance, with particular parents and other adult "influencers," with a particular personality, and a particular set of propensities to succeed (talents, abilities, aptitudes, whatever name you want to use for the raw material with which you were born). The stuff that makes you uniquely you is going to lead you to move in a particular direction that is going to be uniquely fulfilling and rewarding to you. That's the way it's meant to be, in my opinion.

It's not up to you to orchestrate human society as a whole. Leave that up to God. It's only up to you to play your particular instrument in life's orchestra to the very best of your ability. And the starting point is to ask, So what's that instrument going to be? Some are going to choose the tuba. Others are going to choose the flute. Both are valuable instruments. It takes practice to learn both. But you're going to have a propensity toward choosing one over the other. And that's okay. Give yourself permission to be self-absorbed and self-centered in this exercise. It's the only way I know for you to come to grips with what your destiny—your central dream and goal in life—is likely to be.

It's tough for many people to zero in on their number one choice of most important without taking into consideration the opinions of others. Most of us have been so brainwashed through the years—not necessarily in a malicious or intentional way, but brainwashed nonetheless—to think in terms of what other people set as the standards of excellence or even the norms for our lives. In the end, only the choices you make for yourself, by yourself, and ultimately in the best—as in finest and most noble—interests of your life are going to be the choices that are most satisfying and meaningful to you.

Is there a valuable heirloom in your family? Is there something out of all your parents' or grandparents' possessions that you hope to inherit someday? That thing may be a worn-out quilt that your great-great-grandmother brought from the Old Country. Another person might not give two dollars for it at a flea market. But that doesn't make the quilt any less valuable to you.

That's the way you need to view your dreams and goals. What you consider to be valuable and important for your life may not be at all what another person considers to be valuable and important.

Most Challenging

The thing you choose as the most important item on your lists of things to be and do—and even on your list of things to have—is likely to be the thing you find most challenging.

If you aren't challenged by anything on your list, you may be suffering from exhaustion, deep-seated fear, or some type of depression. If that's the case, this exercise may be valuable to you in pointing out that fact. Get some help. Get some rest. Get to the place where you aren't so frazzled or ripped apart by life that you no longer are challenged by anything. A healthy person is going to be challenged by something!

What on your list causes your heart to beat just a little bit faster at the thought? What causes a smile to come to your face but also your mind to start spinning just a little faster?

A genuine destiny for your life will always compel you to get out of your comfort zone. It will challenge you.

As long as you are content to live in your comfort zone, you are going to have a certain amount of disappointment and dissatisfaction. Why? Because a key ingredient that keeps you in your comfort zone is fear—fear of failure, fear of embarrassment, fear of rejection. Fear is debilitating. It holds you back. It drains you of energy. It locks you in. And that held-down, drained-out, locked-in feeling results in a general sense of dissatisfaction.

You may *say* you are satisfied with your life (you may even *think* you are), but if you aren't growing, aren't pursuing a challenge, aren't risking something, I don't believe you can be truly satisfied. Deep down inside, there's going to be a space within you crying out for something more, something new, something better. It may be covered up by layers of insults, failures, put-downs, rejections, or negative thoughts, but that desire for something more is going to be there.

On the other hand, the person moving toward something, trying something new, pursuing something, or learning something is very often deeply satisfied in life, even if he or she has little to show for the effort or has achieved very little thus far. That person has a sense of direction, of motion, of growth. And that is satisfying, rewarding, and fulfilling. It gives meaning to a day.

You may say, "Well, Stovall, aren't we supposed to be content with what we have?"

No, I don't think so. I think we can be content in who we are—content in our relationship with God, content in our sense of value and self-esteem, content in our understanding of our strengths, abilities, and drives. But I don't believe we are ever to be content in terms of sitting on our laurels and saying, "Well, this is it. This is all I'm ever going to be, do, or have. I've arrived." The person who arrives, with that frame of mind, has cut himself or herself off. He has stunted his potential. She has short-circuited her best.

Contentment with our creation, and with our relationship with our Creator, is one thing. Contentment with what we are destined to create in life is something else. The former is the key to real inner peace. But the latter leads only to stagnation, disillusionment, and dissatisfaction.

In the end, the things that you choose as the most important things for you to be, to do, and to have in this life should be things that scare you a little bit. They should cause you to quake in your boots ever so slightly at the thought: *Could I really do that? Might I really have that? Would it really be possible for me to be that?*

The answer, of course, that I hope you will come to is, "Yes." But even so, the choice should be a bigger choice than your current ability can achieve.

Let me repeat that: Your choice should be a bigger choice than your current ability can achieve.

If you can achieve—be, do, or have—what you are currently envisioning without learning something new, changing in any way, growing as a person, or taking any kind of forward-looking risk, your choice isn't destiny. It's a current option.

There's a big difference. Your destiny will always lie in front of you. It will grow and develop as you do, but it will always lie just beyond your reach, calling to you and challenging you and pulling you forward and upward in your life. If the choice you have made is something that you can go out and purchase today, or go out and do today, it isn't a challenge. It's an option you can choose to exercise. It isn't a dream.

> **Your destiny will always lie in front of you, challenging you and pulling you forward and upward in your life.**

Your dream for your life must have a dream element to it. It must be something that calls for you to extend yourself, to push yourself—and in that, to grow or change or develop in certain ways.

A true dream must be challenging! And because it is challenging, and because it is uniquely your dream or goal, it will be motivating. What supremely challenges you and also motivates you is your destiny.

We've somewhat backed into my definition of destiny, but I believe that's the way most of us come to our sense of destiny. We don't start out with a sense of destiny at age three and never stray from it. We come to that understanding after years of experience, including years of living within our skins, our personalities, our aptitudes, our families and circle of friends.

After you have made your lists of things you'd like to be, do, and have in life, and after you have circled the number one thing in each list that is most important and challenging to you, take a look at other top options. You may want to use a different color of pen or highlighter to mark two or three other things in each list that are important to you.

Weigh these choices carefully, and ask yourself several questions about them:

- Do I see a clustering effect? Do all of my top choices seem to be related in some way?
- Do I see ways in which what I want to be relates to what I want to do, and to what I want to have?

Look for connections. In the end, the elements of what you are, do, and have are so closely interwoven in your life that it may be difficult to separate your identity into distinct categories. You are what you have become. You are what you do. You are what you have.

You may see some linkages, however, between items you have chosen as being very important to you. Perhaps you'll gain new insight from the connections or see new ways in which you might capitalize your interests or combine them to create new entities. If that's the case, and if the relationship between two items is true and valid for you, you are likely to feel an even greater surge of creative energy in that area. Look for that to happen as you explore your desires.

In Line with Your Values

I once saw a little sign that read, "Is what you're living for worth dying for?"

Think about it for a moment. Are you spending your time, your energy, and your resources on the one thing in life that you would consider dying for? In reality, you are giving your life for something every hour of every day. You are pouring out your life's blood, your energy, your ideas and creativity, for some end goal. You are likely to be martyred for that thing, whether you have regarded it as true martyrdom or not.

Your values are going to come into play in choosing the things that are most important to you. What you consider to be worth dying for must be what you would desire to live for if you are going to live a congruent, highly fulfilling life.

If there's a discrepancy between what you think you should do with your life and what you choose to do, there's going to be conflict. That conflict will eat away at you.

Your choices about what are the most important things for you to be, do, and have must be in harmony with what you personally believe and have adopted as your values, ethics, and morals. Never leave the basics of who you are. Don't leave your roots; grow up out of them. Stay in touch with what is good about your past. And then move beyond your past into your future. If you cut yourself off from your roots, you'll always feel as if a part of you is missing.

Stay in tune with the basics of all you know to be and do. You'll never become too successful to be honest, to tell the truth, to be kind to people, to follow good business practices, to save money and invest money wisely, or to do and be anything that we know as virtuous, right, and solid.

Never discount the basics of your value system. Never discount your faith, or the beliefs that form the core of your being. Your values and beliefs are like firm footing for your soul. And they'll be firm footing all the way to the top of whatever success ladder you climb, and perhaps most important, they'll provide you with a solid foundation once you are there.

Limit Your Number of Choices

An exercise that I often use when I speak is what I call the numbers game. I whisper a number to a person and then ask him to repeat that number to the person next to him and so on until the number has made it through the entire group present—or perhaps down an entire row of people. If the number is a simple one, such as three or nineteen, the chances of that number emerging at the end of the chain are pretty high.

But if I whisper "five hundred eighteen billion, four hundred eighty-six million, three hundred twenty-seven thousand, two hundred seventeen, point three four," the chances of that number staying intact past two or three people are very low. Why? The 518,486,327,217.34 number is complicated! There are too many numbers to juggle.

In focusing your life and your dreams and goals on one, two, or three things that you desire to be, do, and have, you are also simplifying your life. The more focused you are, the easier it will be for you to stay focused, and the more likely it is that you will achieve your target.

"Be," "Do," and "Have" Are Three Stages

A final (but perhaps the most important) thing to recognize about your "be," "do," and "have" lists is that "be," "do," and "have" are likely sequential stages in your life.

When many people start out toward a successful life, they start with the "have" stage of dreams and goals. They want to have a new car, a new home, a new lifestyle, financial independence. And if they don't find the things coming to them very quickly in their pursuit of a new venture, they abandon ship and move on to another method, or they give up.

Don't start with the "have" stage. Start with "be."

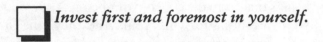 *Invest first and foremost in yourself.*

Invest first and foremost in yourself. *You* are your greatest asset. Your attitude, your intellect, your knowledge, your aptitudes, your experiences, your skills—these are the raw materials for doing. And doing eventually results in having.

Become the type of person you want to be. Start living in your habits, your thought life, your relationships with others, your emotions, and your spirit the type of life you define as successful. Set your goals for what you want to be, and then begin to be that person.

Out of what you want to be, you'll find the strength, energy, and ideas to do something. Since you are already a successful person in your habits and thinking, you will do that thing to the best of your ability, with great diligence, energy, creativity, and motivation.

When you work that way long enough, you can't help having material and tangible prosperity. You'll eventually have all the things you want and probably more.

I heard about a man who had grown up very poor. His big dream of "having" was just like that of many people I meet—to own a car and a house. But he was also a man of high principles and exceptional values. He determined that he would be a man of faith, committed to his church, and that he would work very hard at any opportunity that came his way. He had a tremendous love for missions, and no matter how much he made, a portion of his giving supported missionaries overseas.

A few years ago this man reached a stage where he had achieved substantial business success, and he came to the conclusion that he had too much prosperity. He is one of the few people I know who has reached that place! He said to himself, "I can't take care of all this prosperity. One of these homes or one of these cars I own is always needing something." So he gave what he considered to be his extra homes and cars to his children—and kept only two homes and four cars for himself and his wife. And then he decided to turn over his business ventures to his children and to devote himself to teaching, something he had long desired to do.

But do you know what happened? This man who had developed such strong character traits of being, and had such a long track record of doing, didn't know how to be or do anything that wasn't excellent. Before a year was over, the university where he taught permitted him to teach any course or conduct any seminar he wanted. So he developed a seminar series that was very successful at the university. The second year, the university loaned him out to other universities around the world—and they paid him handsomely for traveling to various nations to teach students and business executives the seminar course he had designed. In each place, the host university gave him a house to stay in and two cars—one for himself and one for his wife.

He said, "I can't seem to get away from having lots of houses and cars. But at least now I don't have to deal with their maintenance!"

Not only that, but when this man went to other nations, the religious denomination to which he belonged would soon discover that he was there. On weekends, this man spoke to people in congregations throughout the area in which he was staying. He became his own missionary, but one who didn't need any support.

When you invest first and foremost in who you want to be, and then give all of your being to what you dream of doing, the things you do will result in the rewards that will represent what you have desired to have.

I've never seen it fail.

7

INSPECTING
THE HEART

Choose to be
the best person you can be.

Greatness—like success, like destiny, like desire—is how *you* define it. There is no external definition of greatness.

If you desire to be the best maid who ever cleaned a hotel room, you will be great in your eyes each and every time you clean a hotel room to sparkling perfection.

If you desire to be the best parent who ever raised a child, you will have an inner knowing that you are great at what you do every time your child spontaneously says to you, "I love you, Dad," or "Thanks, Mom, for always being there."

Primarily because I'm on television regularly, a number of people I don't know will stop me when they see me and say, "You're doing a great job," or "That was a great interview," or "I think you're great."

I could get puffed up about that, but I try not to. I—perhaps more than anybody—am aware that if I came across as great on TV, a good portion of the credit likely goes to the camera operator, the editor of the tape, the director, one of the writers, or the wardrobe and makeup people.

What really matters to me is not someone else saying to me, "You did great." What really matters are the moments in the privacy of my thoughts that I can say to myself, *I did a good job today, I did my best today,* or *I feel as if I hit a home run today.*

And on the days when that is the summation I make to myself about my efforts, I know that these are the only accolades I need. Ultimately, knowing within myself that I've done a good job is all that matters.

If you set yourself up to live according to the praise of others, you'll never be satisfied unless you have their constant approval. And since none of us ever has the constant approval of others, you'll always be set up for a disappointment. If you live according to the praise of others, you'll never be better or think more of yourself than yesterday's press notices.

> **Put your head on your pillow at night and say, "I was the best person I could be today, and that's enough."**

The better approach, in my opinion, is to put your head on the pillow at night and say, "I was the best person I could be today. I did the best I could possibly have done today with what I had, and that's enough."

There's No Substitute for Getting Squared Away

I often stayed up very late in college. That was the best time to study since it was quiet. And it took me longer to read through my assignments than it took most of the guys. I had to take a lot of breaks since seeing the words on the page took intense concentration. So I wandered around the dorm at night, and one of the people I visited was an older man who was in charge of keeping our dorm clean. His name was Jimmy Carter.

I can't imagine a worse job than cleaning the rest rooms in a dorm where 660 college guys live, but that's the job Jimmy had. And he often told people with pride, "We have the cleanest rest rooms in America." He did his job well and he knew it.

Many nights, Jimmy worked down in the room where he kept his supplies. And in my wandering around, I'd visit him. He would always say the same thing to me, "Boy, are you getting squared away here?"

I'd ask, "What are you talking about, Jimmy?"

He'd say, "You have to buckle down. You've got to get squared away."

Jimmy had been in the navy, and apparently, they're big on buckling down and getting squared away. Anyway, before each test, Jimmy would ask me, "Are you ready for that test? Are you squared away?"

One night I found him in the room where he kept his supplies, and he invited me to come into that room for the first time. The walls of the small space were lined with pictures of guys who had lived in the dorm. I said, "Jimmy, who are all these guys?" He said, "Oh, they are just some of my boys who have been here." Then he began pointing out various ones. "This one," Jimmy said, "is going to make it onto the Supreme Court someday. I think he's got a shot at that. This one owns a bank. This one's a college professor. That one's a preacher."

Then Jimmy looked at me and said, "They were no better or worse than you. They just got themselves squared away."

Well, for the next four years, Jimmy helped me get squared away. He came to my graduation, and then I lost touch with him.

A few years ago I was visiting a nursing home in Tulsa, and they rolled somebody up behind me in a wheelchair. He said, "Boy, I've been reading about you, and I think you're about to get squared away."

■ *Being squared away is a good thing to be!*

I said, "Jimmy Carter?" He said, "Absolutely." We greeted each other like long-lost friends. Then as the nurse wheeled him away, she said, "You made it onto his wall."

I have an Emmy Award, a gold medal, and lots of other awards. But one of the greatest things I'll ever achieve is that I made it onto Jimmy Carter's wall. I got squared away.

Today, my understanding of getting squared away is pretty good. I know that it means getting your life in balance and being the best you can be. It means being tenacious—buckling down—and being single-minded and energetic in the pursuit of your destiny. Being squared away is a good thing to be!

Being squared away means, in part, that you have character; you have personal integrity.

Integrity Is Vital in Being, Doing, and Having

Integrity is being who you are at all times and with all people and in all situations, doing what you say you are going to do, and having what lines up with your values and beliefs and *not* having what doesn't. If you don't have integrity, you'll ultimately lose anything you acquire because people won't trust you. If they don't trust you, they won't work with you, buy from you, or give to you. If enough people stop having a relationship with you, your enterprise collapses, no matter what kind of enterprise it may be.

> *Focus more on who you are than on what you do. Ultimately, that's where your value lies.*

I worked for a company that sold a whey-based beverage, a milk substitute product. I became a distributor while I was still a college student, and I went to the top of that organization and owned two distribution centers. However, a lack of integrity and stability on the part of the company leaders destroyed the company itself. Even so, I gained more than I lost through that experience because I learned some basic things about selling and about working with other people. And above all, I learned that if a person doesn't have both competency and integrity, he is at risk and is liable to lose everything he has achieved.

After my experience with that company, I was obviously gun-shy about entering a relationship with another direct-sales organization. And then through working on several corporate boards and speaking at various conventions, I met some people who had both competency and integrity. Their product was a good one. It did what it was designed to do and worked for people in the way it was promised to work. And I began an association with them to help them with their marketing.

Anybody who enters a sales arena enters it knowing that the bottom line is one of money. People go into business for one reason: to make money. There is nothing wrong with that, and I become irritated with people who think otherwise. Nothing that is truly good in our culture happens without funds being expended by somebody. Certainly, families and friendships and other personal relationships are rooted in something other than money—and rightly so. But business is business, and we enter into business arrangements—whether as an employee, a consultant, an owner, a partner, or a consumer—for purposes related to money.

If you're dealing in business, competency and integrity become acutely important because people don't want to purchase a bad product or bad service. And they certainly don't want to deal with ignorant, unskilled, or dishonest people. I don't. You don't. Nobody does.

Focus more on who you are than on what you do. Ultimately, that's where your value lies. Who are you really? What do you value? How do you live your life? What types of relationships do you have? What are the traits and qualities that make you *you*? In the end, these things are the only things. Who you are will determine what you do, far more than what you do will determine who you become and are.

> *Having integrity is doing the right thing in a situation, even if nobody is watching and nobody will ever know.*

Having integrity is doing the right thing in a situation, even if nobody is watching and nobody will ever know. Abraham Lincoln said it well: "Integrity, had it not been invented as the right thing to do, should be invented as the quickest way to succeed."

Integrity, honesty, consistency, persistence, accountability—these traits make a person successful as an individual, regardless of what that person does. In my opinion, they are the finest goals of being.

Do you see yourself as that kind of person? As far as I'm concerned, "being a person of integrity" should be at the top of your dream-and-goal list in the "Be" column.

Give Each Person Your Very Best

A good friend of mine, Dr. Paul Whitman—who serves on the board of Narrative Television Network (NTN)—is an anesthesiologist in Dallas. On most days at the hospital, he is involved in several operations.

Years ago, while I still had some of my sight, I asked my friend if I could go into the operating room with him one time, just to experience what an operating room was like. He agreed and suited me up in a cap, gown, mask, gloves, foot coverings—the whole nine yards—and then we approached the first patient so my friend the anesthesiologist could prepare him for surgery. The man was still wide awake, and while my friend began working, I happened to ask him how many surgeries were on his schedule that particular day. He said, "Seven."

The patient looked at him and said, "Doc, even though you're going to be doing seven of these today, this one here is real important to me."

That's an excellent perspective to have toward every person you meet. Nobody wants to know how you've succeeded with other people or what you've done for other people. Each person cares only about the here and now. Each person wants to know what you are going to do for her and how you are going to perform in her presence and what you are going to give to her.

Each person wants to receive your best. Each person you encounter wants to know he is the only person you have in mind when you are talking to him. It doesn't matter to him that you will deal with a hundred people in a given day. It matters only how you deal with him. A big part of having integrity is giving your very best to each person, no matter who he is or what you are giving.

Treat each person you meet with the utmost respect and kindness. Develop that as a habit.

At the same time, seek the very best of a person. Take the best from everyone. Find the people who are the best in the world at what they do and watch them, listen to them, and mingle with them as often as you can.

My wife, Crystal, and I travel quite a bit to hear performances by gifted musicians or to attend plays being performed by brilliant actors. There's something marvelous about experiencing the work of someone at the top of his profession or at the peak of her performance.

And always, *always*, ALWAYS be truthful with other people. Don't exaggerate—it's a form of lying. Don't hedge—it's a form of deceit. Don't promise something you can't do or can't produce— that's falsehood.

Treat people fairly. Give them good service and a good product for the price you've agreed on. Discount prices, but never discount customers. Give your employees and your colleagues the rewards that are due them.

Surround Yourself with Good People

I travel a lot these days, but I never travel alone. Usually, my associate Michael, my partner Kathy, or my wife, Crystal, travels with me. I'll also travel with Clover, Kelly, Dorothy, or one of many other valued NTN associates.

I wouldn't dream of leaving my office, getting into a limo, going to the airport, and flying to Cincinnati and back with a casual friend or business acquaintance. It isn't that there's anything wrong with that person. I just wouldn't do it—for the same reason I wouldn't let that person take out my appendix. That person isn't trained for the job.

The people who travel with me know how to send me signals that allow me to function relatively normally. Nevertheless, my mobility isn't the greatest. I run into things; I fall down; I bang into things. Being bruised is part of my life.

Even more important than having a good working-together relationship with others is having a mutuality of dreams and goals. If you decide to have a partner in your life—whether it's a spouse or a business partner, or perhaps a spouse who is a business partner— both of you must want to reach the same goals in the area of life that you mutually share. Don't link yourself to a person who doesn't want to be what you want to be, go where you want to go, do what you want to do, or have what you want to have. If you do, each will be at constant odds with the other.

Communicate openly and fully with your proposed partner early in your relationship. Share your heart with the other person as fully as you can. And then do together only what the two of you can mutually agree to do with 100 percent commitment.

Some spouses agree not to pursue the same courses for much of their individual lives, charting a fairly narrow segment of overlap in their lives that they call a marriage. That's fine if that's what both agree to have as a marriage.

Other people need more mutuality in a marriage. That's fine, too, as long as it's what both agree to have as a marriage.

The same goes for a business relationship. Some business partners have very little overlap of their tasks and virtually no overlap in their social or personal lives. Others have a great deal. Either way is fine as long as both agree that is what they want in the business.

Above all, seek to align yourself with people who have your value structure. You will be influenced by them. Choose to be influenced by people of the highest moral character.

Give Away the Credit

If you have surrounded yourself with people who are competent and have integrity—people who are going in the same direction you are going and who have a like set of values—you should find it easy to credit these people often and generously. Appreciate people who help you. Openly acknowledge their contribution and their assistance. Be grateful for their ideas and hard work.

I've discovered one thing about giving the credit away, and it's this: You can't give away credit fast enough. It always comes back to you.

Getting credit shouldn't be your motive for giving away credit. Even so, the principle holds true that you get back in multiplied form what you give away to others. When you thank others, openly acknowledge others, and give respect and dignity to the efforts of others, you are, in effect, giving value and worth to others. The net perception is that these worthy, valuable people are with you.

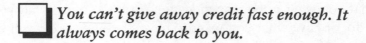 *You can't give away credit fast enough. It always comes back to you.*

You didn't get to your present level of success on your own. Others have helped you, even if you have never stopped to face up to that reality. When you openly admit to yourself, and to others, that you haven't done it all, can't be it all, and don't deserve it all, something excellent happens inside you and in your relationships with other people. There's a mutuality of appreciation. There's a warmth of friendship. There's a sharing of success that boosts the success level of all involved.

Have you ever seen a lock system in operation—the kind that exists in the Panama Canal or the Great Lakes? Ships rise dozens of feet in the course of moving from one body of water to the next, but how do they do it? Nobody raises the ship per se. Rather, somebody raises the tide—the water level. As the water level rises, the ship automatically rises. That's the way it works with sharing the credit. The entire tide of optimism, appreciation, and energy around you increases.

Perhaps because I am blind, I am keenly aware of the help others give me. When I speak, I always try to acknowledge the people who are with me because I am acutely sensitive to the fact that I couldn't be up on the stage speaking without their assistance. Being on television or giving a speech is the easiest part of what I do. Just getting to the studio or to the stage is the hard part! I couldn't get from place to place, or even coordinate the suit and tie and shoes and socks that I'm wearing, without the aid of other people.

Start praising people around you. Voice your appreciation for them. Acknowledge their contributions, and say "thank you" for what they have done for you and perhaps for your company, your department, or your team.

Every quarterback knows that he doesn't win a game by himself. Most quarterbacks have a high regard for the front line that defends them against would-be tacklers. They know that other people make them look good. Those who openly acknowledge that fact are those we most admire because we see in them graciousness and generosity that are compelling.

Every parent knows that she hasn't raised her child alone, even if she happens to be a single parent. The wise parent openly acknowledges the assistance that others have given, be they teachers, pastors, neighbors, friends of the family, aunts and uncles, grandparents. That parent isn't devaluing what she has done. Rather, that parent is opening the child's eyes to see that other people will *always* play a valuable role in his life. She is teaching her child to respect and value others. And along the way, that parent is also likely to enjoy even greater support, cooperation, and positive participation in the parenting process.

Every line supervisor in every factory in this country knows, deep inside, that he looks good because of the efforts of his people. Openly acknowledge that fact! Thank those who put in a good day's work. Applaud their efforts. Speak well of people who support the team effort. In sharing the credit with others, you won't lose the respect of your staff or workers. You'll gain it.

Do What You Do with Sincerity

Finally, do what you do with sincerity. Be genuine. That's really the ultimate measure when it comes to finding your sense of destiny and walking in it. It's been said by countless people through the ages, but it bears saying again: Be true to yourself.

Some time ago I was in Hawaii to be one of several speakers to a large group. After the event, people gathered as they usually do to request autographs or to speak personally with those of us who made presentations.

As the crowd began to disperse, one of the other speakers walked with me backstage and said, "I've got to ask you one thing."

"Sure," I said. "What is it?"

"How do you do that sincere thing you do?"

I was stunned. I said, "Listen, I'm not an actor. I can't lie very well. I tend to show my emotions pretty plainly. When I interview people on TV, I never talk to them beforehand because if I do, I'll know what they are going to say and I'll come across as bored. And it *looks* like I'm bored! What I say I genuinely mean."

He seemed surprised. And I'm sure that what I said didn't help him much. But I was also surprised. I can't imagine doing something that I don't believe in doing.

Ask yourself, Do I believe in the cause I'm working to promote? Do I believe in the product that I'm helping to produce? Do I believe in the message my company or organization is making? Do I believe in the people with whom I'm working? If you don't, there will be a shred of lie in everything you do, even if you don't intend it.

Engage Daily in Self-Accountability

Don't be ashamed of your values or beliefs. Openly embrace them. Values are valuable. Choose to operate out of a strong system of values and beliefs.

> *Choose to operate out of a strong system of values and beliefs.*

Your values determine your character, and they set a framework for the choices you make as well as a framework for evaluating your success. In other words, your values provide the framework for self-accountability. Your personal value structure will tell you that you have done well, or done poorly, based on the decisions of any particular day.

Each night before I go to bed, I review the day I've just lived. And I evaluate it. I say about various things I've done or said, and about the choices I've made, "That was good. That was great. That wasn't so hot." In appraising my actions and decisions, I'm able to make midcourse corrections as I pursue my goals. In appraising my deeds of a day, I can close my eyes and have a sense of accomplishment, of being one step closer to the fulfillment of my destiny on earth.

At one point in my life, I set a goal of losing 150 pounds. I forced myself to be accountable to myself on a daily basis. Each day I would confront myself and ask,

- Did you eat the right things today, Stovall? In the right amounts?
- Did you exercise today, Jim?
- Did you get enough rest today?
- Did you weigh yourself today?

There wasn't anybody else who wanted me to lose 150 pounds as much as I wanted to lose those pounds for myself. I reinforced that desire each day by forcing myself to be accountable to myself.

If there were an eleventh commandment and I could choose what it would be, I'd choose "thou shalt not kid thyself." Perhaps a more formal way of saying that would be "thou shalt not lie to thyself." Either way, the point is that we need to be honest with ourselves first and foremost. If we aren't, we have no basis for being honest with other people.

Accountability isn't limited to what we do. It extends to who we are. It's intricately interwoven with what we hold as values.

In the story of creation in the Bible, we read that at the end of each day of creation, God looked and said that what He had done was "good." He evaluated His work. We are wise to do the same.

I don't believe that God really cared very much if Adam and Eve thought their creation was good. I don't think He cared much if the birds thought He had done a good job in making them, or the fish thought He had done a good job in their creation. No. He was the sole judge of His work.

That's pretty much where we find ourselves at the end of each day, too. For the most part, it doesn't really matter what others think of our decisions, our work, our effort, our motives, our accomplishments. We alone know the full importance and consequences of what we have done. We stand before God on an individual basis, and we are called to evaluate what we have done, in our own eyes, and according to the set of beliefs and values that we hold to be true.

It's nice when other people applaud us. It's nice when someone gives us a compliment, says "thank you," or gives a word of appreciation or encouragement about something we've done or said. But in the end, our evaluation of our deeds counts the most. And most of us make that evaluation based on what we believe and value in the spiritual, or the inner, realm of our lives.

Let me give you an example. If you truly value people, and you want to do everything that you can to help them physically, materially, emotionally, psychologically, and spiritually, you are going to look at your day's work and evaluate closely the things that you have done to help people. You are going to be able to review your day and say, "I did this, and it was a good thing to do," or "I did that, and I should have done something else instead." Your evaluation of your deeds is directly related to the fact that you value people, and you believe that success includes valuing and helping others.

If you truly value earning money, and your definition of success is to make X amount of dollars, you are going to look at your day's work and evaluate the things that you have done to make money. You're going to say, "I did this, and it was a good thing to do," or "I did that, and I should have done something else instead." Your evaluation of your deeds is going to be related directly to the fact that you value money, and again, the value you place on money is part of your belief system.

The invisible, intangible things of your life give rise to the things that become visible and tangible. If you don't value something, you don't desire it.

If you don't desire it, you don't go after it.

If you don't go after something, very likely you'll never get it, become it, do it, achieve it, or have it.

The process is always the same, no matter what your end goal may be:

BELIEFS
    give rise to VALUES
        give rise to DESIRES
            give rise to EFFORT and ENERGY
                give rise to ACCOMPLISHMENT

Making Decisions with Your Head *and* Your Heart

One of the most persistent human beings on the planet is Spencer Wood. For quite some time, my friends Dave Leggett and Carl Duvall wanted me to meet Spencer. Carl never said why—he just wanted me to meet him. Finally, I agreed to have lunch with Spencer. Over the next three hours, I discovered a man who very likely has more ideas than any person I've ever met. He is incredible.

Spencer shared with me his dream of developing a foundation to help abused children. And he convinced me to be a part of his effort. I'm not sure exactly how he did that, but when I figure it out completely, I'm going to present it as one of the best selling techniques ever used.

During a break in our conversation, I turned to my business partner Kathy, who truly makes possible everything I do, and I thought, *How am I going to tell her that we need to be a part of Spencer's project when we can barely keep up with all the commitments we already have?* Just as I leaned over to try to explain to her why I thought we should get involved, she said to me with a little quiver in her voice, "Would you please help these people, Jim?"

I said, "Sure, Kathy, we'll help these people!" It was a relief to me that she, too, saw—and *felt*—the need. And that's an important point. Kathy was convinced in her mind that helping Spencer was the right thing to do. And she felt in her heart that it was a move we needed to make.

When you are making decisions, look for what makes sense to you logically, and also look for the tug of the heart that says to you, "This is worth your time, your effort, and any sacrifice you need to make."

Kathy's agreement was important to me from another standpoint. I knew I couldn't help Spencer alone. I needed her help and that of everyone who works with me. A good leader will seek the consensus of those with whom he works—consensus that is usually achieved by talking over a project and coming to a mental agreement—and a good leader will seek out an eagerness in those with whom he works toward the achievement of a particular goal or a new avenue of commitment. It's not enough to agree. Good decisions are nearly always confirmed by *hearty* agreement—a truly enthusiastic embracing of what is about to be done.

I knew a man who talked about having ideas "leap in his spirit." I like that phrase. To have a decision cause a leap in the spirit means to me that an intuitive enthusiasm takes hold. And when times get tough, as they do in any project or enterprise, the feeling rooted in a person's spirit often gives him or her the fortitude to endure, work harder, and hold the line.

I'm not saying that decisions should be made on the basis of emotions alone. Far from it. Please see the balance in the point I'm making. A person needs to make decisions first and foremost on the basis of hard, cold evidence—as Sgt. Joe Friday on the TV program *Dragnet* used to say, "Just the facts, ma'am."

But then, once the facts line up in a convincing way, check out your pulse about the project. Does it cause excitement? Do you feel energized by the idea and the prospects? Do you feel your pace quickening, your heart beating a little faster, your mind spinning a little more rapidly with new ideas, your eagerness mounting to get started? Do you have a sense that this is truly something that is going to be good, that you are going to enjoy, and that you are going to find fulfilling and rewarding at the deepest levels of your being? If so, you're probably on the right track!

And then see if those with whom you live and work have not only the same mental outlook on the idea but also the same emotional response to it. If you and your family or group of associates have a consensus that something is a good idea and also have a shared commitment that the idea is something worth doing right, and doing right away, you have a running start toward achieving the momentum you will need to launch the effort and to carry it through to completion.

There Is No Magic Formula

Gaining success isn't a con job. Many people think there is some kind of magic formula they need to learn and then use on other people to get them to buy their products, make their deal, or be their friend.

If anything, success is a matter of telling the truth. It's facing up to the truth about yourself—your real desires, your real goals, your real dreams. It's facing up to the truth that you can be more than you presently are. It's facing up to the truth that you are never going to get from where you are to where you want to be without some effort and without some help from others. It's facing up to the truth that your success isn't going to happen instantly, and that you are going to be pursuing your success every day for the rest of your life.

Success involves telling the truth about a product to other people. It's speaking the truth to another person about who you are, what you represent and believe, and what you hold to be true about that other person. Success comes when you follow through on your commitments and you do what you have said you are going to do. Success is found in a life marked by validity and reliability.

Furthermore, success is not the pursuit of a lie or a fantasy world. There is a big difference between having dreams and goals and being deluded. Genuine success lies in finding real solutions to real problems, in helping people in real ways, and in being "real" to other people by being vulnerable, honest, and trustworthy.

Let me elaborate a little on this business of delusion versus dreams. With a delusion, you hope and believe for something that you wish would happen or wish would be true. With a dream, you are willing to work to make something happen that you know is right for you.

Delusions are filled with hot air. Genuine dreams are filled with energy, work, and tasks.

If I set myself a goal of driving the winning race car in the Indianapolis 500, I'd be deluding myself. I might be the owner of a car that wins the Indy. Or I might someday be able to enjoy "racing" a car through some type of virtual reality experience in which cues are fed to my mind in ways that don't involve eyesight. Someday I might be able to drive a car again, given the advances in medical, automotive, and road-engineering technology. But right now, the idea of driving the winning car at Indianapolis would be a delusion, not a dream. No matter how much energy and work I might expend toward being a race car driver, I'm likely to be spinning my wheels off the track far more than I'd spin any wheels on a track.

On the other hand, if I set myself a goal of developing a system or a methodology that would allow a blind person to drive a car, that is a legitimate dream. Energy and work could be put to that goal to make it happen. Not today. But someday. Not by myself. Not without some innovation and invention. But the idea is a conceivable one. That would be a genuine dream.

The basic principle is this: Genuine success is always grounded in truth. It always has its feet firmly planted in reality, and the foremost reality lies in who you are. The greatest reality is going to be who you are on the inside. That's where truth resides. That's the beginning of truth for any project that you undertake or career that you forge.

Work on the truth of yourself. Let your genuine nature permeate all that you do and every relationship that you have. You'll be successful.

Choose to Be Among the 5 Percent

You may think that integrity, honesty, sincerity, and good working relationships are the norm in our world. Not in my experience. The person who truly operates out of personal integrity is a rare breed. On the other hand, I have yet to meet a genuinely successful person—a person living at the peak of performance and fulfilling a personal destiny—who did not have integrity.

Choosing to be the best person you can be—choosing to have integrity—automatically puts you into a special class of people.

Shortly after Crystal and I married, I received information about a special seminar being held in Phoenix, Arizona. It was being conducted by a man I thought a great deal of, and I made a decision: We were going to attend that seminar. The cost was about a thousand dollars.

At the time, Crystal and I had a three-figure bank account. It fluctuated between $999 and $0 about fourteen times a month. We weren't poor. Poor people can't get as far into debt as we were at the time. The idea of paying a thousand dollars to attend a conference a thousand miles away—you might as well have asked us to finance a trip to the moon.

We took our car, which we affectionately named the Old Green Dog, down to the service station where we normally had the car serviced. The mechanic looked under the hood and said, "I won't guarantee that this car will make it off the lot." I thanked the man and said to Crystal, "We're definitely not going to ask him about driving it to Phoenix. Let's go."

We made it to Phoenix all right, and while I was there, I first heard about ducks and eagles. Ducks stay in their pond, never soaring high into the sky but choosing instead to paddle around and quack a lot and periodically migrate as a group. Eagles take the risk to soar above the masses. The speaker made a strong point about how only 5 percent of all people decide to be eagles. I was really inspired by what I heard during that conference, and I said to Crystal as we were leaving, "I'm not sure what we're going to do to get there, but I know we've got to get into the 5 percent."

The 5 percent are people who are willing to do things that other people aren't willing to do. The 5 percent are people who will take risks. The 5 percent are people who are willing to sacrifice some of what they presently have to pursue something more in their lives.

The 5 percent are also people who are willing to live a life of integrity, honesty, and sincerity. They are concerned first and foremost about character and values, and only secondarily about outward trappings.

On the way back to Tulsa from Phoenix, Crystal and I were sleeping in the car for the second night on the trip, and I awoke about three in the morning. Not content to be awake by myself, I awoke Crystal and said, "Look out these windows. Do you see anybody else out here in the middle of nowhere in a three-hundred-dollar car sleeping on the side of the road at three o'clock in the morning?"

She said, "No, Jim. I don't see *anybody* doing that."

I said, "I think we're in the 5 percent!"

We both laughed, although at the time it was more the groaning kind of laughter. And yet there was truth in what we declared to each other that night.

On the inside, Crystal and I had made a quality decision in our lives that we were going to live our lives at the top of the scale. We were not going to settle for second best. We were not going to live as ducks on a pond, just waiting for a hunter to pick us off and turn us into duck soup. No, we were going to soar. We were going to become the people we were created to be and, thus, feel destined to be.

> *Greatness isn't something you acquire. It's something you choose to be. It's a quality of the heart and soul.*

Choose today to live in the top 5 percent of all people—from the inside out.

Greatness isn't something you acquire. It's something you choose to be. It's a quality of the heart and soul.

8

EXPANDING
YOUR VISION

*What more are you expecting
out of your life?*

Visualizing leads to expecting. If you have visualized a new life for yourself and your loved ones, a life flowing out of your beliefs and desires—indeed, a life in keeping with your perceived sense of destiny—you are going to start expecting that life to be forged as you make your plans and follow through on them.

People who live in mediocrity generally expect bad things to happen to them. If something bad happens, they immediately respond, "Well, that always happens to me. I just knew that was going to happen. I was expecting it to happen. And guess what, it happened once again."

☐ *People who live in success come to expect success.*

People who live in success come to expect success. If something good happens to them, they say, "Well, I was expecting that. I was working for it, looking for it to happen, and it did! Now I'm going to start expecting the next good thing to happen!"

Now consider the opposite mind-set. If something good happens to people living in mediocrity, they tend to do one of two things. The first thing is to label the good event or situation as luck, saying, "I had a real stroke of luck," or "That's the first lucky thing that has ever happened to me." The second thing is to dismiss the good thing as something that won't last. People who live in mediocrity rarely see their good fortune as being the first of many steps on an upward ladder. Rather, they see it as a temporary bit of good fortune that they need to hoard, guard, or enjoy while it lasts.

What happens to successful people when something bad happens to them? They consider it to be a temporary setback, perhaps a detour in the road. They rarely see a bad circumstance or situation as the end of the road. It might affect their timetable for success, but it doesn't affect their ultimate goal, dream, or desire.

Most people live at the level of their expectation. They live as they expect to live. And in many cases, that is very little better, if better at all, than their parents or their peers. Most people compare themselves to others, and if they are living about as well as the people they see and know, they are content. Very few people live up to what they *might* do or be. They don't look inwardly to see the difference between who they are and who they *could* be.

Are you such a person? Don't be! Consider what is happening in your life right now:

How did you regard the good things that happened to you today?

- Were you expecting something good?
- Do you have a plan for building on this good thing?
- Do you see it as part of your effort, your goal, your dream, your desire, your destiny?
- How does it fit in with what you value and what you believe?

How do you regard the bad things that may have happened today?

- Were you secretly anticipating the worst?
- Do you see this as signaling the end, or is it just a delay in your plan?

- Do you see yourself as deserving this bad thing? Do you regard it as a form of punishment?
- Did you immediately think of a way of overcoming this bad thing and getting back on track with your goal?

If you look for bad things, you'll find them. If you expect the worst to happen, and expect long and hard enough, it very well may happen!

> **You get what you expect, and I'm here to tell you that you can expect more.**

The opposite is also true. If you look for good things, you'll find them. If you expect the best to happen, and expect long and hard enough, it likely will! The best may not come in the precise form and timing and method that you had envisioned, but the end result will be just as good as you had hoped.

Expect More of Yourself

One of the foremost problems about having a disability is that most people don't expect people with disabilities to do very much. I could have sat for the rest of my days in my house, listening to the radio, and nobody in society would have said, "Jim, you've got to get up and start contributing something." Society feels sorry for people with visual impairments, and it is content to let them do nothing and become nothing.

Compassion isn't a bad thing. We need to have more genuine compassion in this world. But pity is a terrible thing.

Compassion says, "I'm sorry this happened. What can I do to help you help yourself and get through this, over this, or cope with this?"

Pity says, "I'm sorry for you. What can I do for you since you can't do anything for yourself?"

We all have disabilities. We all have weaknesses, problems, and difficulties in our lives.

But we tend to allow people to live in their disabilities more than we try to help them.

We say to the person who is emotionally disabled, "You just rest, dear, and let those of us who are strong handle all the problems."

We say to the person who is physically limited, "I'll do that for you. You just sit there and tell me what you need."

We say to the person who is financially limited, "Let me pay that for you. You don't have to work."

That's wrong. It's pity. It does nothing to build up that person's self-esteem, help that person get through a tragedy, grow in his ability to care for himself, or become a contributing member of society.

Rather than give to people we see as disabled or limited, we need to help them get strong and then help them start giving something of themselves to others. We grow strong through giving, not through taking all the time. When someone starts turning outward to give to others and to embrace the fullness of life, that person who has been hit with a blow of some sort starts to recover fully.

We all live up to expectations—our expectations as well as the expectations of others. Expect something more of yourself. Expect something more from others. Place demands on yourself. Encourage others and assist them, but always with the idea that you are helping them learn how to help themselves.

I have met countless people who admitted to me that they get up each day and go to a job they hate, put in a full day's work, and then go home to a family that isn't happy. Why? They are doing what they say is expected of them. Those people need to start expecting more of their lives. They need to find a career they enjoy, one that will help them get to the place they want to be in life. They need to see their lives and their families from a new perspective. If they don't like the marriage, they need to work on it and transform it into a relationship that brings both spouses greater joy and fulfillment. If they don't like their family life, they need to readjust some priorities and start creating the family relationships they want to have.

I'm not at all advocating that you quit work, leave the family, and go off by yourself. Rather, I'm suggesting that you're probably expecting too little of your work, too little of your marriage, and too little of your family life. Start expecting these areas to improve. Start working out of that expectation to bring your entire life up to a new level of excellence, of fulfillment, of genuine satisfaction.

You get what you expect.

Straw Brooms and Erasers on Pencils?

I once encountered an entire room of people who were getting exactly what they had been told to expect, which they subsequently had decided to expect.

Shortly after I lost the remainder of my vision, a woman came to my house and said, "I'm a social worker with the government. I'm here to help you." I should have known from those two sentences that I was in serious trouble.

She proceeded to tell me that since I was blind, the government would give me a $600 disability check each month and provide me with vocational training. She told me about a place in my city where visually impaired people were working in a sheltered workshop and how the government was helping them become skilled laborers.

She then said, "I'd like to take you to this sheltered workshop." I didn't even know what a sheltered workshop was. It sounded to me like a place to get out of the hot sun and into cool shade.

I agreed to go with her. On the way, she said, "You'll get to meet other blind people and find out what marvelous things they can do." If I'd known then what I know now, I would have said, "Yeah, right." But I was like a dumb sheep being led to slaughter that day.

We went into a room, and her tone shifted. She said, "Now here's where they work." Suddenly, it hit me. She was a "we," and I was a "they." I'd never felt such class distinction in my life. I suddenly was a member of another class of people, a significantly lower class.

I said, "Well, what do *they* do?" trying to keep myself on the "we" side of things but feeling as if I was failing fast.

She said, "They make straw brooms."

"Oh?" I said. "Is that all they do?"

She said, "No, they also put erasers on pencils, using a little machine that clamps the eraser to the pencil."

Neither activity sounded like a lot of fun to me so I asked, "Well, what else do *they* do?"

She said, "That's all they do. That's what blind people do here."

I replied, "That's it? There's no other choice? They either make straw brooms or put erasers on pencils?"

She didn't lose a beat. She said, "Yeah, that's what they do. That's what we have for them to do. That's what we train these people to do. That's what they do."

I tried putting an eraser on a pencil. I tried it only once. Apparently, I didn't work the machine properly because the eraser fell off the end of my pencil. I still don't know how people do that work, especially all day. It's a good thing I can do television programs because I have no aptitude for applying erasers to pencils.

I also learned from her that the government paid by piece at the workshop, which meant that I'd get paid so much per pencil or broom that I made. That would have been a dead-end deal for me! I came away from the outing to the sheltered workshop thinking, *I'd better get some personally fulfilling work.*

It was an important day for me, however, to have taken that tour. It told me what people expect blind people to be able to do. Brooms and pencils.

It told me that was the government's "dream" for my life. It wasn't a good-enough dream. I feel quite certain it isn't a good-enough dream for most of the people in that sheltered workshop. I have a hunch there are some bright, talented people in that room who are going to spend the rest of their lives putting erasers on pencils because someone told them that was the most they could expect from their lives, and they bought into that expectation.

Everything within me wants to shout at them, "NO! There's more! This isn't what you should expect. Don't limit yourself. Expect *more.*"

The trouble is, I've tried that with some people, and if they buy into an expectation long enough, it's virtually impossible to shake them out of that expectation. They've gone from expectation to petrification—turning into solid rock like the trees that are now stones in the Petrified Forest.

Each of us moves toward an immediate dominant thought. If you fall and your immediate dominant thought is, *Get up,* you'll get up. But if you fall and your immediate dominant thought is, *Somebody help me, I can't get up,* you won't get up. You'll lie there until help comes.

Others have planted your dominant thought in you, and they've taught you to make it your dominant thought. It will be very hard for you to change that dominant thought, but you can change it if you desire to change it. You can start thinking to yourself, *I don't need to lie here. I can get up. I don't need anybody to help me. I can start moving upward.*

What is your dominant thought about your life?

Has somebody convinced you that sticking erasers on pencils is the best you can expect?

> *You get what you expect, and I'm here to tell you that you can expect more.*

Listen to a new voice. I'm here to tell you that you can expect more.

Expectation Resets the Dial on Your Dreams

I heard an interesting story about expectation that involved a teacher in New York. She was an excellent teacher, but she had chosen to retire. The superintendent of schools asked her to please teach one more year. The school he had in mind was a difficult one, known for having students who carried guns and knives, and who were grouped into gangs. The superintendent said, "We'll get a police officer or security man to be in the classroom with you if you want."

The teacher agreed to teach another year but said, "I don't need a security officer." Instead, this teacher walked into the classroom the first day and said, "I know we have some discipline problems, but you kids are geniuses and in this class you're going to perform at that level." And they did. They scored at the top of their grade level.

At the end of the year, when the teacher was called on to accept an award from the state commissioner of education, he asked her, "How did you bring these kids to this level?"

She said, "Well, I was given a list of their names and their IQ's. I knew it was a genius class, so all I had to do was teach them like the geniuses they were." The commissioner was embarrassed. He said, "Ma'am, those numbers you were given were their locker numbers."

The students had performed to the level of expectation their teacher had for them.

Once you start expecting something more out of your life, it's as if you have reset the dial on your dreams. You've tuned in to your destiny in such a way that there is no static. You're operating with greater energy and more enthusiasm. The dial has been switched from no gear to high gear!

Put Up Your Umbrella!

Expectation is believing that you can and will achieve your goal.

A farm community in the Midwest was experiencing a severe drought. No rain had fallen for months, and the crops were on the verge of being lost. The need was desperate. Finally, the community leaders called for a town meeting to discuss the situation, and one little girl in the back of the audience spoke up during the meeting and said, "Why don't we meet tomorrow at the church and pray for rain?" Well, the town fathers couldn't seem to come up with any better plan so they said, "We'll do that."

> *Expectation is believing you can and will achieve your goal.*

The next day all of the town's citizens crammed themselves inside the church for a prayer meeting. They agreed to use all the faith and hope they had to believe God would send rain to them. They prayed fervently, and lo and behold, at the end of the service, the skies opened and rain began to pour!

Everybody began hugging everybody else in rejoicing that the prayers had been answered. And then it hit them. How were they going to get home without getting wet? The downpour was so great the streets were already starting to show puddles.

In the midst of this discussion, the little girl who had suggested the prayer meeting walked through the crowd and stood at the back door. There, she peered out, then popped open her umbrella, and walked into the rain without the least bit of concern.

She was the only one who had come to the meeting fully prepared to have her prayers answered. Nobody else truly believed that God would hear and answer.

Expect to find what you're looking for. Expect to achieve what you're aiming for. Expect to enjoy what you will receive.

If you don't really believe that your success is possible, and that you can live the life you dream of living, you won't pursue that success. The likelihood is that you'll never take the first step toward that success.

Breaking the 500-Pound Barrier

A major barrier for me as a weight lifter was the 500-pound mark.

Nearly every athlete hits a wall at some point. It's a number or a play or a level of performance that he or she can't seem to conquer. It might be the speed of a fastball, a shooting percentage, a track time, or a particular height or distance.

I steadily conquered greater and greater weights as I trained: 400 pounds, then 450, then 475, then 490, and 495, and 498. But I couldn't lift 500 pounds. I didn't think I could lift that amount, even though I was saying with my mouth that I knew I could.

When you lift weights at that level, you usually don't load your own bar. If you do, you wear yourself out lifting before you start. A coach or spotter loads the bar for you.

One day my coach said, "Well, let's do just one more lift, Jim, and then we'll hit the showers and go home. Here we go, one more time at 480."

I lifted the bar. And then my coach announced, "Whoops! I think they made a mistake. Sure enough, it's at 506!"

From that point onward, I no longer had a block about lifting 500 pounds.

The real difference was not in my training or in my physical ability. In all likelihood, I could have lifted 500 pounds several weeks earlier, in purely physical terms. The difference was in my mind. I *knew* that I could lift 500 pounds because I had done it. To be sure, there were times I attempted 500 pounds and couldn't lift the bar, but those were for physical reasons, not mental ones. I no longer had any doubt that I was capable of lifting that weight.

Every so often we come up against major barriers—levels at which we don't think we can perform. At times, the levels are real ones. We haven't trained or prepared ourselves to operate at that level. But at other times, the levels are ones that are stuck in our minds. We don't perform at that level because we don't think we can perform at that level.

Why not? We simply aren't expecting.

Expectation Involves Risk

I won't kid you and say that expectation is risk free. On the contrary. When you start expecting new and greater things to happen in your life, there's always a risk involved. If you are ultimately expecting to succeed at what you are pursuing, however, you will be willing to accept that level of risk, and you'll rebound much faster if you encounter problems.

When I was speaking at a convention in Colorado, I had a morning session, and then everybody took off the afternoon to go skiing. Later I had an evening session to conduct. My partner Kathy went skiing, too, which meant I was pretty much in the lodge by myself. I talked to a few people and then made my way back to my room, feeling stuck and bored.

I was also more than a little upset. I figured I must be in one of the most incredibly beautiful places—with mountains all around and people skiing down them—and there I was, stuck in a room in the dark by myself. I finally thought about the mule deer that people had told me they had been feeding all week. Apparently, the deer were tame enough that they'd come right up to the edge of the patios that were located outside the rooms on our side of the lodge, and if a person would throw them bread, they'd come within a foot or two of the person.

I thought, *Well, I'm not experiencing the beauty of this place or the skiing. I might as well experience this!* I figured it would be pretty neat if I could get a deer to come up close enough to where it would actually let me pet it. That sounded like fun. So I made my way to the edge of the patio and began tossing bread into the air. Soon, I could hear a deer coming closer and closer. I figured if I kept throwing the bread shorter and shorter distances, he'd get closer and closer. Indeed, that seemed to be what was happening. I could sense the deer's presence and eventually could feel its breath. I figured it was only about a foot away from me, so I reached out to touch it, and I slipped off the edge of the patio.

I hadn't thought what might be beyond the edge of the patio— perhaps a patch of grass or something. Well, the patio dropped off about a foot, which means that when I slipped, I had a real drop. I went crashing and rolling down the slope at about a forty-five-degree angle. I was rolling head over heels down the mountain, and the deer no doubt took off with lightning speed in the opposite direction— scared to death, which was also the way I was feeling. I knew we were on a 12,000-foot mountain, but at that moment as I was tumbling along, I had no idea where I was in reference to anything. I was rolling over in the blackness four or five times, with no idea about whether I might be close to a ledge or about to tumble hundreds of feet before I came to a stop. I lost all frame of reference.

As it turned out, I probably went about fifty feet from the patio, sliding and rolling, before I finally came to a complete stop. I was a little torn up, bleeding a little, but not too bad. I could tell the incline was steep below me because the gravel I'd been sliding across kept moving, and I could hear the little pebbles falling on down the side of the mountain.

I had on jeans and a sweatshirt, but I really wasn't dressed for the cold. I figured I'd best stay where I was, rather than try to move, but the colder I got, the more I realized I needed to find my way back up to the lodge. I started climbing on hands and knees up the hill, and eventually, I hit a patio. Of course, I had no idea whether it was my patio, and upon climbing onto it and checking the door into the room, which was locked, I quickly deduced that it wasn't my patio. I tried the patio next to it and the next one. Finally, I found a patio with an open door, and it was mine. I was grateful nobody else had left a door open.

I wanted a little adventure in the mountains all right. I got what I expected, but not necessarily the way I expected it!

What you expect is always more important than the means you might anticipate. Set your inner vision toward your goals and dreams for what you want to be, do, and have, and then let the means sort themselves out as you go.

You might tumble down a mountain occasionally, figuratively speaking, but if you expect to reach success in your life, you'll be willing to take that risk, and you'll be able to dust yourself off and climb back out of any problem you encounter.

Expect good things to happen in your life today.

Expect to reach your goals.

Expect to be and do and have what you have envisioned as your personal destiny!

9

BRAVING
THE GLARE

*The first step into your future
is likely to be the most
difficult one. Take it anyway!*

A quality decision changes the very nature of your life. It causes you to move in a direction you haven't gone before to experience greater quality in who you are as a person, what you do, and what you have.

A quality decision leads to visualization, which leads to expectation. A quality decision causes you to reevaluate what you have considered to be the marks of success and of personal greatness.

A quality decision is the true beginning of any positive change in your life.

But the day inevitably comes when you must go beyond thinking, dreaming, visualizing, and expecting greater things. The day comes when you need to take action.

Getting Out of My Room

With the darkness of my complete blindness came fear. The immediate panic I felt gave way to more rational thinking: *This is it. It isn't going to get any worse than this. I'm as blind as I'm ever going to be.* In the wake of panic, however, I had more of a numbing fear.

The numbing fear had this as its message: *This is it. I'm as blind as I'm ever going to be. It isn't going to get any worse than this. But it isn't going to get any better, either. I'll just live in the cave that I've created for myself.*

I was scared to think about going outside my front door. I'm not too proud to admit that. I was more scared than I had ever been in my life. My overriding thought was that I was never going to leave my house again. I had a room in my home in which I had an easy chair, a tape deck, a telephone, and a radio. As far as I was concerned, that was going to be my universe from that moment on.

Living with impaired vision is one thing. There's always a struggle to see and get around. There's always the hope that you're coming across as a normally sighted person. There's frustration at your limitations. There's a sense of helplessness at times. There's a nagging fear about the future.

With total blindness, the struggle and the frustration and the fear multiply beyond anything you've tried to imagine.

For days—then weeks—I sat in my chair in my room in my house. I didn't know what other blind people did. Up to that point, I hadn't given it much thought. That may sound strange, but consider what I had been doing. I'd been conducting my life in as normal a way as possible. I didn't give much thought to what blind people as a whole did or how they lived. I was still among sighted people.

Finally, I came to the realization: *This isn't living. This is only existing. I'm not going to lose any more of my sight, but if I continue to sit here, I'm going to lose my life. Blindness has happened. Deal with it.*

I faced reality.

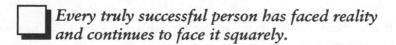 *Every truly successful person has faced reality and continues to face it squarely.*

And reality is an essential thing for any person to face. Every truly successful person has faced it and continues to face it squarely.

If you don't have any money, face the fact.

If your life is without direction or purpose or deep satisfaction and a sense of fulfillment, face the fact.

If your relationships are in disrepair, face the fact.

If you've been rejected by someone—a person or a company—and there's no chance of restoring that relationship by anything you can do or say, face the fact.

If someone has died, face the fact.

If you aren't succeeding in your work, aren't growing as a person, or aren't moving forward in your life, face the fact.

Facing the fact is hard, but it's vital.

The opposite of facing reality is living in a state of denial. And you are denying yourself your future and your potential.

People who live in denial are stuck. They usually don't want to face reality because they see reality as something that can only be bad or worse. Usually, they are already living in a state that's as bad as it's going to get. In facing the worst, they likely set themselves free to see the good that may lie ahead for them.

As I faced the fact of my blindness and my stuck-in-a-chair life, an ache developed within me to talk to people and to be with people. Sitting alone in a chair in a room in a house day after day is just that—sitting alone. I felt a need for people. The need was rooted not in money or success or work but in the desire for involvement with other human beings.

I asked myself a question, *Would I rather sit here until I die or die in trying to do something other than sit here?* Part of the fear I felt was a fear for my physical safety. Would I fall? Would I get run over? They were real fears, as much as any fear of failure.

I decided it would probably be better to die trying to do something than to die from rotting in a chair.

One Call Leads to Another

It's amazing to me in retrospect how quickly things can happen once a person makes the first positive move toward change. It may be one call, one step, or one encounter. And then there are more calls, more steps, more encounters.

Not all the steps or calls lead you directly to your goal. But they are all productive in some way. Each and every call may not pay out big for you. But each and every call brings you one call closer to your ultimate goal.

The first step I took was to call a school in California. I was in hopes that it could supply me with a Seeing Eye dog. I didn't know anything about Seeing Eye dogs, but I figured I'd be told the location of the nearest kennel and I'd pick up a dog and we'd walk away together in total sync.

The school in California informed me that before I could receive a Seeing Eye dog, I had to complete mobility instruction with a cane. Mobility instruction requires having a mobility instructor. The instruction usually takes several months. That wasn't exactly what I had counted on, but I decided to take the next step and call around in Tulsa until I located a mobility instructor.

I found a mobility instructor who worked for the state. She came to our house and said, "If we go out once a week, it will take you months, perhaps a full year, to get through this training. And then, maybe—emphasis on *maybe*—you can get a dog."

I replied, "No, if I'm going to do this, I'm going to get out of here much faster than that. I want you to come every day." I don't know why she agreed to that, but she did. She said, "All right. But as part of your training, you've got to attend some meetings with other blind people, and you've got to start learning some more about how to deal with the thoughts and feelings you're having."

I agreed. "If that's the deal, okay."

We didn't rush right out to a meeting of blind people. Most of our first sessions were in the house.

When the time came to go out in public, I said, "I'm not going out." By that time she was pretty good at manipulating me. When I'd balk at doing something, she'd say, "Well, Jim, if you don't think you can do this, that's fine. If it's too tough, you just tell me, and we won't worry about it right now."

That was usually enough for me to say, "Okay, fine, let's do this."

I may have been blind, but I was determined not to be a coward. It was probably a macho thing, but if so, I'm glad for the macho that was built into me.

I became pretty adept with a cane. I still carry one in my briefcase—a fold-up model. I don't feel at all embarrassed to use it, and I can get around with a cane quite well. But for the most part, I have developed mobility to the level that I can travel with people who are by my side and go virtually anywhere I need to go. As it turned out, a Seeing Eye dog became unnecessary to my lifestyle, but the experience started the ball rolling in many areas.

I occasionally run into things, but I rarely run into people. One reason probably has more to do with my size than my mobility skills. If you see a guy six feet four inches tall and weighing 240 pounds coming in your direction, you generally move out of his way!

In the early days, though, I developed something of a love-hate relationship with Cheryl, my mobility instructor. She was a tiny woman, maybe weighing 115 pounds, and I would yell and scream at her and call her every name imaginable. It's a wonder to me that she returned day after day. I hated what she was doing to me, but at the same time, I appreciated what she was doing for me.

Out to the Mailbox—and Back!

My first venture outside my house was to the mailbox. At the time, we were living in a house that had a mailbox out by the street, and the driveway sloped down to the street. No matter what I achieve or do in life, I will always remember my first walk out to that mailbox and back to the house. It was a monumental experience for me.

A year later, I was in Hawaii doing an eight-day speaking tour, and when I called home to talk to Crystal, she reminded me that it had been exactly a year since I made it out to the mailbox and back. I realized how far I had come. I don't recall if I got the mail that day. I just walked out to the mailbox, about forty feet from my front door. But in retrospect, that mailbox seemed a lot farther away than Hawaii.

The first step you make toward the realization of your dream may be a very small one.

The first step you make toward the realization of your dream may be a very small one. It may seem insignificant to others and even to you. But the first step is always the first step. And that makes it important, no matter how small it is.

When Cheryl and I first ventured out of the house together, we went to an empty church on a Tuesday afternoon. We walked a little in my neighborhood. And gradually, we began to go to places with more and more people.

A big day came for me when Cheryl said, "You're going to be on your own tomorrow. I want you to call a cab, tell them to pick you up at your house, take you to city hall, and I'll meet you on the second floor of the library."

I did it! It was a major milestone for me.

Yet even with that hurdle behind me, Cheryl kept insisting that I attend a meeting with other blind people. Finally, I agreed. She went with me to the first meeting of a group she recommended. The group held meetings once a week, and the people talked about what it is like to be disabled. As Cheryl and I sat there with forty or fifty blind people, I couldn't help thinking, *This is some kind of charity thing.*

I heard a man say to another person about the group as he was passing nearby, "These are the blind people." Again, I felt an artificial barrier. The world was one of "us" and "them," and I was part of "them." I had known the man speaking in years past, when I was a part of the "us" group, but suddenly, I was in a different class. I said to Cheryl, "Get me out of here. I'm not one of the people taking the tour of this building, and I'm certainly not going to be one of the people in the cage. There's got to be another place I can go."

Please understand that I believe there are many tremendous organizations of and for blind people. I am very proud of the work we do with the Lions Clubs and other national organizations. My greatest desire for blind people is that they have quality lives and live and function as independently as possible. Although I am very proud of many skills I have acquired that enable me to function in my environment, I am still in awe of many blind people with respect to the manner in which they function independently in the real world.

At that time in my life, however, I found it frustrating to be considered an "exhibit" for others to view.

Cheryl sent me to a meeting of another organization of blind people. I was on my own. I put on a suit and tie, used my cane, got to the meeting place, walked into the room, and found a seat. The meeting was in a private room in a restaurant, so I ordered my meal and waited for the program to begin. A few minutes later, a young woman came in and sat down next to me, and we exchanged names.

Then she asked a question that I thought was incredibly stupid.

She said, "Why are you here?" After all, I was at a meeting for blind people!

I said, "Why do you think I'm here? Do *you* just like to hang around with blind people?"

It turned out that Kathy was legally blind but still had some of her sight. She hadn't seen my cane, which I had already folded up and put on the floor next to my chair, and she didn't think I was dressed like a blind person would be. Kathy was a paralegal and legal studies instructor. It was also her first meeting.

She admitted that she thought I was the speaker for the day, and I was a little flattered by that. Apparently, a lot of blind people don't dress up for meetings or use good table manners. In the end, I was encouraged that she didn't perceive me to be blind, especially when the speaker turned out to be a physician who spoke about some new training methods.

I didn't gain much from the meeting that day other than meeting Kathy, but for that, I'll be forever grateful.

Most of the meeting was irritating to me. Much of the time was spent talking about government subsidies and how inadequate they are. Although there may be some legitimate complaints, I didn't hear any that day. The government subsidizes cabs to pick up blind people and take them where they need to go. The cab fee is very low to the blind person. Having been in business, I thought it was a pretty good deal to be able to get a cab for about $1 when the fee would normally be $10 to $12, but mostly, I heard complaints that the cab was always late or that the cabdrivers often stopped to pick up another person.

Overall, I was there only because Cheryl, my mobility instructor, insisted that I go. My deal was with her. I was doing double time to try to qualify for a Seeing Eye dog.

In the course of introductions during the meeting, I told the group that I owned my business and did various things. I also introduced Kathy and told them a little about her, including the fact that she was also a first-timer. I quickly realized as the other thirty to forty people introduced themselves that Kathy and I were just about the only two people in the room who worked.

Kathy and I met a couple of times after that to share our sense of frustration and to talk about her condition, which was degenerative but seemed to have hit a plateau.

Then one afternoon, I put on the tape of an old movie I had enjoyed while I could still see. It was a Humphrey Bogart film, *The Big Sleep*, and I thought I would remember enough of the movie's visuals to be able to follow the story. About an hour and a half into the movie, however, somebody shot somebody and everybody screamed and the car sped away, and I didn't have a clue what was going on. I could no longer follow the story, which was really frustrating to me. So I did a little research.

I discovered that there are thirteen million blind and visually impaired people in the United States. If I couldn't follow the movie, even having seen it as a sighted person, there was a good likelihood that the other thirteen million people might have a little trouble following the story, too.

I thought, *Somebody ought to do something*. And friends, that's a critically important statement for anybody to make. If you say, *Somebody ought to do something* about a particular situation, sit up and take notice. You are very likely the *somebody* who should do it.

The next thought led to the next along the track, *How could I make that happen?* Finally, the idea came, *I'm going to make videos and put an extra sound track on them to describe what is happening visually.*

I called Kathy and told her about my idea, partly to find out what a visually impaired person who wasn't fully blind would think of it. She was so enthusiastic about it that she left the law firm and came to work with me as a partner in the business we are in today.

At the time, I didn't realize what a gutsy move that was for her. She was a single mother, teaching law at a university, with a twelve-year career of working for one of the best trial lawyers in the area, making her way through life. She suddenly quit her job with very little hope for immediate income. As it turned out, we scraped by for almost a year with virtually no money coming in to the company, but Kathy hung in there.

I also didn't realize at the time that probably what I needed most as a partner was someone who was fully sighted to help me get around and put the project together. Instead, I chose to be in partnership with somebody who could hardly see anything. Kathy didn't drive, but she could read a little. Even so, we have since traveled the nation and the world putting together a television network.

We started out with an idea but very little else. My wife, Crystal, was encouraging, as she always has been, but the two or three other people I casually mentioned the idea to weren't impressed. Television for blind people? I quit talking to people about it and concentrated solely on doing it. I was in a pretty fragile state at that time, emotionally and psychologically speaking. I had just lost my sight, was finally starting to get out of the house a little, was struggling to learn how to get around in a black void, and the last thing I needed was rejection or cynicism.

In retrospect, it was a good move on my part to concentrate on doing my idea rather than talking to people about it. Most people can't accept most new ideas, regardless of what they are. If you have an idea that you truly believe is worth pursuing, you are probably better off to keep it mostly to yourself and to the people who truly believe in you and save yourself a lot of "jaw" from other people. Their opinions are likely to be negative, or at least not very enthusiastic, and you don't need negativity to launch something new. You need positive energy around you.

Nothing was complicated about my idea. The idea has remained consistent from the beginning: put a program on a television screen that blind and visually impaired people can enjoy "watching."

Within a matter of weeks after I had decided to make the move out of my chair and into the world, I had a direction for my life. I had a sense of my destiny again. I had ambition, energy, and a feeling of expectation.

I didn't know how I was going to turn the idea into a reality, but I was determined to do it.

I had taken the first step—the toughest one—and I was ready for the next steps.

After the *What* Comes the *How*

At that point, and only at that point, the questions of *how* began to emerge. I'm thoroughly convinced that this is the time when *how* questions should emerge.

Decide who you want to be as a person.

Decide what you want to pursue.

And then start asking, How am I going to make this work?

> **Once you've taken a positive step forward, you are out of a failure mode and into a remedy mode.**

Once you've taken a positive step forward, you are out of a failure mode and into a remedy mode. And once you start thinking about remedies, you begin to think in practical, concrete terms, asking such questions as:

- What do I need to make this happen?
- Whose help do I need?
- Where can I go to get the help I need?
- What might be available that I'm not tapping into?
- What changes do I need to make, and how do I make them?

No longer did I spend my days sitting in a chair in my room in my house. No longer did I spend my days learning how to get around. I was going somewhere!

Once you have a direction to go, go!

And that's just what Kathy and I did.

10

KEEPING YOUR EYES
ON YOUR GOAL

Don't let the experts

trip you up.

Someone asked Conrad Hilton when he knew he was successful. He said that he knew he was successful while he was still sleeping on a park bench because he knew that once he had made his mind up to become successful, he had taken the first step on the journey to being successful. He started thinking of himself as successful with that first step.

People who travel a great deal internationally tell me that they set their watches to destination time as soon as they board an airplane. They start living in the time zone to which they are traveling. Success is much like that. Once we've set ourselves toward a particular goal, we start thinking of ourselves in terms of having accomplished that goal. On the inside, we live as if we have already reached our goal. We become successful people in our thinking, even though nothing about our external lives may have changed yet.

Kathy and I started thinking of ourselves as having a video production company that produced videos for visually impaired people. We didn't have much in the way of equipment, skill, or product. But we began to think and operate as if we did.

We did have an idea, and we were totally idea driven. Over the years, I've come to the conclusion that most truly innovative ideas are quite simple. They tend to be the ideas that people look back on and say, "Why didn't I think of that?" The idea seems too obvious, in retrospect.

Our idea was and is simple: add a narrative sound track to an existing piece of film. The narrative sound track describes the setting, sets, scenery, props, subtitles, costumes, and the action taking place on the screen. In other words, the narration describes all the things that a visually impaired person cannot see. For example, the narrative sound track might say, "We see a large white building and then a sign in front of it that reads, HOSPITAL." Or "We see the skyline of New York City and the words *New York City 1943.*"

This narrative sound track must be added to the film in such a way that the current sound track of the film—with all the existing dialogue, music underscore, and sound effects—remains intact and in sync with the visuals. The narration fills in the blank spaces on the sound track with useful information.

In my mind's eye, the process for doing this was as simple as the idea—just peel off the sound track, add to it, then put it back together and reel it up.

That didn't turn out to be as easy in reality as it was in my mind! Nevertheless, we began our pursuit of the idea.

Videos for Blind People

Today, we are a television network, but we started as a home video company known as Narrative Video Network. Our first office was in the basement of a condominium building in downtown Tulsa. And we used some equipment we borrowed. The guy who owned the equipment didn't think my idea would work, so even though I wanted to buy the equipment, he said, "I'll just let you use it, and when you need to [in other words, when you discover that your idea won't work] you can bring it back."

We had that equipment sitting on a card table outside a broom closet under the stairs. We hung boat cushions on the walls in the broom closet to create something of a sound studio. We wrote seven narrative scripts for various television shows, and then we chose the specific materials to create our first two videotapes. Our thinking was that if our idea worked, we could duplicate the tapes and make them available for distribution directly to blind and visually impaired people. With the proceeds, we'd do more tapes.

The process was slow and laborious.

Kathy could see the screen well enough to prepare a script, which I contributed to from the vantage point of a person who couldn't see what was going on. Kathy ran the equipment, and she kept an open line to the toll-free troubleshooting expert at Sony, which had manufactured the equipment we borrowed. My job was to go into the little sound booth we rigged up and record the narration. Kathy would say, "Here's the segment," and she'd play the tape. Then she'd say, "Right after this sound, you say this, and right after this sound, you say that." And then I'd record the narrative sound track completely from memory, according to the sound cues she had given me. I'd say a line, wait a count, say another line, wait four counts, say another line, and so forth. Then we'd play back a segment to see if the timing was right. If it wasn't, we'd redo that portion. It takes a long time to do a ninety-minute movie at that pace.

It never dawned on me then to get a narrator who could read the script and see the monitor at the same time. Not all good ideas come instantly and up front. In many ways, we were clearing ground like pioneers, by hand, totally unaware that heavy earthmoving machines might be available.

Today, we have a team of writers and production people. Kevin Meyer, our narrator, is among the most talented and dedicated professionals I have ever met. We can do a program in a matter of a few hours, but back then, with only the two of us working, and one of us fully blind, the process took several days.

After what seemed like an eternity, we completed our two tapes, and we were ready to put the narration back onto the broadcast master tape. We quickly discovered there wasn't any room on the master tape for the additional track we had created.

We had to mix our sound in with the existing sound, but the time codes on video equipment don't allow a tape to take sound only. This posed a massive problem, one we couldn't resolve on our own.

I called the best broadcast facility in our part of the country at the time, and I said, "I need your help. I need your best person to help us with a problem." Looking back, I should have said, "I need your most creative, innovative engineer."

The manager gave us his *best* person, however. An expert.

Watch Out for the Experts

As you make decisions and pursue your dream, watch out for some of the most dangerous people I know: experts. Experts usually don't know anything about what you are going to do and be, but they are convinced that you can never do it or be it. They'll give you at least a couple of dozen reasons why what you've decided to pursue won't work and can't be achieved.

> ▢ *As you pursue your dream, watch out for some of the most dangerous people I know: experts.*

I didn't know at the beginning how my idea was going to work. I just knew that if I could imagine the idea, it could work. And I knew that if I stayed with the idea long enough and tried enough things, I'd find what did work.

The same goes for your new idea. If you can visualize fully how your idea works as a finished product, there's got to be a way for it to work in reality. You may not stumble on the exact *how* the first time out. You may have to spend weeks, months, even years figuring out the *how* part. You may need to try many methods. But eventually, you will find the key if you stick with your goal and are true to your idea.

Experts rarely believe your idea will work. I can't tell you how many times people have said to me, "Don't try that, Jim, because you're going to hurt yourself or you're going to be disappointed."

For the most part, the people who tell me that aren't vicious. They truly believe what they are saying. But if your best friend feeds you poison when you're starving, you'll still die, regardless of the fact he is your best friend. The same principle applies to your ideas and dreams. The best-intentioned person can feed you poison that will kill your ideas, and all the time, she'll think she is doing you a favor.

It's up to you to keep your mind shut to that poison and keep your idea alive.

Well, there we were in our fine television facility, and an expert came to talk to us. He sat down next to me. My little machine was in a cardboard box on the floor between us. That was my entire television network at the time—a little machine in a cardboard box. I told the man what I wanted to do to create a narrated program. He started in, "Jim, I've been in this business twenty-one years. I've been everywhere, seen everything, and done everything."

All the while he was telling me his credentials, he was kicking my box. He was kicking my entire television network, and he didn't seem to realize he was kicking it!

The man concluded, based on everything he knew as an expert after twenty-one years in the business, that our idea wouldn't work. And he walked away.

I went back to the manager of the broadcast facility and said, "Do you have anybody else back there I can talk to—preferably somebody who doesn't already have his or her mind made up that our idea won't work?" The manager said, "I'll see."

In a few minutes, a twenty-year-old kid came out, and I said, "Will this work?" He said, "I have no idea. I'm just a college kid trying to work my way through school, but I can wire it up and give it a try."

That was good enough for me.

He agreed to work with us, and we started in on making it work. He'd read the manual, and then we'd work our way through it, step by step. We would wire things up, give it a try, second by second, frame for frame. If it didn't work, at least we knew what didn't work. We stayed late a lot of nights to try the next idea and the next. And I learned a great lesson in that process: There's great freedom in just trying out possibilities.

If there is a prescribed way that something is supposed to be done, there is a certain amount of pressure to do the task that certain way to the best of your ability. But if you are just trying out various possibilities, you can do virtually anything you want. There is no pressure. It's a very creative feeling, and it's rewarding in its own way even if you don't succeed. At the very least, you have an understanding of what doesn't work as well as a sense that you are one step closer to discovering what will work.

While we were experimenting with ways to put the extra sound track on the video, I embarked on a campaign to write some of the top people in the television industry, telling them what I was doing, and asking for their help, usually in the form of an interview. One person I wrote was Ted Turner, who wrote back immediately, saying in essence, "That's a great concept. Let me know what I can do to get involved."

I discovered in the course of contacting various people that the visionaries, the people who have an ability to visualize something, didn't have any problem with my idea. They thought it made sense. They were all encouraging. Only the people who got bogged down in "how's this going to work?" details raised caution signs.

The day finally came when we wired it up, we gave it a try, and it worked! Truly without realizing it at the time, we had pioneered a new technology for television.

You might think I had learned my lesson about experts, but I hadn't.

After I had a program that would work, I had to figure out what to do with it. That meant, I presumed, entering the video business. I thought, *Well, we'll duplicate a few tapes and get them out there and see what happens.*

Frankly, my dream wasn't big enough. It's one of the few times in my life when I didn't have a big-enough vision for what could be done.

Always remember this: A big dream doesn't cost any more than a little one.

Always remember this: A big dream doesn't cost any more than a little one.

Our Next Step Was a Major Leap!

When Kathy and I had our first two videos, we were thrilled. I can't tell you what an accomplishment that was to us at the time.

The product we had in hand wouldn't have been all that impressive to a casual observer, however. We had two two-hour video masters. The first video had an opening in which I briefly interviewed the man who was the producer of *Matlock* and *Perry Mason*, and the interview covered the difference between Matlock and Mason as attorneys. Then we had a *Matlock* program with a narrative sound track on it, followed by a *Big Valley* episode with a narrative sound track.

The second tape opened with a segment of *The Andy Griffith Show*, followed by a program called *The Guns of Will Sonnett* featuring Walter Brennan, followed by a *Gomer Pyle* segment with Jim Nabors and a *Branded* segment with Chuck Connors.

These first two tapes are still out there. We get calls periodically from libraries and other organizations that have the tapes, have worn them out completely, and want more copies.

We had gone through a round of letters with the syndicators of the programs we put on video, of course. That process had taken about the same length of time as our technical challenge of creating the tapes. But in the end, the owners of the programs were willing to cooperate with a company called Narrative Video Network.

Duplicating tapes and distributing them directly to people who were blind, however, loomed before us as a major new organizational challenge. How could we get our precious tapes directly into the hands of the people who would want them?

If we duplicated them and sent them through the mail, we would need a huge mail-order business, with a sizable warehouse. When I visualized thirteen million copies of a videotape, I quickly concluded that the tapes weren't going to fit in the basement room of a condominium building!

Mail order was not the way to go. What then?

It seemed logical to distribute tapes through outlets where people could pick them up, view them, and then return them.

So where do blind people get materials? They go to public libraries, primarily to borrow books on tape, records, tapes, and compact discs. And they get some materials from the various organizations of blind people.

These became our targeted outlets.

We duplicated our tapes and sent them to these outlets, but we soon realized that we weren't going to be able to keep up with the demand. Duplicating and mailing out tapes were taking all of our time and all of our money.

We had sold advertising to cover the production costs of the videotapes we had produced, but that money didn't cover the expense of duplicating and shipping out thousands of tapes. We had originally anticipated that the users would pay something for each tape, but libraries and organizations of blind people don't spend money for tapes such as ours. The bottom line was that the more tapes we duplicated, the more we were digging ourselves into a financial hole.

Television.

The idea hit me like a bolt of lightning. If we could get our tapes onto a television network, people would have immediate access to them, and we'd bypass all of the duplicating and mailing. Our costs would be covered by the advertising, and we'd truly be in business.

Everything about the idea seemed right to us.

But since I didn't have a clue how to get a program on television, I turned to yet another so-called expert.

The Gorilla of Cable Television

Shortly after I said to Kathy, "We need to be on television," I had a meeting with the people in the public relations firm we had hired to promote our tapes. When I told them my idea, they said, "We know a man, right here in Tulsa, who has a reputation as the gorilla of cable television. We'll arrange for you to meet him next Monday, and you can see if he'll go for this idea."

Fortunately for me, that meeting was four days away. Also fortunately for me—at least at times—I'm not a patient person. Patience may not make my top ten traits.

I started thinking, *There's a cable television company right here in my city. I pay it eighteen dollars a month for thirty-two channels. The least the company can do is let me be on one of them since there's a lot of garbage on there that isn't as good as my stuff.*

The more I thought along these lines, the more impatient I became about meeting the gorilla of cable television the following week. So I loaded up my TV network in a box and took a cab to Tulsa Cable Television. I didn't know very much about cable television at the time. I didn't know that there were a thousand cable companies in America, or that Tulsa's cable company was the twentieth largest. I didn't know that Tulsa was the largest city in America with only one cable company, or that Houston has seventeen cable companies and Dallas has eleven. I didn't know any of that. I just took a cab and went over to my local cable company with all my stuff in a box, and I got an appointment with the guy in charge of programming.

I wired up our system and showed him one of our tapes. He said, "That's the most amazing thing I've ever seen." And then he said, "We'll carry you guys." We made a deal. I returned to our basement office a few hours later and announced to Kathy, "We're on!"

I thought to myself, *That was easy enough. Maybe I don't need to meet with the gorilla of the cable television industry.*

Still, I thought there might be something I could learn, so I kept my appointment. For nearly three hours, I sat at a conference table with this guy and told him about my idea to create television for blind people. He listened patiently, never interrupting, until I was finished. Then he said, "Jim, I've been in this business a long time, and I can tell you, you'll never get on one system anywhere."

"Not even one?" I asked.

"Not even one," he said with all the confidence in the world.

"Never?" I asked.

"Never ever ever," he assured me. He went on to say, "And, Jim, even if you did manage to get on one station, what corporation in its right mind would want to run its commercials with your programs?"

I thanked him for his time, picked up my little box with my tape, and walked out.

All the way back to the office, I had a conversation in my mind with this man. It went pretty much like this: "Thank you for your opinion. I don't know who gave you the title gorilla of cable television, but I'm not sure you deserve it. We may never get on more than one cable system, but I've already got our programming on one cable system and I believe I'll be able to get us on other systems as well." By the time I got back to the office I wasn't the least bit discouraged; rather, I was greatly encouraged. I had a sneaky hunch I knew more about my success on cable television than he did.

Today, 1,028 cable systems and broadcast affiliates carry our programming into twenty-five million homes in North America. NTN is currently shown in eleven foreign nations. We have about twenty hours a week of programming, and we're on seven days a week. Our advertisers have included major companies such as Sears, Kmart, and AT&T. They buy our commercial time not because they like me or because they feel sorry for blind people but because it's good business.

The people who produce commercials know something that regular television producers don't seem to know. The people who produce commercials design them to be heard more than viewed. In many instances, the commercials run on both radio and television, and the images on TV only enhance what is being said. The commercials that run on our programming seldom need to be adapted in any way.

Many people listen to TV more than they watch it. Many people engage in some other activity while supposedly watching television. It may be ironing, working in a shop, or doing chores or handwork of some kind. These people respond to our programming with enthusiasm because they can watch less and understand more. And then there are people who simply seem to enjoy this style of programming. Perhaps the narrative track calls their attention to certain visuals, or perhaps they find it a fuller experience. Whatever the reason, an amazing 60 percent of our nationwide audience is made up of people with full sight who enjoy the programs.

I wouldn't have known all of that to share with you today if I had listened to the experts.

11

REFUSING
TO BLINK

Stare down the big lies.

When a crisis strikes, people generally ask, "Why me?"

I admit to having asked that question on a few occasions. But I believe the more realistic question to ask is, "Why *not* me?"

Whoever said life is fair? Fairness ultimately involves comparing yourself to other people. And that's a surefire way to achieve mediocrity as far as I'm concerned. When we compare ourselves to others, we decide in some cases that we're better off than others, and we settle down at that spot and start to stagnate. On the other hand, in cases where we decide we're not better off than somebody, we can let jealousy and bitterness bog us down to the point that we lose momentum and never pursue our dreams with all of our energy.

Assume that life isn't fair, but your life is your life.

Don't resort to the fairness argument. Assume that life isn't fair, but your life is your life. Make the best and most of it!

The Big Lies

This issue of fairness, however, is only one of several lies that are likely to be fed to you as you pursue your personal destiny. One of the biggest lies that people seem to swallow in the course of their self-appraisal about what they want to be, do, and have in life is this:

Lie #1: That's for other people to be, do, or have, but it's not for me to be, do, or have. I can't have that great a destiny.

I can't count the number of people I've met in the last decade who hold to that lie. It's a cop-out. Rather than say to themselves, "I really want that"—and then go for it—they make an automatic assumption that they are going to fail if they try. They cover for their lack of focus and effort by saying, "Only certain people can be, do, or have that, and I'm not part of the elite group."

Such people divide the world into two classes of individuals:

- *Category #1:* Healthy, wealthy, happy, successful people—people who get everything they want out of life. Things come easily and naturally to these people. The "fortunate ones" get all the breaks, know all the right people, and have all the best luck.
- *Category #2:* Those who work hard, never seem to get anywhere, live their lives in mediocrity, struggle to get by, and never achieve or do anything spectacular. The "unlucky souls" never have any breaks or any luck, don't know anybody, and never succeed.

When the people who lump folks into these two categories drive past a luxurious home or pull up next to a limousine or watch the people depicted on *Lifestyles of the Rich and Famous,* they make an automatic assumption that these people had a head start in life and that they were gifted in some way. They never see life as a level playing field. They always assume that successful people get what they have because life is somehow stacked in their favor.

This division of people into the "lucky fortunate" and the "unlucky unfortunate" is a big lie. That isn't the way life really is. And if you believe that lie, you'll always be looking for excuses to justify your paltry existence. You'll never get beyond where you are.

You've put yourself into the pile of people who are "destined" to live just below the level of success.

In reality, very few things are beyond your capacity to be them, do them, or have them.

"Well," you may say, "I can't walk on water." Oh? At least two guys in history—one named Jesus and one named Peter—walked on water. And a whole lot of water-skiers might tell you that they routinely come close to that feeling.

"Well," you may say, "I can't fly." Oh? Maybe not without a mechanical device of some kind, but try telling a woman on a hang glider that the experience she is feeling isn't one of flying. Not to mention, of course, that when you are in an airplane, you are definitely moving through the air on wings.

"Well," you may say, "*you* can't see, Jim." Oh? I may not be able to look through my physical eyes at this present time and see visual images, but I have a great ability to "see" things. Not only that, but I'm not willing to concede that there aren't new horizons just around the next experimental and technological or medical bend that might not enable me to "see" in some way in the very near future.

Seeing involves perspective, and I've got that. Seeing involves focus, and I've got that. Seeing involves interpreting cues for meaning, and I've got that. I see in all kinds of ways, though not perhaps as a person with a working cornea, retina, and interocular nervous system.

> *Face up to the reality of what you can do, and you'll likely discover that there are, indeed, very few things you can't do.*

Face up to the reality of what you can do, and you'll likely discover that there are, indeed, very few things you can't do. And they are things you probably don't need to do to fulfill your deepest desires and dreams.

Lie #2: You shouldn't be, do, or have what you are dreaming about as your personal destiny and goal of success.

The first lie deals with whether you can have success and achieve your personal destiny. It's a matter of *can*.

The second lie deals with *should*. Some people are going to tell you that you shouldn't dream big, set higher standards, or seek to get more out of life than you already have.

You need to face this lie head-on.

If, through your efforts and focus on a new and bigger dream, you begin to take yourself out of Category #2 and put yourself in Category #1, you will be subject to scrutiny, ridicule, and rejection. Those who remain in Category #2 are likely to think that you have turned into someone with an "attitude" who, in their opinion, needs to be brought down a notch or two. That may not be at all the way you feel or in any way related to the reality of the situation or your motivations, but it is likely to be the way many people perceive you. Be prepared for it. It's part of what happens when people begin to enjoy some success.

Accept at the outset of your pursuit of your personal greatness that not everybody you want to help you in your push toward your full potential is going to help you. That's life. Don't become angry or disillusioned with them. Recognize that they have their agendas and they are exercising their options of choice, and move on in your life.

Grudges, resentments, and bitterness will only hold you back.

This holds true for people you supervise or employ. As much as you might try to hire people who are on your team and who want to achieve the same goals you desire to achieve, you have to face the fact that nobody is going to be as motivated to reach your dreams and goals in life as you are.

You can motivate these people, but ultimately, you need to accept that nobody is going to run as fast as you are to your goal. Accept that. And keep moving. Even though others may not be fully up to your speed, you must continue to set the pace. If you slow down to accommodate their speed, eventually, you'll be stopped. Keep running. Keep people around you on their toes trying to catch up to you.

If others tell you that you shouldn't do something, take that advice with a big grain of salt. How do they know you shouldn't? And what do you know about yourself, what do you believe about yourself and about God, that leads you to believe you should?

I can't begin to tell you how many very successful people I've met who were told at one time in their lives that they couldn't do something or shouldn't try something. If they had taken that advice, they wouldn't have become the successful people they are.

Just when you have pretty much decided that you are going to pursue your dream or goal anyway—apart from the hurtful remarks or rejection you may have experienced from people you thought were your friends—you need to watch out for a second wave of assault.

This assault comes in the form of fearmongering.

Lie #3: You can try, but you won't make it.

When they see that their initial efforts to hold you down or keep you at their level aren't working, those who desire to keep you in their circle of mediocrity are likely to turn to fear as a tactic. They'll begin telling you, often using a host of statistics and rationales, why your idea may be dangerous or detrimental for you to pursue.

The tactic often employs personal assaults on your character, background, or dignity as a person. You may be told that you can't succeed in your area of choice because of the following:

- Your sex
- Your family history
- Your personal mistakes of the past
- Your face
- Your social class
- Your age
- Your lack of education
- Your personality flaws
- The character flaws of your family members
- Your physical inabilities or limitations
- Your mental inadequacies
- Your past record of low achievement

And the list goes on. No insult seems too low or too cutting to a person who seems intent on separating you from your dream.

Why are people so vindictive? Envy, mostly. Why are people so envious of the success of others? Nearly always because of their low self-worth.

I've found that the people who attempt to alienate you, manipulate you, or instill fear in you tend to do so because they have been using you in some way to increase their sense of self-worth and self-identity. When you begin to achieve something on your own and thereby increase your self-worth or develop a new dimension of your identity apart from their help or prior approval, they feel threatened. They feel less important.

Sometimes the attacks aren't personal, especially at the outset. Rather, they are linked to the consequences the people think you will experience as a result of pursuing your idea. You may very well hear such comments as:

- "You're going to look stupid when . . ."
- "I hate to see you invest all of this time and effort in something that is such a long shot."
- "Why put yourself through all this grief for something that you aren't certain will succeed?"

Don't listen.

Think about the farmer who spends days preparing the soil for planting a crop and then planting his seed into the ground. After he has finished planting, he is going to appear to have an empty field. The field is likely to remain that way—to the naked eye—for some time. And sure enough, not all the seeds may sprout. But just as surely, some of the seeds are going to sprout, and if the crop is tended well, a good portion of the seeds are going to reproduce and create a harvest.

A person could very well say to the farmer, "Just look what you've done. Burying all that seed into that field, sweating and busting your back, and for what? You have nothing to show for it except a bare field."

> *There's a seed of life in every dream or goal that a person sets for himself.*

But the farmer knows the real fact of the matter—that he has planted seed, each kernel of which bears life inside it.

The same principle holds for the person pursuing a dream or goal. There's a seed of life in every dream or goal that a person sets for himself. The person who doesn't share the dream or goal can't see that life, can't experience it, and doesn't believe it's there. But the person with an ardent inner motivation knows that the life is in the seed of her idea or dream, believes it will grow and, therefore, expects it to grow. The person motivated toward the achievement of a personal dream or goal feels, knows, and believes in the life of that dream, and the capacity of that dream to grow, develop, expand, and eventually manifest itself as a reality.

Success Doesn't Envy Success

I've discovered in recent years as I have met more and more successful people, as well as those aspiring and working hard to become successful, that truly successful people don't envy the success of others.

Eagles wish all birds could fly at their level, see the world from their vantage point, and enjoy the life they lead. Pond-bound ducks become upset when one of their own begins to soar like an eagle.

Those who enjoy success rarely have animosity toward another person's success. They know there is plenty of room in the sky for more successful people. They know there is no limit on the number of people who enjoy win-win success.

Who resents the success of others? The person who bears one of three opinions:

1. Another person's success detracts from him and lessens his worth.
2. There is only so much success possible so that another person's success lessens opportunity for success.
3. One becomes successful only by trampling on other people.

Let's discount and dismiss these opinions one by one.

First, one person's success does not mean that anybody else is lesser in value, lesser in importance, or lesser in worth. Truly successful people are usually magnanimous toward others—generous, considerate, and thoughtful toward those who have less than they have or who are doing less than they are doing. This stems, in part, from the fact that truly successful people know that success is defined individually. What is success to one may not be success to another. Therefore, what successful people have achieved is regarded as a personal dream, goal, or endeavor. Successful people don't expect other people to live their lives, to pursue their dreams, or to have their definition of value.

> **There is plenty of success to go around because success is always determined individually.**

Second, there is plenty of success to go around for precisely that same reason: Success is always determined individually. If person A wants to be the president of a company and person B wants to be the president of a company—well, more than one company exists in this world! If person A wants to be a movie star and person B also wants to be a movie star—well, the movie industry has room for more than one star! Success is not limited in quantity. Success is determined by quality, and quality has no limitations.

Third, truly successful people don't use others or step on others as they climb the staircase toward success. How can I say that? Because truly successful people seek success in every area of life—and they can't malign, destroy, use, or hurt others and be successful on the inside. Those who are malicious and ruthless, attempting to destroy others, know deep inside who they are and what they are doing. That knowledge is often embedded in their deep-seated feelings of inferiority. I'm not a licensed psychologist, but I know enough about human nature to know that. People who try to destroy others nearly always have low self-esteem. They think by destroying others they are going to appear big or tough or important. But they appear mean and, very often, petty.

I've had conversations with literally dozens of people at the top of their fields, and not once have I heard them speak maliciously or with evil intent toward their peers or their competitors. They may want to win on the playing field of competition, but they don't want to see other people destroyed. They know that to be truly successful, one must forge win-win situations and have a feeling of success at the end of the day, or the end of the campaign, that rests peacefully in the depth of one's soul.

No, truly successful people don't become successful by riding roughshod over others. Only greedy, hurtful, or evil people do that. And greedy, hurtful, evil people are not successful in the arenas that ultimately count most.

What Response Can You Make?

Perhaps the best response you can make to people who try to put you down, discount your dreams, or instill fear into you is no response. Ignore them.

I remember watching Muhammad Ali trying to regain the heavyweight championship. In the early rounds, he was beaten badly. After the fight, physicians discovered that he had been badly injured. I still had some sight at that time, and I watched the fight on television. I remember that there were three rounds to go in the fight, and at that point, the camera zoomed in on Ali as he sat in the corner on his stool between rounds. His manager, Angelo Dundee, was asking him, "Do we stop the fight, or do we go on?"

Ali said, in essence, "I don't want to talk about it." He refused to speak directly to Dundee. Rather, he sat on his stool talking to himself, saying things that we've all heard him say more times than we can count, "I am the greatest. I am the greatest of all time." And when he came off that stool, Ali got up with strength, and in the course of punching his way through the next three rounds, he won back his heavyweight championship belt!

Lie #4: You don't really want that.

There's a fourth lie you may hear. It seems to come from those who fail in talking you out of a dream by using the traditional tactics of fear, discouragement, and envy. It's the lie that says, "Oh, you don't really want to do that, do you? That's not really who you are. That's not really what you want."

A popular country song some time ago had a lyric that has stuck with me. The song was about a couple whose relationship had soured, yet they seemed to be sticking together for lots of wrong reasons. The line I recall is this: "We tell ourselves that what we found was what we meant to find."

I meet dozens of people every month who are feeding themselves that same line—that the career they found, the general lifestyle they found, the level of success they are enjoying in their lives, is what they *meant* to find.

In virtually all cases, I know they have bought into the lie that says, "What you have is fine. Why would you want anything more? Surely you don't expect more than this, do you?"

How do I know this is a lie? Because if I give these people an opportunity to dream about what they'd do if money were no object and they had no obligations, they eventually tell me what they'd rather be doing.

Even Little Lies Can Immobilize

Have you ever heard how elephants are trained? When we see elephants in a circus, we are watching beasts that weigh thousands of pounds—they are the largest land mammals on earth. They frequently are kept in their pens with a small piece of cord around one ankle, the cord attached to a small wooden stake. Any thinking person would ask, "Why doesn't that huge elephant just yank that little string and stake up out of the ground and walk away?" A beast that size can do pretty much whatever it wants to do and go wherever it wants to go!

Look closer. A small yearling elephant, maybe weighing only one hundred to five hundred pounds, is probably secured nearby. His cord will be a large chain, and his stake in the ground will be a large spike driven into concrete. The little elephant will strain and pull until he can't move anymore, all to no avail. In the end, he won't try to free himself. And at that point, the trainer can trade in the heavy chains and spikes for a piece of cord. The elephant no longer will try to free himself as long as he senses a tether around his foot.

People have been immobilized by far less physical means. A little fear. A little doubt. A little hopelessness. Wham! They're chained, afraid to move and unwilling to try.

Even a little lie can immobilize you if you let it. Don't listen. Walk away from these lies, and walk into the truth of your success and greatness.

Face Up to Your "Ifs"

"Ifs" are lies that say you can't be the success you envision yourself to be because or unless certain people cooperate, certain situations arise, or certain circumstances fall into your favor.

Face up to your ifs. Ifs are things that you are already anticipating as possible obstacles in your path even before you begin your trek toward success.

I'll do this, be this, or have this . . .

IF the economy is good and interest rates don't rise.

IF I don't get laid off.

IF the car doesn't break down.

IF the bank will give me a loan.

IF IF IF.

Ifs are endless. Once you are in an "if" mode, you aren't likely to get out of it because ifs become a mind-set. And that mind-set will hold you back to the point that you'll never arrive at your desired destination in life.

People may hide out in a place I call If Only. This is the place where people don't take responsibility for their actions and where excuses ranging from the weather to bad parents are used to account for failure. If Only is a terrible place to live. It has a very high tax called regret. And people who live with regret very easily become bitter and disillusioned. Such people have virtually no chance of getting out of the rut they've dug for themselves.

You can live and die in the land of If Only. And your life there is likely to be miserable from start to finish.

I had a few bad experiences in college with people who thought I would be healed if only I had more faith.

Some of them couldn't pay their bills, had weak marriages, and were abusive to their children. As far as I could tell, they didn't have much going for them in their lives, but their advice to me was, "Have more faith and you'll get healed."

I could never understand how they attached faith and healing only to the physical realm. I also came to realize that very few of the people who said this to me had truly read the Bible.

I've read the Bible cover to cover four times, not for any other reason than just to read it and find out what it says. And one thing

I've concluded from my Bible reading is that not everybody who was sick or injured or disabled in some way during the first part of the first century was healed. It seems to me that the apostle Paul was losing his eyesight at the end of his life because he speaks of writing in a large hand.

Healing involves so much more than the physical. From my perspective, physical healing is probably the least significant aspect of a total healing of who we are as individuals—spirit, mind, and body—since a physical healing is going to last only a brief period of time, whereas an emotional healing might last the rest of our lives on this earth and a spiritual healing may very well last into eternity.

I finally said to people who encouraged me to believe for healing and to have more faith for healing that if God wants to restore my eyesight, He knows where I live and He knows that I'm entirely receptive to having my eyesight restored. But in the meantime, I'm going to be about my life. I'm going to be and do everything I can be and do. Above all, I'm going to be a whole person in my mind, my emotions, my relationships with other people, my spirit, and my general physical health.

This issue of healing raises another question that pertains not only to my life but also to yours. I phrase the question this way:

Which Is the Greater Miracle?

People sometimes ask me if I believe in healing—the direct intervening healing miracles of God. I do. I see *all* healing as divine. If you cut your thumb with a knife, it will heal itself. Ask a doctor how that happens, and the doctor will shrug her shoulders. Nobody knows exactly how the body heals.

When a cut finger heals itself in a day or two, or a broken leg heals itself in several weeks, we don't think anything of that. If that finger heals in seconds or that broken leg heals in a few minutes, we'd call it a miracle. The fact is, we're hung up a little bit about time. All of healing is a miracle. I've personally experienced hundreds of healing miracles because I've recovered from hundreds of illnesses and injuries through the years.

The other thing we seem to be hung up about is whether a person "recovers" from an accident, especially if that accident causes severe injuries and there's a likelihood the person won't recover any or very many capabilities.

The real question as far as I'm concerned is this: Recover what? I've seen people recover physical abilities, yet never get over emotional trauma after a serious accident. I've seen other people overcome the psychological and emotional trauma of a serious illness, even though they may never regain fully their physical capabilities. Which is the greater healing? Which is the better recovery?

> ▪ *If I had the option of living a mediocre life with eyesight or of living the life I have today, I'd stay blind and keep the life I have.*

If I had the option of living a mediocre life with eyesight or of living the life I have today, even though I am blind, I'd stay blind and keep the life I have. I'm far healthier and stronger and more able today in so many ways than I once was, and I'm still growing and becoming more and more and more.

The ideal would be to have my sight and develop on the inside, too. But if I had to make a choice between the two, I'd choose the greater recovery I've had on the inside of my life. To me, that is a genuine healing miracle.

You'll face this same issue to some degree in your pursuit of your success. The ideal for you, naturally, would be for all of the "if only" situations to stack up in your favor.

But what is the greater miracle? Is it a greater success if you don't have everything going your way or if you do?

Do you become a better person by coming up against certain obstacles and challenges and overcoming them or by not having to deal with need, trouble, or difficulty?

Is it a greater fulfillment if you have smooth sailing all the way and everything works in your favor or if you have to fight your way to the pinnacle of your success?

I suspect a part of any person's success is this matter of dealing with "in spite of" situations, people, and circumstances rather than waiting for "if only" perfection to appear.

Healing to me is obviously a matter that involves the whole person, beginning and ending on the inside. The same goes for success.

Your success involves your whole person. It's not something tied to externals. It begins and ends on the inside. "If only" situations and circumstances are nearly always on the outside. They really aren't the issue.

Overcome Your Set of Excuses

"If only" statements and the big lies ultimately are excuses. You need to face your set of excuses, in whatever form they appear.

Once or twice a year, I speak to groups of blind people. One year I spoke at the annual convention of one of the largest organizations of blind people in the nation. About three or four thousand delegates were present, and I told them, "If many of you miraculously received your sight again today, you would have to come up with another excuse for the lousy way you live your life."

I doubt if I'll be invited back to speak to that group anytime soon, but I firmly believe what I said to them. Most blind people have given up trying to lead successful lives. They are willing to let other people define their lives and establish the ceilings of their success. They're willing to do degrading, demeaning, demoralizing things because they have lost their sight. They're willing to rely totally on others to give them things and do things for them.

But the even sadder fact is that this is true for most people, not just blind people. Most people I know live under a dark shroud of excuses. They let other people define who they are, what they can do, and what they can become. They allow themselves to become boxed in. They rely totally on others to hold them up.

It doesn't need to be that way.

I don't go to many meetings for blind people, not because I don't like them, but because I don't have much in common with them. With many blind people I meet, the only thing I have in common is that we are both blind. I rarely meet a blind person who is in business for himself or herself, who travels extensively, who is involved in the television industry, who does a lot of public speaking, or who is involved in marketing or direct sales. I'd like to meet some blind people who are involved in these areas, and if I did meet them, I suspect that we would discuss business, travel, television, public speaking, and marketing—not our blindness.

What excuses are you living under? What do you think gives you a disadvantage? What do you think keeps you from moving forward and upward in your life? What do you believe is holding you down or holding you back?

Whatever that something is, or whoever that someone is, I'm here to tell you that there's a way around that thing or that person. There's a way over that limitation, around it, through it, or under it. And no excuse is good enough for not making the effort to get past that thing or that person and moving on with your life.

To a blind person who says, "I'm not successful because I'm blind," I would say, "No. The truth is, you aren't successful because you think you can't be successful because you're blind. You're not trapped by your blindness nearly as much as you are trapped by how you think about your blindness."

Whatever your excuse is today, substitute your excuse for blindness. I'd give the same speech to you!

Face up to your excuses. You may want to use a technique that a friend of mine calls "list and dismiss." She advises people to list all of their excuses for not doing a certain task and then to go through them one by one very objectively, saying, "But that's no excuse."

If you really want something in your life, there are no excuses for not pursuing it. If you really believe you have a destiny to be somebody, do something, or have a certain thing in your life, no excuse is good enough for not making an all-out effort to achieve that dream.

Associate with Other People of Destiny

There's another aspect to this, too. You've got to be very careful who you hang around. We're influenced by other people. That's part of our human makeup. The old saying, "Choose your friends wisely," is an old saying, in part, because it's true!

You're going to end up like the people with whom you associate the most.

If you're a member of a club, you're expected to attend meetings. That's especially true for Rotary Clubs. If you miss too many meetings, you're out. Why? Because there is a mutuality principle at work.

I don't hang around groups of blind people very often because I don't want to be like many of the blind people I meet. I don't want to be limited in my thinking. I don't want to have my dreams quenched by their negative thinking and discouraging talk. I don't hang around any group of people that is continually moaning and groaning. I want to be around people who are thinking, achieving, talking about ideas, pursuing goals, and laughing along the way. I want to be around positive, upbeat, forward-thinking people.

This may sound strange coming from someone who is in the television business, but I don't want to hang around most television show characters. By the time the average student graduates from high school, he will have seen approximately twenty-five thousand people murdered on television. He will have witnessed countless abuses and rapes. He will have been fed a near constant barrage of sexual innuendos and sexual jokes. He will have witnessed untold numbers of relationships that, in the past, would have been considered illicit or immoral.

Researchers are quick to say, "Well, that doesn't mean that students will do those same things or commit those same crimes." Granted, research is based on correlation, not cause and effect. We can't say with certainty that people will act a certain way because they see, hear, or experience certain things. But even correlations tell us that there is a greater likelihood that people will act a certain way through repeated exposure to certain messages.

That's the basic premise underlying the advertising dollars that drive the TV industry. If people buy thirty seconds of TV time and spend $110,000 to air a commercial to sell us a particular brand of cereal, they are counting on that commercial to be effective. They are counting on a person changing her opinion and then her behavior based on a thirty-second message. After six hours of television a day for nearly eighteen years, our children have been exposed to thousands upon thousands of hours of messages that say rape, violence, adultery, and other forms of immorality and uncivil behavior are acceptable or normative. And then we complain that they buy into the messages? We need to get a clue.

We become like the people we hang around. And if the people we hang around are TV characters on sitcoms, we're going to become like them. We're going to do what they do, dress and talk the way they dress and talk, and follow the values they profess or display by their scripted behavior.

That's why it's vital to choose your friends and your groups very carefully. You'll find it nearly impossible to be a positive person if you surround yourself with negative people. You'll find it nearly impossible to continue to put out extra time and energy toward accomplishing your goals if you hang around people who aren't going anywhere in their lives.

If you know no positive people right now, avail yourself of positive messages in books or on tapes. At the time I was trying to turn myself away from a negative outlook on life to embrace a positive outlook, there weren't a lot of people I knew to call or to be with apart from my immediate family. So I occupied myself by listening to literally scores of tapes, many of them tapes of books. I hung around positive people, even though I hadn't met them face-to-face.

You Have More Than You Don't Have

Living with excuses means that you are looking more at what you don't have than what you do have. Turn the picture upside down. Start concentrating on what you do have. In all likelihood, you have far more than you don't have.

An Irish family came to America at the turn of the century. They were very poor. They worked hard and scrimped and saved for more than three years to earn tickets on the boat to America. When they were shown to their sleeping quarters below deck, the family assumed that they were being told to stay below deck the entire voyage. And they did, eating from the meager supply of cheese and crackers that they had brought on board with them.

Day after day, they watched with envy as the first-class passengers up on the deck ate from sumptuous banquet fare. Finally, just before the ship docked at Ellis Island, one of the children in the family became ill. The father made his way to the steward and said, "Please, sir, could I have some of the leftover food for my child?"

The steward replied, "Why, of course. This food is for you, too."

"It is?" the man replied. "You mean to say we could have been eating well during the entire voyage?"

"Of course!" the steward said in amazement. "This food has been for you and your family, too, during the entire voyage. Your ticket determines only where you sleep, not what you eat."

That's true for many people. They assume that the place they are "shown" is where they must spend their entire lives. They aren't aware that they can partake of many of the same privileges as others. Success is there for the asking, there for the partaking, there for the accessing.

Face Down Your Fears

Staring down lies is one thing. Dismissing your excuses is another. Finally, you will need to face down your fears.

Meet them in the middle of the street at high noon and confront them. When you do, you'll have victory over them.

When I first began speaking and making special appearances at conventions, I went to some out-of-the-way places. Sometimes the only way to get there was by flying on a small commuter plane.

Traveling in large planes is fairly easy for me. I find the terminal, then the gate, and then walk down a little hall until I am on the plane. I count the rows to my seat and sit down. I always travel with another person, but I could probably manage large-plane travel by myself because it's a pretty straightforward process. There is no way I can get lost once I've moved into the passageway that connects the terminal gate to the plane.

Commuter planes are a completely different story. I usually have to walk outside, across pavement, and then go up stairs into a plane. Upon arrival, I have to walk down stairs and across pavement into a particular door. And the entire experience is usually noisy and windy. Once an environment gets noisy, I'm in trouble. Even when someone is with me, the experience is disorienting and frightening, in part because I often can't hear my traveling companion.

On one of my first small-plane flights, I fell down the stairs while disembarking from the plane. I sat there on the pavement with the wind and noise of airplanes all around me and literally cried. I felt utterly humiliated, frustrated, discouraged, angry—in a word, defeated.

I went home and sulked, but eventually, I got my attitude squared away. One fall down the stairs wasn't going to put an end to my life. Nor could I allow it to put an end to my travel.

Three years after that experience, the Narrative Television Network moved into Canadian markets. Our publicist told me, "You've got eight cities to do in eight days."

Well, I figured that was no problem. We were ready to go! But then I realized that we had fourteen flights to take, and most of them were going to be on little commuter planes.

Fear hit me.

It wasn't a rational thing. It was irrational, which is what most fear tends to be. We're frightened by what doesn't make sense, by what we don't know, don't understand, or don't see clearly.

I logically tried to talk myself into feeling no fear about getting on one of the small commuter planes, but when the moment came, I was scared stiff. I realized that I had to take on my fear one step at a time. First, I had to get to the door of the terminal. Then I had to cross the pavement. Then I had to climb the stairs. Then I had to find my seat. In getting off the plane, I had to go through the same step-by-step process. First, get to the door of the plane, Jim. Then find that first step. Then find the second step. Take each step down one at a time. Then cross the pavement.

And we made the journey. All eight cities. No mishaps. No falls. For me, that was a tremendous victory. It almost was as important a victory as the fact that I had eight very successful speaking engagements in the eight cities, including a major press conference in Toronto. Part of the trip involved the announcement of our program on the Family Channel in Canada—which meant an addition of two hundred affiliates to our network at one time. And yet, to me, even that fabulous news was on par with the fact that I was overcoming my fear of flying on small planes.

By the time we returned home, I realized that I was having fun. I was elated when I got on the last flight home. I had made the trip!

Fear is debilitating and paralyzing.

But winning over fear is empowering and exhilarating.

A Way Through It

There is a way through your fear. I don't know what that path may be, but I believe it's there. Fear is irrational, but there is always a rational solution for what causes your fear.

As a speaker, I have had a different kind of fear from what many people have. Giving a presentation is not a fearful thing for me. I don't have stage fright. I enjoy speaking before groups and always have.

Fear tended to hit *after* a presentation.

After a presentation, there always seemed to be a press of people who wanted personal contact. If I was speaking to ten thousand people, I'd find myself surrounded at the close of the event. I had no idea if the press of people around me indicated that there were only a few people seeking to shake my hand, tell me their story, or ask for an autograph—or if there were hundreds of people. The latter, of course, represented a potentially dangerous situation to me.

After one of the first few large conventions of this type, I told Kathy, "I'm not comfortable. Get me out of here." And she did. Once we were in the back of the staging area and away from people, I said, "There has to be a way to do this so that I can be comfortable and meet the people who are nice enough to want to say something to me personally." I especially needed to meet those who were promoting our network or who were among the VIP guests we had invited to the event.

The solution we found was for Kathy to usher people into a one-on-one fifteen-minute meeting with me.

People come into these encounters very relaxed. They know that because I'm blind, I'm not boring into them with eye contact, and that I'm not appraising their personal appearance. Talking to me is more like talking to a person on the phone. And in that setting, people seem to relax and speak freely. Also, because they know that we have only fifteen minutes together, we often get right down to the point of the conversation, and we get a number of serious things done during these fifteen-minute appointments.

What started as a fear has turned out to be one of the most enjoyable aspects of the work I do!

There is a way through your fear, and when you find it, you may unearth a real benefit to your quest for success.

Many Packages

Fears come packaged in many forms. Just as I can't define greatness, success, or destiny for you, I can't begin to know your personal fear.

I do know from talking with literally thousands of people in recent years that many times people are afraid of making a fool of themselves. They are afraid of what others might say.

Sometimes people are afraid of what they might lose—such as money put at risk or a position they have acquired.

Sometimes they don't think they can perform at a higher level, usually because they have been told by someone that they can't perform at that level.

I heard about a young woman who was told by a college counselor during her first semester at a junior college that she wasn't college material. He advised her to go into a line of work that didn't require a college degree. Fortunately, she didn't take his advice. She completed that year of junior college and then transferred to a four-year school where she found a major in which she could not only perform but also excel. She discovered that she had a difficult time taking certain types of tests, so she worked around that by taking courses—in fact, an entire major—in which performance was evaluated by means other than multiple-choice exams.

Regardless of the source of your personal fear, recognize it as a fear and throw it over the wall.

The story is told of a group of boys who lived in Ireland where the fences are often made of stones. When the boys would run through the fields and come to a stone fence that was too high for them to jump over, they'd stop and throw their caps over the fence. That was a signal that they had to find a way over the fence because no self-respecting Irish boy loses his cap! Having their caps on the other side of the fence was a way of saying to themselves, "We have to get over this. There is no other option."

Regain Your Childhood Bravado

Think back to when you were five years old. At that age, everything is possible! If you ask a group of five-year-olds if they can draw a picture, they will raise their hands and say, "Yes, I can draw a picture!" The same goes for singing a song or telling a story or learning something new. But if you ask a group of forty-year-olds the same questions, virtually nobody will respond. Someplace along the line they've allowed themselves to become infected with can't-do-itis. They have a stronger belief in what they can't do than in what they can do.

If you ask a group of children, "How many of you could be a professional baseball player, president of the United States, a millionaire, or any other position of success you can name?" virtually every child will respond that he or she could be such a person. Everything is possible to a young child.

But somewhere between childhood and adulthood, we seem to have that ability to conceive our success beaten out of us. It's still possible for you to be, do, or have what you dream about, want, or conceive.

Be a kid again, at least when it's time to dream.

You Aren't Alone in Your Fear

Truly successful people have the same fears and doubts that unsuccessful people have. They get scared. They wonder about things. But they don't let their fears and doubts stop them from pressing forward. They do something with their lives, and they take risks in spite of their fears.

One of the first actresses I interviewed for the Narrative Television Network was Katharine Hepburn. I asked her, "What makes you so special?" She said, "Most actresses of any skill look at my work and find themselves saying, 'I could have done that.' The difference is, I did it, and they didn't." I believe what she said is true for most great people. Others can always look at their work and say, "I could have done that." But, they didn't.

Successful people overcome fears and do what they set out to do, no matter how scared they may be while doing it.

Clearing the Cobwebs

When you get past the big lies and past the "if only" statements and past the other excuses you are using and past your personal fears, you are likely to feel free. It will be as if the cobwebs have been brushed away and you are unencumbered to walk freely into your future success.

Your capacities to think and to feel are your two greatest assets. They propel you forward. They also can hold you back and keep you down. Choose to get rid of the baggage that lies, "if only" statements, excuses, and fears represent.

Walk boldly into your tomorrow!

12

CORRECTING
YOUR VISION

Tackle each problem as it arises—
and refuse to give up!

Once an idea has been launched, it begins to grow. That's true for babies. It's true for companies. It's true for projects. Managing growth is what life is all about.

With growth come problems. Some of them will be small, some large. The person with his or her eyes set on greatness and destiny must learn to tackle each problem as it comes up—and never, never, never give in to a problem!

After we had our first two-hour block of time on the local Tulsa cable station, I started contacting other stations. I found a network that had a format similar to ours—the Nostalgia Channel. Nostalgia is a nationwide network, which had about five hundred affiliates at the time. I showed people in management what we could do—and told them that we intended to do a narrative track mostly for classic films—and they said, "We'll take you." Every one of the affiliates picked us up. In addition, we picked up about a hundred other outlets. And suddenly, we were just sixty days away from going on national television into some six hundred outlets with our two-hour time block, and we had only two hours of material ready to air!

We screened movie after movie and started immediately to do narrative tracks for them. Things were hopping.

Almost simultaneously, we moved into a real office—one above ground—and hired a couple of people to work for us. One of our employees was a real negative guy—the bigger the problem, the more he loved it. He came into my office at about that sixty-day mark and said, "Jim, we have a really serious problem. We're out of business. We're bankrupt. We're done."

I said, "What's the problem?"

He said, "The movies are too short."

"What do you mean the movies are too short? I screened every one of them, and they're great."

He said, "Well, they average about an hour and a half in length, and you've got a two-hour time block. You have to deliver two hours to every one of these stations by means of satellite, and you're just going to have a blackout for about thirty minutes or more if you do only a narrative track for these movies."

And then he added, "What are you going to do about that?"

At that precise moment I didn't know what I was going to do about that, but I wasn't about to tell him that I didn't know what to do. So I said, "I'm going to host a talk show. I'm going to interview the movie stars who are in the movies that we select for narration, and I'm going to do an opening and a closing for the movie, and that will fill out our two hours."

He left my office pretty upset because he thought he had a surefire great problem, and unfortunately, I sounded as if I'd already resolved it.

I went to Kathy, however, and said, "We have a serious problem." We got in a cab and went to the Tulsa Central Library, where we found a book titled *Addresses of the Stars*. I didn't know such a book existed, but we borrowed it. I wrote to Frank Sinatra, Jimmy Stewart, Katharine Hepburn, Jack Lemmon, Chuck Connors, Helen Hayes, and many more. In my letter I told them what a wonderful career opportunity I was prepared to afford them on my talk show and on my network (neither of which actually existed yet). And then I waited. I decided that we'd do a narrative track only for the films whose stars responded to the idea of an interview.

About six or seven days later I received a letter from Katharine Hepburn. It said that if I'd call a certain number, she'd be happy to discuss the interview idea with me. So I dialed the number, scared to death, and not at all expecting Katharine Hepburn to answer the phone. I knew that she hadn't done an interview in several years and that she wasn't granting interviews to anybody. That was back in 1989. Since then she's made several movies and she's done interviews to promote them, but at the time, she was pretty reclusive. To my amazement, she answered the phone. I said, "Miss Hepburn, this is Jim Stovall. I'm surprised you answered your phone."

She said, "Jim, don't you answer your phone?"

I said, "Well, yes, I do."

She said, "I've always felt that when one's phone rings, one should answer it."

"Well, of course, they should," I said, feeling a little stupid at that point, but forging ahead nonetheless. "I'd like to interview you for this program I'm doing for blind people."

And she said, "It makes perfect sense to me." So we agreed on a time for the interview, and a few days later, I called her back and we conducted the interview over the phone. We talked for nearly an hour about her career and about the production of the movie we were going to screen.

The next person I interviewed was Douglas Fairbanks, Jr. He went to Dallas, and we flew down there and videotaped an hour-and-a-half interview with him in a hotel suite. He is a fascinating individual. His father, Douglas Fairbanks, Sr., virtually invented movies as we know them today. His father also started United Artists with Mary Pickford, Charlie Chaplin, and D. W. Griffith. He also knew Harry Houdini and Charles Lindbergh, and he had stories to tell about them.

The interviews grew from there. When people knew that Katharine Hepburn and Douglas Fairbanks, Jr., had appeared on the network, they were more willing to accept our invitation to be interviewed.

We're doing more and more of these feature interviews all the time—including interviews with famous people who aren't necessarily movie stars—and there is a good possibility that the interviews themselves may be syndicated to cable companies. Several of the stars

I've interviewed—such as Helen Hayes, Chuck Connors, Cesar Romero, Ralph Bellamy—have since died. I'm hopeful that our full interviews with them can see some airtime since they were such outstanding artists and had intriguing stories to tell. At the outset, however, we had the task of editing the interviews down to fit our movie packages—primarily to fill up our two-hour block of time.

I'd like to be able to say that I planned all this at the outset—that I sat in my room and thought all this through and then emerged with the announcement, "I'm going to interview major stars, package their classic movies and interviews together, and build a nationwide television network." But as I indicated previously, things evolved.

Projects Evolve—and You Need to Change with Them

Some people say that certain projects seem to "take on lives of their own." I'm not sure that's exactly what happens, but I can understand that expression. The idea developed. And every problem that emerged in our pathway became a challenge and a means of developing the idea further.

At the time, I didn't have a vision for being on television. I had a vision for producing programs that would be of special interest to visually impaired people. Nothing more.

Two of the most foreign-sounding things to me at the time would have been that I might do television or speak publicly. I just couldn't imagine at the time how blind people could do either.

I had enjoyed both activities as a sighted and partially sighted person. I'd been a guest on a financial TV show a couple of times, and I had given a few speeches. But once I lost my sight, I figured those opportunities were over forever.

One thing I've discovered through the years is, your vision grows as the things you envision develop.

There was a time when all I could envision for myself was getting out of my room. Nothing more. Just stepping outside was a major challenge, and once I had done so, it was a major accomplishment.

Then once I was outside, I could begin to envision going to a meeting or two and being around a few strangers. Nothing more. Just attending that meeting where I first met Kathy was a major step for me.

Then once I had done that, I dared to envision with Kathy the possibility of doing a videotape or two and distributing them through a few outlets. Nothing more. Getting to that step was a giant step.

And then I could envision our programs on a cable station or two. Now I can see us being a big network, expanding our programming, and even going international.

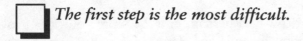 *The first step is the most difficult.*

I've become convinced that

1. *The first step is the most difficult. The second step is the next most difficult, and so forth.* I've heard that a law in physics relates to this—something to the effect that it takes more energy to get a ball rolling than it does to keep that ball rolling. That's the way it is with life and dreams, too. Taking the first step is often the most difficult and requires the most courage. The good news, however, is that the next two principles are also pretty sure bets.

2. *The more steps you take toward the total fulfillment of a dream, the faster those steps seem to fall into line.* There's a momentum in success. You don't go from being in dire circumstances one second to fabulous success the next. Success comes in increments—a step at a time. But the more steps you take toward accomplishing a goal, the faster those steps seem to come.

3. *The more steps you take toward the total fulfillment of a dream, the easier it is to take the next step that presents itself.* If someone walked into my office today and said, "Jim, I want you to triple your hours and introduce two new programs on your network," I wouldn't hesitate more than a second or two in responding to that challenge.

I'd want to make certain that the deal was sound and that all the numbers lined up favorably, but the challenge of increasing our output, or of diversifying our programming, wouldn't faze me in the least. Three years ago, I might have been brash enough to say yes to such a challenge, but I would also have known that I had just taken on a monumental task, one that may very well have created too much stress for our company and certainly more stress for me personally.

The good thing about incremental success is that the person who walks this upward path tends to be ready for the next step when it presents itself.

Infants drink formula.

Babies eat baby food.

Adults eat steak.

The more you grow as a person, and the more your idea grows into a reality, the more you and your idea are ready to expand further.

That doesn't mean that a successful person can't suffer a reversal. However, when a successful person fails, the reason seems to lie in one of these two categories:

- The person diversified outside his talent. In other words, he began pursuing things that weren't truly a part of his central dream for his life.
- The person misread the marketplace, dramatically outstripped her resources, or overextended herself financially.

This second type of error is what I call a technical error, a business mistake. Any person can make such a mistake, and most people can reduce these mistakes dramatically by surrounding themselves with sound financial advisers.

The first type of error is far more serious. It's a personal tactical error—taking on something that isn't central to your identity or your perceived reason for being. It's the result of taking on something that isn't part of your vision for your total life.

If you've suffered a reversal in your success, I suggest you take a look at these two areas. I've suffered from both of them.

Separate Technical Errors from Identity Crises

Shortly after Crystal and I married, we decided to pursue a deal on some lakeshore property about an hour's drive from Tulsa. In the early 1980s, banks in Tulsa were pretty free with lending money, and if you had a good story and a little collateral, you could get fairly decent money from a bank board. I told the bank about the half mile of shoreline I wanted to develop into a vacation community on Grand Lake, and I liquidated everything I had to come up with the earnest money. I leveraged my way into the deal, and we were given a loan at 2 percent over prime.

Prime at the time had never been above 11 percent, but six months later, we were paying 22.5 percent interest on more money than I knew existed in the whole world! The interest payments began to kill the deal. I had borrowed enough money to get the roads built to the lots and down to the lake, but we didn't have enough money to make the final hundred-foot road connection to the main highway. Crystal and I went down early one morning with a wheelbarrow, a pick, a shovel, and a saw, and we literally cut down trees and dug up stumps until our hands were blistered and bleeding. But we got a road cut to the highway, and we drove our car back and forth across it until it was pretty smooth. A couple of days later we had a road. It would have taken a bulldozer about twenty minutes to do what we did, but we didn't have the money for a bulldozer.

Another time, we found ourselves with a house on the lake and an office in Tulsa, but we didn't have enough money for an apartment in town. So I had to make a choice about whether to have a place to live or an office. For nearly two years, we slept on the floor of our office every night. As far as everybody else was concerned, we got to work early each day.

Both Crystal and I have been willing to work hard and to sacrifice for what we have and are doing in our lives. We never dreamed that we would have success without work. Work is not only a means of achieving success; it embodies success. I can't imagine a personally fulfilling life without work.

As it turned out in our situation, we eventually were able to get out of the property deal and the high interest payments without taking a hit, but without making any money, either. We jumped at that chance. We felt very lucky.

Sometimes you have to know when to cut something loose that isn't working for you. In most cases, that's also the time that you need to focus anew on what *is* working for you.

Technical errors can be far more devastating than the one we experienced, but it was tough enough for us, thank you. My error was that I hadn't foreseen the possibility of a downturn in the market or a dramatic increase in interest rates. That technical error is one I've vowed I'll never make again.

I trust I'll never make an identity crisis error again, either. I came very close to making that error during the years that I worked as a stockbroker. But even then, I had a deep inner understanding that I was working as a stockbroker only to accumulate the money I needed to do something else—something that I didn't fully envision at the time but that I realized intuitively would be what I really wanted to do in my life.

Being a stockbroker was not a part of the central dream I developed for my life. It was something I could do, and do well, but it wasn't my desire for my life. And therefore, even financial success didn't bring me the sense of fulfillment and joy that I feel today in the work I do.

Stay on Track!

To achieve incremental success, you need to get started on the right track for you and then stay on that track. Only you can define that track. And after you have defined your track, you need to persist in it.

That first step may take weeks, months, even years—and it may take a tremendous amount of patience and effort. Sometimes the first step toward your success can seem as if it's twelve feet high. But once you're up at that first-step level, you're likely to find that the next step seems only eight feet high. It likely will take you less time and even less effort than the first step. The third step will be easier.

Are the steps any less difficult or major? Probably not. Going from step four to five may involve hundreds of thousands of dollars, whereas going from step two to three involved only thousands of dollars, and going from step one to two involved only hundreds of dollars.

The risk may grow. It usually does. The higher you go on the staircase of success, the greater the fall you are risking.

But, you are no longer the same person as you climb higher and higher on that staircase. If you've taken full advantage of the lessons to be learned at each increment of success, you are stronger, smarter, and bolder.

The first time I stepped out of my house and walked to my mailbox, I was tentative. Barely moving and scared stiff might be a better description. The five hundredth time I stepped out of my house and walked the length of my driveway, I was anything but tentative. I didn't even think about being nervous. I just went to the mailbox and came back to the house.

I could just as easily have stumbled on the five hundredth trip as I could have on the first. A neighbor may have left a tricycle in my path or a small limb might have blown into the driveway from a tree, but by the time I'd made five hundred trips, I also knew that if I tripped over something, I could get up, dust myself off, and still get myself to the end of the driveway and back to the house.

Nothing about the driveway or the potential hazards had changed. *I* had changed. And that's the way it is with any success.

The problems and obstacles and challenges may not be any different. They may be bigger. But you and your ability to take on that challenge have grown even greater proportionally. You are better able to take the next step, and in that lies all the difference in the world.

Rocky Fields or Stone Fences

Some American farmers returned to the Old Country for a visit in the late 1980s. They had been born and raised in the United States, and they were unfamiliar with the stone fences, hedgerows, and other farming practices in Europe. One of the men noted, "You men must have spent a lot of time building these elaborate stone fences."

The European farmer replied, "We didn't set out to make stone fences. This ground was very rocky, and as we cleared the fields, we piled the rocks at the edges of the fields. Our aim was not to build a fence but to clear a field. The result, however, was both a clear field and a fine fence."

In your pursuit of a goal, you are likely to find this same principle at work. Your mistakes, your errors, the problems you overcome, the obstacles that you remove from your path, tend to form a boundary of sorts. This boundary is of what not to do.

Research in education has shown in the last twenty-five years that students need two types of examples to learn a concept well.

They need examples of what the concept is, and they need examples of what the concept isn't. If I'm going to teach a person about the concept of focus and the way it relates to a television camera, I need to give that person examples of a camera being sharply in focus and examples of a camera being out of focus—perhaps just slightly out of focus as well as severely out of focus. If I'm going to teach a person how to sing in tune, I'm going to want to train his ear so that he hears the true note and then give examples of that note being sung just slightly flat or sharp as well as severely flat or sharp.

The mistakes you make as you pursue your goal are examples of what doesn't work. They aren't failures. They're points of learning!

You can perceive them as failures and allow them to form stone fences that completely surround you so that you feel trapped and begin to wallow in your mistakes. Or you can perceive them as stone fences along a road that you continue to travel—a road ever more free of stones, and a road more clearly defined.

> *In most cases, successful people consider their failures to be important lessons that prepared them for success.*

Most successful people I know can point to one or more serious failures in their lives. In most cases, they consider the failures to be important lessons that prepared them for the greater success that lay ahead of them.

Scientists can point to a string of failed experiments before they found the one ingredient or one method that worked.

Actors frequently tell of the many times they have auditioned for parts and failed to get them before they landed the one role that catapulted them on their way.

Highly successful businesspeople often have serious setbacks, and some have complete financial failures and bankruptcies in their pasts.

Great cooks know that many a pot has been scorched or a particular blend of spices didn't work as they learned the techniques of creating a fine meal.

The point is not that we fail or that we strive only for perfection. The point is that we refuse to sit down in our failures and stay there. We haven't truly failed until we give up!

Pitchers and batters may hit slumps, but they keep playing ball.

Investors may hit snags and the market may slide at times, but they keep trading.

Salespeople may have doors slammed in their faces nine out of ten times, but they keep ringing bells to find that tenth-call sale.

Don't see the stones in your field as immovable. Virtually all of them can be moved with sufficient effort over time, and sometimes with the help of others.

If necessity is the mother of invention, adversity is the mother of success. Endurance through adverse times is vital.

The imagination of our entire nation was captured by the story of Captain Scott O'Grady, the fighter pilot who was shot down over Bosnia and survived six days before the daring rescue that flew him to freedom. O'Grady said in press conferences and interviews that he spent most of his time hiding, sometimes with Bosnian soldiers only a couple of yards away and sometimes with weapons firing at fairly close range. Through it all, he kept his head, stayed poised, and eventually, he was rescued.

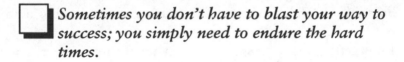 *Sometimes you don't have to blast your way to success; you simply need to endure the hard times.*

While O'Grady couldn't seem to understand why so many people were making a fuss over him, the fact is, he overcame adversity. He endured it. He came out alive. He was successful in outwitting and outlasting his adversaries. He became an example to all of us that sometimes you don't have to blast your way to success; you simply need to endure the hard times.

Don't Get Locked into a Methodology

There are countless ways to get to any goal that you set.

Our public relations firm advised us to make personal calls on the television affiliates that chose to carry our program—to meet the people face-to-face, thank them for carrying our program, listen to their comments, and so forth. It sounded like a great idea. I agreed that it was a good move to make.

Once I made that decision, however, I did the math.

At the time, we were on about six hundred affiliates. I thought, *If I visit one system a week, that will be about fifty a year. At that rate, it'll take me twelve years to visit each system—and that's assuming that we don't grow beyond six hundred affiliates and all these system managers don't die first!*

We sought a new *how*—a new way of getting to our *what* goal. The idea developed that I'd do some public speaking, and as I spoke at various events across the nation, I'd invite these system managers to come to them.

I remember the first convention speech I gave after we made that decision. Kathy was with me, reminding me of the details: "Make sure to recognize these people . . . don't forget this . . . don't forget that . . . try to remember what city you're in."

I was trying hard to stay focused and remember all these details, and then I sensed that someone had walked up to me and was standing right in front of me. Even though I couldn't see him, I had a sense that someone had entered my space. I leaned over to Kathy and asked, "What's going on?"

She said, "There's a man standing in front of you, holding a note in your face."

I was getting ready to speak publicly for the first time in about three years, and I was struggling to stay focused. I didn't need any more things to think about. I said, "Well, what does the note say?"

She replied, "It says, 'I'm deaf. Can you help me find the front desk?'"

So, I looked in the direction of the man I sensed was standing there and explained, "No, sir. I'm blind. I can't help you find the front desk."

He didn't move.

So I said, "Kathy, what's he doing now?"

She said, "He's holding the note closer to your face."

I told him in a little louder voice, "Sir, I'm blind. I can't help you!"

We never could get together on that one! He saw my lips moving and assumed I could see. I couldn't see him, and even though I heard the word *deaf*, my mind didn't calculate that he couldn't hear what I was saying. Poor guy. I hope he found the front desk.

Generally speaking, however, our shift in methodology worked. System managers were delighted to come to the VIP speaking events and to spend a few minutes with me afterward. I was delighted both to speak to the groups and to meet with the managers. It turned out to be a win-win deal for all involved.

Adjust the *How*, Not the *What*

In another very different situation in my life, my wife requested a change in methodology. Again, I didn't change my goal—only my methodology of achieving it.

My goal was to be physically fit. The *how* of reaching that goal evolved.

After we moved back to Tulsa and into my childhood neighborhood, I decided to renew a daily habit of running. I knew as an athlete that roadwork was the best way to get in shape and maintain my weight. I've run more miles than I care to recall. And since I knew the neighborhood well, having thrown papers there as a kid, I decided that it would be safe for me to run the streets when there was no traffic.

I typically awaken very early in the morning. My alarm is set at 5:45, but I wake up and shut it off before it ever rings. Most days I'm up by 4:00 A.M. so I decided that was a good time to run down the middle of the streets in my neighborhood. If a car did come, I felt I'd be able to hear it in plenty of time and veer toward a curb until it passed. Basically, I knew I was in the middle of the road because the center of the road is higher than the edges of the pavement—almost like a hump. Oh, occasionally I'd bump into a parked car or get a little off and stumble on a curb, but for the most part, I had no problem.

One day, however, I had been running about a mile and was almost to the point where I turned around—I was about as far away from the house as I dared go—and I was doing pretty well. I was starting to enjoy the morning run a bit. Running and walking were never things I enjoyed. They were things I disciplined myself to do.

So I was running along that morning when WHAM! I ran into the back of a car. My knee immediately began to swell, and I could tell that I had a deep bruise in my thigh. The force of the hit knocked me to the pavement, and as I lay there, I had a few serious thoughts about whether I was going to be able to get up, much less get home. The first thing I said to myself after the pain subsided to the point that I could speak was, "This isn't fair! I'm doing everything I know to do. And here I am."

I was hurting. I was frustrated. I was angry. Not at anyone in particular, but if someone had emerged and taken blame for the situation, I feel sure I could have beaten him to a pulp. I finally gathered myself together, got to the curb, and walked along the edge of the curb until I got home.

Every time I have had a mishap like that, fear creeps back in. It may last only a few hours or days, but it comes calling nonetheless.

And at those times I need to take stock of things once again—almost as if I'm back at square one but not quite—and remind myself of who I am and what I'm doing and what I have. A little fall in the middle of the road can't be the reason I quit pursuing what I truly want out of life. Now, it could be a reason that someone could quit. But I'm determined it's not going to be a reason for me.

You're going to have moments in your pursuit of excellence when you bang yourself up, perhaps pretty badly. You can cry, moan, fight the air, and sit down in defeat. But don't stay there. Get back on track. Separate your mistakes, your hurts and injuries, and your errors in judgment from the real you—the you destined for something better.

If you lose the capacity to get up and get back on the horse that just threw you, you lose your nerve, and when you lose your nerve, you lose everything you might do and become.

What did happen in the aftermath of that serious fall in the early-morning darkness was that Crystal asked me to please find another way.

Several times prior to that, I had misjudged a turn in the road and had ended up running into trees or tripping over curbs. Most of the time I was all right, and fortunately for me, the sanitation workers looked out for me. They were the only people up at that time of morning, and somehow they figured out that I was blind. So as they would run around with their little carts and ferry the trash back and forth to the big truck, they'd yell to one another, "Watch it! This is the blind guy, so move over!" They were pretty decent about it, although the people in the neighborhood were probably awakened by their yelling more than once. For my part, the sanitation workers and I got along just fine out there.

After I ran into the back of that car and injured myself, Crystal brought the matter to a head. She had been upset for quite some time about my running and getting hurt. She'd awaken when I got up, and then she couldn't go back to sleep, worrying about if I was okay out there in the dark. As much as that, I think, she resented being awakened at all!

Crystal is not an early-morning person, which is putting it mildly. She'd just as soon get up at the crack of noon every day. She holds to the belief that if God had intended people to get up in the morning, He would have started the clock by putting the "1" at dawn.

And so it was that one Christmas, I bought a treadmill. A wonderful invention. I built a room onto the back of my house to serve as an exercise room, and then I went to a guy who sells equipment to health clubs and said, "I want the best treadmill that you have."

He said about one machine, "This one does everything. It has a computer on board and it does all this stuff. Everything you need is on this treadmill."

I said, "It has to be simple. I'm blind, and I can't see this thing to read all its gauges or to program it."

He replied, "I'll preprogram it for you so you have a workout every day. All you do is push the button, and this treadmill will take you through hills and valleys and curves. It will tell you how far you've gone, how fast you went, how many calories you burned, and it will monitor your heart rate along the way."

I bought it, and he set it up in my house. The first day I got on it for my twenty-minute workout, I pushed the button and the thing fired up and I started moving. Up hill. Down hill. Kept going. I had my radio on and I was listening to the news and then to some music, and then the news came on again, and then some more music, and then the news came on again. I was starting to get pretty tired. I thought, *I'm in better shape than this. I've been running every morning, and I can't do a twenty-minute walking workout?*

I called to my wife, and she said, "Well, Jim, you're going through this the third time! The workout program is automatic, but the machine doesn't stop when it gets to the end of the workout. You've got to push the button again to stop it."

If I hadn't called her, I'd probably still be on that treadmill!

Methods may change. But problems don't disappear with a change of methods. They also change.

The other side of that coin is this: Don't be afraid to change methods. You can get to your goal—in my case, physical fitness—using many methods. Find the one that works for you and for those who are important to you.

What If Your Dream Changes?

What happens if you start out pursuing a dream and then you find yourself dreaming about something else?

That's possible. One dream often leads to another dream. And that's okay. You need to give yourself permission to make a switch. We've all heard stories of people who pursued one dream and made it to the top of that field, and then seemed to take a flying leap in another direction and began pursuing another dream. Fine with me! And, I hope, fine with you. My guess is that the person who pursued one dream and made it to the top in that field is very likely to make it to the top of the next thing he or she tries.

What about the successful Wall Street investor who decides to trade business suits for overalls and become a farmer in rural New England? That person may very well become a successful farmer in rural New England.

What about the corporate manager who decides to trade his stock options for a small bed-and-breakfast operation or a small-town business? So be it. That person may very well become a successful B-and-B owner or small business owner.

What about the CPA who decides to trade in his ledgers for a Bible and become a member of the clergy? Or the pastor who realizes that he wants to become a mechanic? I'd suggest both make the switch if that's truly the heart's desire.

One type of career, one job description, isn't necessarily more valuable than the next. Success is defined by what you want, and your wants may change. Your definition of success may change. And that's okay.

You also need to recognize that you have more choices than you may think you have. So often people get locked into thinking that in any particular situation, the only choices are A, B, and C—or however many categories they think exist. In reality, there are virtually countless options in just about any situation. Not only are there options that you haven't thought about yet, but there are options that nobody has thought about yet!

As you pursue a dream, you may stumble across an option that you hadn't remotely anticipated. Suddenly, that opportunity is right in the middle of your path. Do you take it? Evaluate it just as you would any other choice. It may be just the thing for you, or it may be an obstacle in your way. Either way, the choice is yours. As much as I encourage you to focus on the pursuit of your dream, I also encourage you to be open to the possibility of new and even greater dreams.

When I was a kid in first grade, I couldn't imagine all of the opportunities that might be there for me once I had a high school diploma. The opportunities unfolded as the years went by. Once I was in college, I didn't imagine all of the opportunities that are before me today. The opportunities presented themselves while I was pursuing a prior dream and goal.

That's the way dreams and goals work. They get you to a point where a new, more expansive, greater goal presents itself. You see new horizons. And when you do, don't be afraid to switch gears and direct your energies in that new direction.

How can you tell if the new goal is a potential detour or obstacle or a new goal worth pursuing? Check your motivational level about it. Do you really want this new thing? Has it become the foremost desire of your life? Does the new dream last? Does it grow, or does it fade after a few days of thought? Can you see this new dream more clearly than you've seen previous dreams?

Then consider your new dream or goal objectively. Does it fit into your broad understanding about who you are and who you are destined to be? Does it fly in the face of values you hold to be true and worthy? If the new dream represents a radical departure from your basic understanding of yourself and your values, you aren't likely to sustain that dream very long. Give the dream time. It may still be in development.

Look for the Sign: Dream Under Construction

Dreams and goals develop over time. The more you give wings to a dream, the greater the possibility that dream will move in a direction you hadn't anticipated. Dreams rarely stay fixed very long. Dreams flow from our creativity, and because they do, they change with the flow of our lives. They are like water moving over hard ground—they form channels and rivulets and take on direction.

Don't pounce on a dream or goal too quickly. Give it time to sink deep within your being. When you find the dream or goal that recurs, go with it.

Does the dream settle into you, or do you settle into the dream? I don't know. That's something like the old philosophy question: Which came first, the chicken or the egg? Our dreams and goals that define our personal sense of destiny become so much a part of us that we cannot be separated from them. They define us, even as we pursue them. What we do gives us definition for who we are. Who we are drives us toward what we do and have. We may be able to write our goals and dreams on paper, but if a dream or goal is truly linked to our personal sense of destiny for our lives, we don't need to write it as a statement. That dream or goal will be so much a part of us that we'll think about it, ponder it, and put our imaginations to it from waking moment to sleeping moment. We'll live and breathe that dream. We cannot run from it, hide from it, or escape it. We can never take a vacation from it. It will always be there, central to all of our decisions and, therefore, central to all our activities.

Be Encouraged—Your Dream Isn't as Fragile as You May Think

For many people starting out in pursuit of a greater degree of success, success may seem fragile. I've seen people worry about one meeting, one event, one sale, or one interview as if it was a make-or-break moment.

In reality, there are few make-or-break moments in your path toward personal greatness. You certainly want to have as many successful moments as you can have and keep the unsuccessful encounters to a minimum, but success rarely hinges on just one moment or just one personal encounter.

I discovered this early in our promotion of the Narrative Television Network.

Despite my success in selling commercial time for our programs, the first few months we were on television were a struggle. Part of that was due to the lead time necessary in selling advertising. Most people make their budgets a year in advance so we were convincing people to buy commercials that weren't going to air, and thus weren't going to be paid for, for many months. Some agencies producing commercials wanted to test the market, which meant that not only did we need to produce good programming during this time, but we also needed to make a concerted public relations effort to get our name known.

We felt a real break came for us when *Good Morning America* asked me to come to New York to do a feature segment with Charlie Gibson. We saw that as a major step for us, and we called all of our advertisers and cable systems to tell them that we were going to be featured on the show. In some ways, we hung our hat on the few minutes of national exposure.

Kathy and I flew to New York and prepared for the segment, and then the show went long for some reason. We were sent away and told to come back the next day. No big deal to them. I was devastated. I thought, *Our credibility is shot. We've told all these people that we were going to be on and now we aren't.* We immediately got on the phone and called the people we thought would be watching, saying that there had been a mix-up and that we'd be on the next day.

The next day I was all set to go on when one of the floor producers announced that the president was coming on with a live remote from the White House—I think it was an announcement related to the crisis in the Persian Gulf—and Kathy and I were once again sent back across the street to our hotel. This time I thought, *We're dead for sure. Nobody is going to want another call from us telling them that our feature segment on this show has been postponed a second time.*

I worried about it all day. Kathy encouraged me at that point. We were standing at a street corner in New York City, and I was feeling as if I had totally blown everything. I was ready to fly home and forget all about being on *Good Morning America*. Kathy said, "We didn't come this far to get tripped up by something this minor." I'm glad I listened to her.

We did the interview later in the day, and it turned out great. The segment aired some time later, on Valentine's Day as I recall. The next time I called our advertisers, they said, "Hey, we saw the feature," or "We heard you were going to be on *GMA*, but we missed seeing it. It was great that you got to be on that show." Nobody really cared that we hadn't been on the first day we had said or the second day.

I learned a lesson out of that: Success isn't nearly as fragile as many people think. If you're out there doing all you know to do to the best of your ability each and every day, success is pretty durable.

In a good many instances, if you are headed in the right direction for you, and you are doing everything you know to do to treat people well, provide good service and good product, and build your life on sound principles and solid values, things very often seem to have a way of working out.

This came home to me in another interview experience.

As good a guide as Kathy has been to me, accidents still happen. This particular time we were on our way to San Antonio, and we were both enthusiastic about the trip. I had been invited to appear on another cable network to discuss our show, and it seemed like a break for us. We were rushing through the airport on our way to meet the man from the network who was picking us up, and Kathy was doing her job perfectly. I was paying attention the best I could, but the place was very noisy, and noisy places are always difficult for me. As it turned out, four-foot concrete pillars hold up the roof of that airport, and I hit one of them squarely and hard right on the side of my eye. Almost instantly, my eye started to swell and turn black. By the time we got to the station, it was throbbing with pain and looked even worse.

The woman in charge of makeup took one look at me and said, "Well, I can't fix that." I didn't know what to do. I hadn't come all that way to back out of the interview.

About that time the interviewer came in to talk over the show format with me. I was sitting in semidarkness, almost in profile to him, as he explained that he did his show format a little differently from most hosts. He informed me that he would sit in the middle of a semicircle and have one guest on either side of him so that the three of us would form a three-way conversation.

I said to Kathy, "Somehow this is going to work."

I was in profile virtually the entire program. The side of my face that was swollen and discolored was off camera. I did the entire show, talking straight to the host on my right, and my bad eye was never seen by the audience.

Running into posts is part of the price I pay for getting out of my little room at home. I could still be sitting there. But I'm willing to fall or run into something or injure myself in some way to have the freedom of getting out of my room and into the mainstream of life.

You may injure yourself as you pursue your goal—dent your reputation, suffer a bruise to your ego, get a black eye for a mistake you make. But don't let it stop you. Don't let it send you back to a place of fears, doubts, and discouragement.

Refuse to give up.

Keep moving forward.

You'll get there!

13

DEVELOPING AN EYE FOR EXCELLENCE

Become the most competent person in your field.

Competency means that you know how to do what you do. If you don't have the knowledge or skills at the outset of a pursuit, acquire them—and do so as quickly and with as much excellence as possible. If you aren't competent, you won't get very far in your pursuit of your maximum potential, no matter how charming or glib you may be. There is no substitute for knowing your business, whatever that business may be.

Being competent isn't the same as becoming an expert. As I have used the term in this book, being an expert has more to do with attitude than with competency. Those who are truly competent rarely advertise themselves as experts or claim to know it all. Rather, competent people know enough to know that they don't know it all, and competent people are willing to tell you they don't know.

Although I would never encourage you to adopt the attitude of an expert, I encourage you with all my heart to adopt the goal of becoming competent at what you choose to do.

Invest in Your Skill Level

Dr. Warren Hultgren, the retired pastor of a large church in Tulsa, is one of the most well-informed, best-read men I've ever met. A number of years ago he asked me, "Do you know anything about the South African tree frog?"

"No, I don't," I said, a bit stunned.

He said, "You probably don't want to know anything about the South African tree frog, but if you did want to know, and you began to read only five minutes a day about the South African tree frog, within five years you would be recognized worldwide as the most knowledgeable person in this field. People would call you, fly you to their corporate headquarters, and pay you handsomely for the advice you could give about the South African tree frog. Granted, that is a very narrow specialty and your audience would be narrow, but you could be the world's foremost authority on the South African tree frog if you read and studied about it only five minutes a day for five years."

I've often thought about what he said.

Most people I know don't spend five minutes a day, much less five hours a day, becoming the person they truly want to be.

Woody Allen said that 90 percent of life is showing up. That's the level at which most people live. They show up at breakfast. They show up at the bus stop. They show up at work. They show up at home in the evenings. They move from place to place and task to task, going through the motions of their lives but rarely investing quality time in what they truly want to be, do, and have by the time they reach life's end. I suspect that most people are surprised to find themselves at retirement and thus are ill prepared for it.

The margin between success and no success isn't a giant chasm, as many people imagine. It lies in the five minutes a day, the added phone call, the bit of extra effort, the nice gesture at the right time, the added energy given to a performance, the additional research, the one more experiment in the laboratory of life.

You don't have to be light-years better than anybody else to be successful. Comparison isn't a part of the process. You need to pursue the goal within yourself of being a little bit better tomorrow than you are today.

A little more competent.
A little more alert.
A little more prepared.
A little more aware.
A little more energetic.
A little more creative.

You Alone Know If You're Competent

I can tell if you are competent, but usually only after the fact. If you're a surgeon and you botch my surgery, I can tell that you are incompetent, but first I had to suffer at your hands. If you're a cook and you prepare a lousy dish, I can tell that you are incompetent as a cook, but probably only after the first bite.

> *The person who is the best judge of your competency isn't a teacher, a consumer, or a friend. It's you.*

The person who is the best judge of your competency isn't a teacher. It isn't a consumer. It isn't a friend. It's you.

You alone know prior to any action whether you know something or can do something. You can do your best to wing it if you're incompetent and hope and pray that nobody discovers how little you know or how unskilled you are, but in the end, you know that you are incompetent and you need to face that incompetency and rectify it.

There is no excuse for prolonged incompetency. You may not know anything on day one, but by day two you should know something. You may not be perfect at a task the first time you try it, but you should be better after a day or two of practice than you were the first day.

There is also no way that someone else can judge accurately—in advance of behavior—whether you are a person of integrity. Only you know your motives and your intentions. Only you know if you are an honest, truthful person. Only you know if the deal you are offering is a fair deal.

People who con other people know it. If they no longer know it, they have become pathological liars, and they are in serious trouble indeed.

Force yourself to become competent at whatever you desire to pursue.

Study your field. Read and watch and listen to those who are the best in your field. Learn from them.

Practice. And then practice some more. And then practice some more. Never give up practicing. Never give up learning and then applying what you have learned.

Keep up with the latest innovations and techniques and research related to your field. Attend the new performances, the conventions, the conferences, the fairs. Find out what's new and what's on the drawing boards. You'll discover what's currently possible, and that is exciting because in knowing what's possible, you'll likely see new horizons for your effort.

Become competent.

A Wealth of Information Free for the Asking

Most of the information you need to have to become competent is free for the asking. It's available to you at no cost. Honest.

Shortly after I lost my sight completely and made my way out to the mailbox and back, I ventured to the park. We had moved back to Tulsa, and we had bought the house I grew up in. I knew the house and the neighborhood, and I could visualize myself in that environment. There's a park about two blocks from that house, and I also knew that park well.

I walked over to the park one day using my cane, and I found a park bench and sat down there to rest. I had prearranged with my wife, Crystal, to meet me at a certain time, so I had some minutes to sit and do nothing until she arrived. I can't tell you what a big step it was for me. To go to the park by myself, to navigate the street crossings, to feel confident as I walked—it was a milestone.

Before long, I sensed that another person had sat down next to me on the bench. I had already adopted my goal of attempting to meet at least one new person a day—which was part of forcing myself out of my comfort zone—so I said to this person, "Hi, I'm Jim Stovall.

It's a nice day, isn't it?" We began conversing about various things. I knew that it was close to the time I was to meet Crystal, so I asked this guy if he would look down the street for me to see whether my wife was coming. I figured he had to realize I was blind since I was sitting there with a blind person's cane, and it seemed obvious to me that it should be obvious to him that I was blind.

The guy laughed a little. I said, "What's so funny?"

He said, "Well, I don't know if you're trying to make a bad joke or what, but I don't appreciate it."

"Don't appreciate what?" I said. I was clueless about his reaction.

We talked a little more, and the upshot was, he was also blind! The odds of two blind people sitting down on the same bench in that park must be astronomical. Neither of us could hardly believe the other was telling the truth, but we both were.

I told him that I had lost my sight recently, and he told me that he had lost his sight seventeen years earlier. He had been the pastor of a church. I asked him, "What do you miss the most?" He said, "The ability to read. I used to enjoy books a great deal, but it's been seventeen years since I've read one."

I said, "Don't you know there's a National Library Service that functions as part of the Library of Congress? The NLS will give you a free tape recorder and send you, free of charge and postage paid, any book that is available in the Library of Congress on tape. All you have to do is call and request a title."

He had never heard of that service, and he was thoroughly delighted at the prospect. I suspect that the first thing he did after he returned home that day was to order some books.

I couldn't imagine then, and I certainly can't imagine now, going for seventeen years without reading a book or hearing a tape of new ideas. And yet, I realize millions of people will go through this entire year and not read a book in its entirety, hear a tape of a book, or hear an inspirational or educational tape of any kind. In so doing, they will have shortchanged their lives. They will have failed to avail themselves of a tremendous opportunity for growth.

As you pursue the success you desire in your life, make certain that you take full advantage of every resource available to you. Many of the resources are books at your local library.

I encourage you especially to read biographies. The stories will teach you about life and about living. I read about five books a week and probably half of them are biographies. In many ways, these people have become my mentors without any intention on their part of mentoring me. I've learned very little from them about television or marketing. In the vast majority of cases, I don't learn one practical thing from the story. But I have learned, and I continue to learn, what it means to be a successful person.

I didn't read Lee Iacocca's book, for example, and say, "Now I'm going to structure my business a different way." What I learned was more about how to be a successful businessperson.

I've read two of Ted Turner's books. His work in television paved the way for some of the things we've been able to do with the Narrative Television Network. But when I read Ted Turner's books, I didn't learn anything new about television. A first-year student in any television program in the United States knows more about television than he or she is going to learn from Ted Turner's books. No, I learned principles from Turner's books that I could apply to any life and to any profession.

The library is also a tremendous source of factual information that can help you, regardless of your area of interest.

As I have shared in previous chapters, we began the Narrative Television Network as a home video company. To pay for the production of the first videotapes, we decided to sell advertising.

To my knowledge, that hadn't been done before, but it worked for us. We knew we couldn't pay for the project with rental or purchase fees, and I was determined that NTN was going to be a for-profit company. So we took a different route. We decided to sell commercial time on the videos and then distribute the finished products as widely as possible to outlets that could lend them to viewers at no charge. I am proud to say that NTN is owned and operated by blind and visually impaired people, but I am even more proud to say that we are a business, not a charity. We receive revenue from a number of traditional sources, and in our sixth year of business, we also began doing work through a cooperative agreement with the U.S. Department of Education.

In selling advertising, we needed to work with national companies since the tapes were going to be distributed nationally. So where did Kathy and I go? To the library! There we found a book that listed all of the national companies in the United States. I focused on the ones located in Tulsa, and I called them all.

One company I called on was Bama Pie Company. It sells pies nationally through McDonald's and also through grocery stores and its own outlets. I told the managers my plan for distributing tapes to libraries and to organizations for blind people, and I convinced them to buy commercial time on the video.

We learned quickly that the people who heard the ads on our tapes purchased pies. Most people don't know who sponsors their favorite shows. They watch the show, and they watch the commercials, and they often don't associate the two. But visually impaired people associate sponsors with the programs developed exclusively for them, and they show their appreciation to the sponsors by purchasing their products. We received letters from people who told how they had gone out of their way to buy Bama pies in appreciation for Bama sponsoring the tapes.

Become Acutely Aware of Your Surroundings— Literally and Figuratively

A big part of being competent is developing the ability to know where you are—both literally and figuratively. Have a context for your life and for your efforts. Know where you fit into the market. Have an understanding of how you relate to other people and the work they are doing. Study the trends.

As a blind person, I've had to process information in new ways. I suspect that's something every person needs to do if he is going to reach his potential and realize his dreams.

Let me give you an example of what I mean by processing information.

It's one thing for someone to feed me a line, tell me where to focus, and then say, "Jim, you have fifty-five seconds to regurgitate that line on camera two." That's a matter of visualization and focus.

It's another thing for me to visualize the entire television studio in which I am seated. To do that, I need to process information in a different way.

Not too long ago I was interviewed by a man in a hotel suite. I had never been in that hotel before, much less that suite, but after I'd been in that room about thirty minutes, I knew the room. I knew how to get out of the room if I needed to. I knew where the bathroom was located, where the furniture was placed, what style of room it was, and much more. Things may not have been the colors or patterns I was envisioning them to be, but in my mind's eye, I had developed a clear picture of that room. I wasn't a blind person sitting in a dark hole, talking to a voice a few feet away. I was a total person sitting in a complete environment, talking to a total person.

How do I develop that sense of understanding about my environment? In part, I process sounds. Where is the traffic sound coming from? From which direction do I hear water flowing? Is a room service cart rumbling down a hallway, and if so, from which direction?

I process space. I know which direction I'm moving in and how many steps it takes to get from space to space. If the other person in the room is moving, I follow her voice. How long does it take for the voice to move from place to place?

I process texture. What kind of flooring am I walking on? What is the feel of the furniture around me?

I process aromas. I have a sense of whether another person is present in a room and about how far away that person might be. If I'm eating, I process taste.

All of these cues give me a sense of where I am, of the space I'm occupying.

Once I'm out of a room, I can describe that room more accurately—especially when it comes to spatial dimensions and locations of certain objects—than a sighted person who was in the same room with me. The sighted person wasn't processing nearly as many cues, or monitoring nearly as many senses, as I was.

My hearing and my senses of taste, smell, and touch aren't more acute or sensitive than those of a sighted person. I don't believe that's the case. But I'm accessing and using these senses more than most sighted people do, and I'm taking in more information about my environment than most sighted people take in.

I've heard about research studies in which people who were involved in accidents or crimes were asked to recall details of the scenes in which the accidents or crimes occurred. They couldn't seem to remember a thing. And yet, when put under hypnosis, they were able to recall minute details about objects, people, and activities. The information was there all the time—they weren't able to access it and bring it to the forefront of their conscious minds.

You have around you at any given moment a great deal of information. But most of it you don't take into consideration. And as a result, you aren't using all the information available to you, and as a secondary result, you may not be able to recall that information if you need it later.

What does this have to do with success and your ability to achieve your goals in life? Virtually everything!

The decisions you make about which directions to move, and about which opportunities to pursue, depend to a considerable extent on information. How you get information and process it, therefore, determine to a great extent the moves you make in life, and whether the moves are forward and upward moves, or unproductive moves that keep you marching in place.

■ *There is no substitute for homework. It's critical to every successful venture.*

When I walk onto a stage, I continually visualize the audience before me. How can I do that? Because I've rehearsed. I've accessed that information prior to speech time. I've practiced walking to the lectern and moving about on the stage. I've walked through the auditorium. I know where the seats are located, what kinds of seats they are, how big the room is, where the aisles are situated. And on and on. I know where I am. Not because I just imagined the scene. But because I did my homework. I researched and studied the situation thoroughly. I know how to move around in that environment, and I know how to use the environment for my purposes.

There is no substitute for homework. It's critical to every successful venture.

You don't make good grades in school if you don't do your homework. You don't succeed in business if you don't do your homework. You don't develop a successful marriage or relationship with your children if you don't learn about what's important to those with whom you are in relationship.

Once you've defined for yourself what you want to be in your life, and do with your time and talents, study the path you've chosen for yourself. Learn as much as you can about it.

You may not need to earn a formal degree in the field. On the other hand, a course in the subject may be helpful to you. And if it's a profession such as nursing, medicine, law, or a similar field that you've chosen, by all means get as much formal training as you can.

Even with formal training, you face the need for learning continually how to apply that information. You need to keep current with your knowledge of the field. You need to be listening, reading, and at all times learning so that you can recognize trends and take advantage of them, so that you can use new discoveries and innovations to your advantage, and so that you can adjust what you are doing to better meet the needs of the people you are hoping to serve, impact, or sell to.

Fortunately for us, Kathy is one of the greatest researchers I've met. At the outset of our television network, she determined how much to charge for our commercial time. I sold the time, but Kathy set the pricing schedule. She got price sheets for various networks and then created our price sheet based on that information. We were market-competitive, not because we picked numbers from thin air, but because we analyzed where we were in the industry. We did our homework.

Competent People Have a Plan

Part of being competent means developing a plan.

A plan puts your dream onto a timetable. It literally sets your goals into time like a jewel is set into a ring. What you dream about becomes a plan when you start putting dates to it. Rather than say, "I want to live on a mountaintop, take photos, and write novels" as a dream life, you say with a plan, "Within X years, or months, I expect to be living on a mountaintop, taking photos, and writing novels."

Your plan is the how-to that you attach to your goal. It sets out the things you need to do to make your goal come to pass. Here are just a few things that might be involved in a plan to make a living-on-the-mountain dream a reality:

- Find a mountain (including housing on the mountain of your choice).
- Get a start in writing. (If you haven't written a novel or anything for publication before, you'd best start writing!)
- Gather gear. (You'll need certain equipment to run the lodge-style operation you are dreaming about.)
- Build a savings account of X dollars to make the transition.
- Sell current home and unwanted material possessions to make the move.

And so forth.

A plan is a step-by-step guide toward reaching your goal. Each part of your plan should have a date attached to it; that way, you know with much greater clarity in any given month or year where you are in comparison to where you want to be. You have a method, a direction, a focus. And you have a gauge against which to plot your progress.

Most plans need to be broken down to daily components. Ask yourself, What can I do in a day—and do day after day after day—to reach my goal? That is the most important question you can ask, in my opinion, in your development of a plan that will carry you to success.

You must be able to hold yourself accountable for pursuing your dream on a daily basis.

If you dream of writing a screenplay for a movie, you must write every day. Set a goal for how many words or pages you want to produce in a day.

If you dream of making a quilt by hand, you must spend some time working on that quilt each day. Set a goal for how many minutes or how many stitches you intend to produce in a day.

If you dream of being a top salesperson, you must make a certain number of calls a day.

If you dream of being an expert with a computer, you must spend some time every day working at your computer.

Success is measured not by what you achieve on a daily basis but by what you do toward achieving your ultimate dream. And that activity must be daily.

Note this subtle difference. Success isn't measured by a single day's output. But getting to success is a matter of daily discipline and daily effort.

When I was making investment-related calls, I measured my success not by how many sales I made in a day but by how many calls I made. Did I make my two hundred calls? If I did, I knew the sales would be in there somewhere—perhaps not that day, but eventually.

A Plan Helps You Isolate the Detours

If you have a plan, you have a much better understanding of when you are working your plan or when you have embarked on a detour or side trip.

Think for a moment about what it would take for you to drive to the nearest major city (other than the city you may live in). How many hours do you think it would take? What would happen if that road was suddenly closed due to a major natural catastrophe—perhaps an ice storm, an earthquake, a flood, or damage from a hurricane or tornado? The fact that you need to get to the city doesn't change. Your overall direction doesn't change. But the route you take to get to your destination may alter, as may the amount of time it will take you to complete your journey.

The same principle holds true for the goals you set for yourself on a daily basis. You may not make your hundred calls or write your five hundred words or complete your quilt block or study the full hour you had intended to study. The first question to ask yourself on days when you don't complete the goals you set for yourself is this: What did I allow to interrupt me, and was it a productive interruption?

If you were interrupted by an incoming call from a person who wanted to make a fairly sizable investment, or if you didn't complete your quilting or your writing because your child was sent home from school with the measles, you have a legitimate reason based on a situation over which you had no control. Ultimately, you are headed toward your goal. You may be delayed by an unexpected detour, but you are still on track. You can easily get back into high gear the next day, and sooner or later, you'll get to your overall goal.

However, if you allow yourself to get sidetracked by every

butterfly that floats in front of your eyes, flit from chore to chore that is unrelated to your life goals, or spend your time in idle gossip at the office watercooler, you have no excuse. You have allowed yourself to be benched by minutiae.

Being Competent Means Gaining an Understanding About How People Respond

You must also become competent in your understanding of the people you choose to influence. They may be people you want to reach with a product or service. They may be people you are hoping to entertain in some way. They may be people you hope to hire. Become a student of people.

Especially focus on what they need or want to know about you. Zero in on your common points of interest. Let everything else fall to the wayside. Focus on areas of mutuality. Look for ways you can help or benefit each other and create win-win situations and relationships.

In my experience with literally thousands of salespeople over the past two decades, I've come to the conclusion that many of them are too product focused. They need to shift their concern about the product they are selling to the people to whom they are selling.

The average car buyer doesn't remotely need to know all that the car salesperson knows, or should know, about the car in the showroom. Someone can happily drive a quality car for five or ten years and never know all that the salesperson knows about that car.

People who are successfully "in the groove" of their destiny have learned this lesson: Tell others what they need to know, give others what they desire to have (to the best of your ability and according to your desire to give what they request), and leave it at that. Don't oversell yourself or your accomplishments. You'll be far more influential.

Let's take an example. If you are selling furniture, you are going to need to know certain things about the items you sell to be able to answer questions about them, such as questions about the construction, the materials used in fabrication, and any special features. But to sell furniture to someone, the only thing you really need to know is this: What is the person looking for?

A recliner for under three hundred dollars? In what type of fabric? Bingo. You have just the piece of furniture for her!

No matter what area of life you are pursuing in your personal quest, you are going to be dealing with people, and in some way, you are going to be giving, offering, or selling something to them. Concentrate your efforts on what they need, not on what you have to give.

Mother Teresa is a nun. Her primary goal in life is to be a representative of the Catholic church and to be a representative of Jesus to the people she meets. But the people with whom she works don't come to her, saying, "Mother Teresa, please give me a sermon," or "Mother Teresa, please pray for my soul." No, the people with whom she works are dying. They are in the last days and hours and minutes of their lives. They need her tender touch, her care, the love they see in her eyes. And that's what she gives them. In doing so, she is giving them her purpose simultaneously. She is showing them the church; she is representing Christ to them.

Let's take a radical leap here and assume that your desire is to be a song-and-dance man on stage. Why do you want to be that? Because singing and dancing make you happy, and at some point in your life, watching people sing and dance gave you happiness.

What will make you a successful song-and-dance man? It won't be the precision of your moves or the clarity of your voice or the way in which you technically deliver a song. Your success will start with your recognition of the person in your audience who needs to smile. Visualize that audience member as coming to your show for a few minutes of escape. Give that person what he or she needs. Sing to make that person smile or feel or get momentarily lost in a fantasy. If you do that—no matter the quality of your voice or the coordination of your feet—you will enjoy success. You'll know you have made a connection. The other person will know it. And in the end, you'll be rewarded for it.

Another leap! Let's assume that your desire is to be a college professor. What do your students truly need from you? Granted, they need a certain amount of skill or information, which you are in a position to give them. But they need more than that. They need to have a feeling that they can and will succeed in life. They need confidence that they are understanding what you are conveying to them. Some of them need to get over the fear they feel about their inadequacies and possible inability to comprehend what you will be teaching.

Address these needs in your students—even as you convey information to them—and they will not only consider you to be one of the finest teachers they have ever had, but they'll actually learn more of the material you desire to convey to them.

The principle holds true in every walk of life. Find out what the people need who are in the path of your destiny, and do your best to meet their needs. In meeting their needs, you'll find your true success.

> **Find out what the people need who are in the path of your destiny, and do your best to meet their needs.**

See the Person Inside the Person

As part of becoming competent, you need to develop an ability to see the person inside the person.

If I met you today for the first time, within a matter of minutes, I'd have a picture of you in my mind. It may not be at all what you look like, but that picture suits my purpose. It's the same process you, as a sighted person, go through when you talk to a stranger on the phone. You tend to develop a visual image of what that person looks like, and the next time you hear that voice, that image comes to mind. And the image of that person suits your purpose—until the day comes when you meet that person face-to-face, and then you may have to alter your image significantly. One thing about being blind—I don't have to adjust my image of you over time. You can look like you do right now for the rest of your life.

The point is, when you are talking to me, I'm hearing you with my ears, and I'm seeing you in my mind. In some ways, I'm reading more into your identity than I have a right to do, based on the evidence at hand. In another way, however, I'm developing a picture of you based on evidence. The tone of your voice. The inflections you use. The content of your speech. Your accent. Your laugh. All of these things convey meaning to me. I see you more completely than your outfit, your hairstyle, your gestures. I begin to see a personality. And the image I develop of you is really an image of your personality—your whole personhood.

How does this relate to success?

Well, all people you meet are going to affect your life in some way. They are going to take up a certain amount of your time or occupy a certain amount of your space. They are going to give something to you or take something away from you. They will benefit you or keep you from meeting someone who will benefit you.

The more you are able to size up a person—and do so intelligently and accurately, based on firm evidence—the more you are going to be able to help that person, and also the more you are going to be able to help that person help you (which is another way of saying that you will be able to keep yourself from being hurt by that person).

Become Acutely Aware of Your Personal Strengths

Being competent includes taking a brash, unapologetic look at your strengths. Become a student of your assets. Know what they are, and then work to develop them.

> *Become a student of your assets. Know what they are, and then work to develop them.*

When a person has a disability, the disability tends to loom large, not only in the individual who is affected, but in everybody else around him. The tendency is to focus more on the person's *dis*ability than on the *ability*.

In facing my blindness, I fortunately also came face-to-face with some of my assets.

I have an excellent memory. I've always had it, but until I faced my impending blindness, I didn't fully develop my memory or see it as the great asset that it is. I learned that part of my success in college was going to be directly related to my ability to go to a class, listen intently to a lecture, and remember in detail what was said. The same was true when a reader read textbooks and other materials to me. I honed my already good memory into a highly efficient tool.

Along with my memory—perhaps as a part of my ability to memorize—I have a good ability to concentrate and to focus on things. I can shut out everything, except what is vital to hear. I can sift through ideas and get right to the heart of what I need to know.

I know these are my strengths. I don't take them for granted. I work all the time at developing them into greater strengths. They are key parts of my being a competent—and successful—person.

Take stock of your sensory skills, your aptitudes, and all of your mental, emotional, spiritual, and psychological strengths. Build on them.

Keep Track of the Details

Many people assume that successful people see the big picture and rarely involve themselves in details. In my experience, I've found just the opposite to be true. Although successful people have the ability to envision the grand picture for their lives, their companies, their ideas, they are concerned that the details be nailed down. Successful people follow through. They demand excellence at the detail level. They may not do all the detail work, but they are concerned that it is handled well.

> **Successful people follow through. They demand excellence at the detail level.**

As I have already mentioned, I face a few unique challenges in traveling. But even on my worst day of traveling, I have never experienced what happened to my friends Richard and Ted. We were in a meeting in Dallas. It started at one o'clock, and they told me that they would need to leave at three o'clock. They had a private jet, and a three o'clock departure would allow them to keep their later commitments that day. I figured their timing was just about right for me. I had a flight at 3:45, and their schedule would give me plenty of time to make my flight with a few minutes to spare.

About 2:30, however, I heard them talking, and suddenly, there was a little commotion. Someone finally asked, "Well, where *is* our plane?"

"What do you mean, where's your plane?" I asked.

As it happened, Richard and Ted had flown in the night before, had rushed to a waiting car and then to their hotel, and they had never given thought to which airport they landed at in Dallas. Never in my worst day of traveling have I lost a jet!

Keep track of the details. They can make a big difference in getting to your destination goal.

Taking Inventory

A part of keeping track of the details is keeping track of what you have. This means keeping an ongoing inventory of material assets as well as what is available for you to use or to put at risk.

For several years, I have helped The Nanci Corporation with its marketing. This corporation does business in the United States, Canada, Mexico, and Japan, and I travel frequently with Nanci Masso, the chairperson of The Nanci Corporation, in speaking to sales groups. Because of my heavy speaking and traveling schedule, I usually go through a set of luggage about every six months.

One time as I was preparing to leave on a weeklong trip, my wife, Crystal, made a special point before I left home of going over with me exactly where everything was in my new suitcase. When Michael came to pick me up, he took the suitcase and put it in the back of the limo. At the airport, he checked my luggage with the curbside baggage handler, and on I flew to Chicago, switched planes, and then met Nanci at the Toronto airport.

On the flight from Chicago, I flew in a jumbo plane, so when we arrived, the terminal was crowded, and the baggage claim area was equally crowded. We were on a fairly tight schedule, and in an effort to retrieve my luggage as quickly as possible, Nanci asked me, "What does your bag look like?"

I didn't have a clue. I could have described for her all of the contents and their arrangement inside the case, but I didn't have any idea what the luggage looked like—either its color or style—or even what it was made of. I didn't know its brand or anything about it. So we waited and waited and waited until only one bag was still going around and around the baggage carousel. We opened it just to make sure it held my possessions before we left with it.

Since that time, I'm very concerned about knowing my inventory when I travel!

An Ongoing Concern for Quality

You will never outgrow your need for monitoring the quality of your life, your activities, and your possessions. Quality control is an ongoing part of every person's life, no matter how successful he or she may become.

Some time ago I was in Hawaii. Now, part of the way a person adjusts to changes in time zones is based on patterns of light and darkness. When the sun goes down, the brain's normal signal is to say to the rest of the body, bedtime is coming up. I'm told that frequent travelers often use a technique called the jet lag diet in which they trick their bodies by using caffeine, protein, carbohydrates, and eye shades. Eye shades don't work for blind people, so those of us who are blind often have more trouble with jet lag.

I love traveling to Hawaii, but I'd just as soon somebody move Hawaii to the central time zone. That would be truly beautiful!

I was up at three o'clock one morning in Hawaii, and given the nature of my business, I decided to turn on the television set in my hotel room and see if I could find the local Narrative Television Network station. I struggled for two hours and never did figure out how to turn on that TV set. I couldn't help thinking, *Here I am, with twenty-five million households connected to a television network that I own, and I can't turn on the TV set in this hotel room!* It was an interesting problem. But my point to you is this: Monitor the quality of what you are doing at every step of the way.

If you are producing or selling a product, use that product. Watch how others use it. You should be the first person to note if there's something that can be improved about your product, its packaging, or its promotion.

Become an Expert in Analyzing Emotion

Every issue has an emotional component to it, just as every person has emotions. Every dream and goal has emotion tied to it. That's good! Without emotion, few of us would have much motivation because we'd never be able to feel rewarded or excited or intrigued by a dream or goal.

The people who watch the Narrative Television Network are emotional about NTN. It's not just an idea to them. It's not just a program format. It's hope. NTN opens a new door for them. It gives them a new means of enrichment for their lives. It sends a message to them, "Somebody in television cares about me."

Emotion in our viewers is something we not only recognize but also value.

Ask in your quest for success, How do people feel about what I do? They don't necessarily need to like you as a person, but what you do for them needs to evoke an emotional response. They need to have a feeling about what you do that involves them.

In terms of the Narrative Television Network, because our viewers have an emotional response to our programming, they become loyal viewers as well as loyal purchasers of the products sold by our sponsors. That's a fabulous advantage for us. And I suspect this principle holds true for any enterprise that compels a positive emotional response in the people related to it.

If an employee feels good about working for you, he is going to give you better effort.

If a customer feels good about the product you are selling or the service you are providing, she is likely to give you repeat business and positive referrals.

If a reader feels something while reading what you've written, he is likely to read on.

The principle is universal.

The feeling need not be one of syrupy sweet niceness. It need not be a heavy dose of happiness. The feeling may be one of intense challenge or conviction. It may be one of too-deep-for-words joy. Whatever the feeling, it does, however, need to be one that would be rated as positive—a feeling that the person would like to have again.

Work to give a positive feeling to others.

Competency Is a Tall Order

You may be saying to yourself, Competency is a chore!
You're right. It is. But being competent means

- knowing what you need to know to do what you want to do at a top-notch level.
- knowing yourself—your strengths and the assets you bring to the task at hand.
- knowing people—and how they respond to you and what they do.

Take that information and put it into a plan. And then work your plan. Stay concerned with quality and details. Stay involved with people. Step back occasionally to regain sight of the big picture of what you are trying to do. And I have no doubt you will become a competent person.

You can be successful for a time without competency. But you can't be successful consistently without it. And you certainly can't live and work at the peak of your potential without becoming competent!

14

STAYING FIXED
ON YOUR FOCAL POINT

Become the most productive person you know—

not just the busiest!

One of the most counterproductive principles in business, as far as I am concerned, is the practice of paying people by the hour. When people are paid by the hour, they can confuse activity with productivity.

Have you ever seen a gerbil running around the little wheel in a cage? That little animal is putting out a lot of energy and engaging in a lot of activity, but it isn't going anyplace. Many people are just like that gerbil in the way they pursue a dream or a goal.

If you have been productive, you'll be closer to your goal. If you have been busy, you'll just be tired.

How can you tell if you are being productive or if you are engaging in a lot of activity? An effective technique is to take your daily planner and look back over the last thirty days. Note all the things you have done and all the things you have crossed off your to-do list. Then ask yourself, How many of these things directly affected my getting from where I am to where I want to be in life?

If you have been productive, you'll be closer to your goal or to the realization of your dream. If you have just been busy, you may be tired, but you won't be closer to your goal.

Because of my speaking schedule, I have an opportunity to converse with many people. Some of them share with me their dreams. I always try to encourage them to go for their dreams, and I sometimes ask, "What progress are you making?"

Ones who are truly productive nearly always respond, "Good progress." Ones who are just active—just running on wheels in their cages—often answer me with silence.

Dreams don't turn into reality by accident. Plain old-fashioned work is required to turn dreams into reality. And by work, I mean productive work.

Start Moving!

The universal laws related to success lie in the emotional realm, but they affect every area of life, especially outward behaviors.

Consider, for example, the issue of being overweight. I share the challenge of fighting weight gain like millions of people in our nation. I am fortunate in that I am tall and large-boned and can carry a lot of weight. I've taped television shows and still looked good at 300 pounds. I've had female cohosts who were five feet ten inches and weighed 128 pounds and were told by their agents or producers to lose 4 pounds. In general, we men have it a little easier, I think, when it comes to weight. Our culture accepts more weight on men than on women. Even so, millions of people struggle with losing weight, and from time to time, I've had to be very weight conscious, especially when I was lifting weights competitively and needed to stay under a weight limit to qualify for a particular weight class.

I've discovered several things through dieting, and one of them is that there are many reasons for people to be overweight. One reason might be an addiction to certain types of food. Another might be habitual overeating; yet another might be chronic lack of exercise.

But there is only one way to lose weight, and that is to take in fewer calories than you expend as energy. It all comes down to math. Eat more calories than you burn up and you'll gain weight. Burn up more calories than you eat and you'll lose weight.

There is also only one thing that causes people to be successful in a weight-loss plan, and that is this: They must first deal with the problem in the emotional realm. They must make a quality decision: I am going to do this. I am going to lose weight. If they don't make that decision and see it as a primary goal, they won't succeed, regardless of which diet plan they follow.

On the other hand, once they make that decision, it really doesn't matter which plan they follow insofar as that plan tells them which foods to eat at which time. All plans will work if people stick to them—as long as they burn up more calories than they take in.

Burning up calories involves exercise. And certain universal rules are related to exercise, too.

The exercise component of any weight-loss program is vital. Research has shown repeatedly that obese people—those who are 30 percent or more overweight—cannot lose or maintain a significant weight loss over time without consistent exercise. In one study, chronically overweight people who weighed between four and five hundred pounds, and who were being monitored by a physician, consumed as few as eight hundred calories a day and they still didn't lose weight. Their metabolic rate continued to shut down to almost no activity at all. Obese people actually have the most efficient metabolic systems of all people. If there's ever another Ice Age, obese people have the best chance of being among the survivors because their bodies store fat efficiently. And even if they virtually starve themselves, they lose weight slowly. Without exercise, severely obese people have little hope of losing any pounds, even eating what would be considered for thin people to be a very strict intake of food.

In sum, motivating obese people to exercise regularly is vital to their weight loss. In the first place, exercise burns calories while they are exercising, but more significant, exercise increases the metabolism so that the amount of calories they continue to burn for the next twelve hours is increased, even though they may be resting or doing routine work. That's the residual benefit of exercise that most people don't know about. Not only do they burn up extra calories while they are exercising, but they put their bodies into a mode to continue to burn up extra calories for hours after the exercise period.

The last thing most obese people want to do, however, is to exercise. It's the hardest part about any weight-loss plan for them.

Thin people seem to think that if obese people will just eat less or eat different things, they will automatically shed the pounds. That's rarely the case. In the vast majority of cases, obese people are not obese because they eat huge meals, binge on junk food, are lazy, are stupid, or don't care about themselves or life. Obese people are obese primarily because they don't move very much. But unless they know that and unless they then act on the knowledge, they are probably going to remain obese. Obese people need to develop and maintain a plan of exercise.

They don't have to run a marathon, lift three hundred pounds, or take a special course at a gym. They need to get up, put on some comfortable clothes and appropriate shoes, go out for a walk, and get the heart rate up into the target zone for their weight. That's the number one key to losing weight.

This same principle holds true for all areas of life. Most people aren't wallowing in mediocrity in their lives because they are lazy, are stupid, or habitually do the wrong things. Most people are unsuccessful because they don't do certain things they need to do. They don't understand the basic rules, principles, or universal laws that make the difference between being successful and remaining unsuccessful. In most cases, one of the first laws is this: *Start moving.* Make a beginning. Get going. Start doing something that will move you toward your goal. And then the next day, do something more.

I've also learned another principle in my work counseling chronically overweight people around the world. Many obese people put off doing certain things because they are obese. They say, "I'll take that cruise . . . I'll get a different job . . . I'll move . . . I'll seek a relationship . . ." or achieve some other goal for their lives . . . "when I'm thin." They live in the mythical place that my friend Denis Waitley calls Someday Isle. Someday Isle is a place where everything's possible and nothing ever happens because you never quite get there.

Don't wait for some magic moment to begin your pursuit of your goals and dreams. Get moving today. Going for a walk every day is not a big thing, not even to an obese person, in theory. But doing it can be a big thing. And doing it can make a tremendous difference in losing weight.

In your particular area of goals and dreams, you can start doing something right now to put yourself on the road toward fulfillment of your desires.

What is it? Name it. And then, start doing it. Today. Tomorrow. And every day after that. Get going.

In sales, that something you can do is likely to be to increase the number of calls you are making. If you are making no calls, start making calls. If you are making a few calls, make a few more. Set a goal for yourself and get with it.

If you want to change your profession and need more training, enroll in a class. Pay the fee. Buy the books. Start attending class. Do the homework.

If you want to learn to paint with oils, find a teacher. Get the equipment you need. And start painting.

If you want to take a trip, pay a visit to your local travel agent. Develop a plan. Start working it.

> *No matter what your goal or dream, you can start doing something today. Get with it!*

No matter what your goal or dream, you can start doing something today. Get with it!

Activity Alone Is Not Productivity

Although you can't have productivity without activity—without work, without effort, without expenditure of energy and creativity—it's true that activity alone doesn't equal productivity.

You can be very active and yet be unproductive. Productivity is related to what you accomplish, not what you do.

In sales, you don't get paid or rewarded for reading manuals or for sharpening pencils. You get paid for the number of sales you make.

In performing, you don't get paid for reading scripts or having your nails done or shopping on Rodeo Drive. You get paid for the performance you give on stage or in front of a camera.

Weigh your activities against what they produce in you and through you.

Productivity is not always measured by external things, such as dollars, titles, or possessions. For example, you can be productive in your studies and have nothing to show for that productivity; the accomplishment is an internal acquisition of knowledge. On the other hand, if you are just going to the library and putting in time staring at the shelves or browsing through books, rather than reading and studying with the intent of remembering and using what you are learning, you are wasting your time. You're being active, but you aren't being productive because you aren't accomplishing anything.

> **Productivity is related to what you accomplish, not what you do.**

Ministers spend periods of time praying, reading the Scriptures, and reflecting on what they have read. To many people, these activities may seem to be just that—activity. But most ministers I know will tell you that they are, indeed, being productive. The time they spend praying and reading the Bible accomplishes something deep inside their spirits—it gives them new perspective, new wisdom, new strength, and renewed ability to help others. Their activity accomplishes something in them, and it helps them accomplish something on behalf of other people.

Name any pursuit in your life, and you can discern a difference between activity and productivity. You know what you don't need to be doing. You can name things that are a waste of your time.

It's critical that you learn to separate busyness from achievement. Pare away what doesn't produce, what isn't fulfilling, what isn't in keeping with your talents, desires, or dreams. Trim down your associations, commitments, and relationships to ones that are vital to who you are and who you want to be.

Take Control of Your Time

Time is the only commodity you truly have. All other things are owned or have been owned, at least in part, by other people. That goes for the air you breathe, the space you take up on earth, the ground you walk on, the possessions you own (which you own only temporarily). Yet many people squander the only thing they truly have.

◻ *Time is the only commodity you truly have.*

Many people spend a substantial portion of any day or week or month or year doing things that are unrelated to the accomplishment of their goals or that are not directly related to their dreams. Don't be among them! Make your days count. Don't just count your days.

Too many people spend 80 percent of their time with people who are creating only 20 percent of their success. Employers spend the majority of their time with the 20 percent of people who cause the most problems. Agents spend the majority of their time with the 20 percent of performers or models who don't show up prepared for the assignments they've accepted. Politicians spend the majority of their time passing laws for the 20 percent of the population who are in need or who have problems or who *are* problems. In many cases, these people aren't even the people who voted for them!

I do some marketing consulting, and part of what I do is to talk to people about how to build their businesses. A piece of advice I always give them is to find others who will help them build the business and give these people their serious time. Their casual time they can spend as they want, but their serious time should be spent only with individuals who are serious about succeeding and about helping to build the business both have.

Avoid unnecessary phone calls and appointments whenever possible, especially during your peak performance hours in a day. Save your serious time for tasks and appointments that are going to help you reach your goals and dreams.

Find More Time

Where's the number one place to get the time you think you don't have to better yourself or to do more toward achieving your personal goals?

This is going to sound odd coming from a man who makes his living in the television industry, but the source of that time is likely to be TV time. Turn off the set, and get to work on the serious business of building your life.

Stop watching others maim, entertain, and proclaim, and start living out your dreams. Get out of the fantasy world that has you vegetating in front of a TV set night after night, and start claiming the real world as your own.

Set Boundaries with Your Time

As you pursue your road to success, don't be surprised at what people ask you to do for them along the way.

People make the most amazing requests of one another. Few people stop to think that what they are asking might be offbeat, inappropriate, or rude. They simply ask. It's up to you to set boundaries for yourself. If you don't set these boundaries, you are likely to get distracted and lose the focus you must have to reach your goals.

That doesn't mean, of course, that you can't accommodate some requests.

I recall a time when my friend Sam came into my office and asked with a hurry-up tone in his voice, "Can you do an hour?"

Just like that, he wanted me to speak with him to a group of people—a presentation expected to last about an hour. I said, "Great." I could accommodate that request. It wasn't something I had planned, but it was certainly something I could do and was happy to do.

He talked. I talked. Everything went well. After the presentation, a nice woman came up and said, "I have one picture left on this roll." And she then handed me her camera and asked me to take a picture of her standing next to Sam!

The woman knew I was blind. She had just heard me speak. But somehow it didn't compute to her that a blind man is not the best person to take a photograph of you!

I figured she was going to get a close-up picture of me or perhaps a somewhat acceptable picture of herself and Sam. On the other hand, if she was willing to take the risk, I was willing to snap the shutter. Her request was certainly not one that was going to delay me, keep me from my goals, or occupy my thoughts. Her request—which I still consider to be fairly offbeat—was what I call an innocent and brief little detour. I'm not sure how her photo turned out. I was sorry it was the poor woman's last frame on the roll of film.

At other times, people will seek to spend time with you, and even though that is not something you've planned or scheduled, spending time with them is to your benefit.

Sam came to me one evening and said, "Let's take ten minutes." Over the months and years, I've come to realize that when Sam talks about ten minutes, he is using a different clock from what other people use. His idea of ten minutes usually means half the night.

On that occasion, he said, "Let's go into this restaurant and take ten minutes." The restaurant was closed. A waiter told Sam, "We're closed," and what did Sam do? He responded, "Yeah, I understand that, but all we want is food." I'm thinking to myself, *What else would we want? Snow tires?* But amazing me, the waiter said, "Oh, you just want food. Well, come on in and we'll get you some food." And so, some food was brought to us, and Sam and I started to take our ten minutes together.

Sam started talking about destiny. That's not a topic that can be covered in ten minutes. I chose to invest my time in talking to Sam about destiny for several hours!

> *If you don't choose what you do with your time, somebody else will.*

The word *choice* is critical to your understanding of time. If you don't choose what you do with your time, somebody else will. It's your destiny. It's your success. It's your greatness. Choose what you will do with your time and with whom you will spend your time.

I recommend that you evaluate closely these areas in your life:

- Are you involved in some things you aren't supposed to be involved in? Are you doing some things you aren't supposed to do? Are you involved with people you shouldn't be involved with? Are you going for a goal that truly isn't important to you or perhaps is counterproductive to what you want to achieve and be in your life?
- Is there something you should be doing? Is there a goal you should be pursuing? Are there people with whom you believe

you should be working? Is there a cause you should be supporting or a project with which you should be involved?

Time ultimately is all you have that you can never increase. If you let others rob you of time, you have let them rob you of something irreplaceable.

Getting Paid for Your Time

On several occasions, people have said to me, "I can't spend my time doing things I don't get paid for. I work, I get paid, I work, I get paid. What I make barely covers my expenses. There's no point in my doing work that isn't going to be rewarded."

I agree with that viewpoint, but only to this extent: None of us does anything we don't get paid for.

Ultimately.

Eventually.

We all get paid for what we do. If we're lazy and do nothing, we likely get nothing. Our reward is linked to our effort.

But if you invest effort in furthering your dreams and goals in life, you *always* get paid. That's a principle of life. I don't know when you'll get paid for your effort, or when the return on your investment of time and energy is going to come back to you, from whom, or in what form, but I can guarantee you that it will come back to you. If nothing more, your expenditure of time, energy, and talent will have made you into a different person. It will have altered you in some way. And as your identity changes—which usually means not only a change in the substance of who you are but also a change in the way you perceive yourself and your worth—things around you will change. The reward may not be in tangible things that come to you. The reward may lie in what happens inside you—and therefore, what is capable of flowing out of you to others. Either way, you are rewarded.

Give, and you receive. Fail to give, and you don't receive. It's a simplistic formula, but it's one of life's basics.

Combine Your Efforts

Most people don't fail because they don't work hard. Just about everybody I know works hard. The janitor who cleans our offices at night works hard. The person who owns the building and from whom we lease our office space works hard. If working hard in and of itself made a person successful, just about everybody would be successful.

Success doesn't lie solely in effort, and I don't want to leave the impression that it does. There are two other key ingredients. The first is understanding the rules. The second is having a chance.

Some people who work hard—and pursue their dreams and goals with gusto and diligence—don't arrive at their goals because they don't know how the game they are playing is meant to be played. They don't know the rules they are violating—the violations of which are keeping them from the success they desire.

Life has rules. Every career and every job has rules associated with it. You may call them skills or laws or procedures or principles. But in the end, they are all variations on the theme of rules.

A rule that can help you in your quest for success is this: Combine your efforts whenever possible. Find ways to get more out of a single encounter. Always be on the alert for ways in which you can multiply your efforts.

If you are sending a letter to one person, perhaps you can personalize it slightly and, in the same mailing, send it to a dozen people.

If you are speaking to a group of people, record your message. That way when others ask you later to repeat for them what you said, you can direct them to the purchase of your tape!

A friend shared her secret for giving dinner parties. When she wants to pay back her friends for various invitations, she plans back-to-back dinner parties. When she cooks, she prepares two of everything, and she gives one dinner party on Friday night and the other on Saturday night. It's far less work than doing two separate cooking sessions several weeks apart. She buys one floral centerpiece for the table, cleans house one time instead of two, and polishes the best silver only once. A little more effort at one time, but double the benefit.

As I have already mentioned, shortly after we started the Narrative Television Network, our public relations firm advised me that I needed personally to contact the affiliates that were carrying our programs—to thank them for carrying the shows and to make myself available for personal appearances and promotional activities. The firm booked me as a public speaker in an area, or at a particular meeting, and then invited local affiliate and program managers to attend as our VIP guests.

That approach did two things simultaneously. It allowed me to meet more than one affiliate operator at a time, and it also gave me a means of reaching more people with the news that the Narrative Television Network was on the air.

A traditional way to get viewers to watch your programming is to go on television with a ten-second spot and say, "Watch this show at 7:00 P.M. tomorrow." But blind people didn't routinely watch television, so spots of that type didn't really work for NTN. I had to find a way to reach people with the news that the Narrative Television Network existed and to tell them a little about our programming. The public speaking engagements were a means of multiplying my efforts.

This book you hold in your hands is an extension of that same idea. I realized one day after speaking that I had shared some of my thoughts and experiences with thousands of people in recent years, but that one way to share more of my life with more people would be in written form.

In my work with NTN, I soon realized that it took me just as much time and energy to do an interview that was going to be seen on one hundred affiliates as it did to do an interview that was going to be seen on one thousand stations.

I don't know your dreams or goals, but I do know that you can multiply your efforts in some way. That's one of the basic rules of success. Think about it!

Taking Possession of Your Entire Life

Taking control over your encounters. Taking control over your tasks. Taking control over your time. All of these point to an overriding principle: You need to take possession of your entire life.

Through my months of working with obese people, I've concluded that it's vital for them to take possession of their bodies, to take ownership and to visualize that they are now in control of their bodies just as if they had acquired a tangible possession.

We live in our bodies. But many of us haven't taken possession of them. We don't see our bodies as habitats in which we are going to have to spend the rest of our lives. We don't invest in our health. We don't engage in the routine maintenance that will keep us strong and healthy for decades to come. Most people take better care of their automobiles and their homes than they do of their bodies. And yet our bodies are our primary means of transportation and our most primal dwelling place.

When it comes to your success, I'm asking you to take possession of your life and your future. If you don't take possession of both, somebody else will.

I struggled most with my weight during the time I was losing the last bit of my eyesight. You see, I couldn't control what was happening in my eyes. That was very frustrating for me. But I did have control over what I could eat. I had the power to walk to the refrigerator, open it, pull out more calories than any person on the planet needed in a day, and eat until I could eat no more. Eventually, I had to say to myself, "Stovall, you think you have control over what you eat, but what you really need is to have control over your total body."

When you take control over your total body, eating is just one part of that control. It's a system that you control, just like the system of rest and relaxation, cleanliness and hygiene, good grooming, exercise, and all other systems that relate to bodily functions and appearance. Most of us don't need a control plan for our eating nearly as much as we need to develop a plan for our bodies—a plan for total well-being and fitness. When we develop that plan, we develop a plan for eating. We see it as part of a whole.

The same goes for your success in achieving your personal destiny. You need to take control over that destiny. Nobody else is going to make it happen for you. It's not up to fate, luck, or the alignment of the planets. It's not up to the whims of others. It's not even up to the Creator by Himself. (He has already given you desires, abilities, energy, and all of the other raw resources with which to find, develop, and pursue your destiny.)

Take control of the dials. Put your hand on the joy stick. Sit down in the command seat. And start flying your life in the direction you want to go!

You'll only become as productive as you determine you will become. Your productivity is subject to your will and your choices.

■ **Make today the most productive day of your life.**

Make today the most productive day of your life. Set boundaries. Focus your activity. Make choices that are aimed at your goal.
I suspect you'll like the way you feel at the end of the day!

15

FOCUSING ON THE GOAL, NOT THE MEANS

Consider money a tool—

not an end in itself.

Eighty percent of the workforce in our nation get up on Monday morning and do something they absolutely hate doing for someone they don't respect for less money than they need, and they do it for forty to fifty years of their lives! That's an amazing statistic and an alarming one. Are you part of that group? If so, I'm here to say to you, "Don't be."

You'll hear it said often that you have to pay a price for any success you enjoy. I'll say it to you, too. But my first concern is to get you to recognize that you are already paying a price for *not* having the success you want in life. You are paying a price for *not* leading the life that you truly want to lead or that you feel is your ultimate destiny to enjoy. You are paying a price for *not* being the person you want to be and doing the things you want to do.

Don't do it. Not for another day.

Many people consider being successful as having a lot of money. Money isn't the mark of success. It's a tool. You can use money to become successful as a person, but having money—in and of itself— doesn't make you a success.

Ultimately, money by itself cannot buy your success. Being successful isn't a matter of reaching a point where you can lie down on a comfortable bed of soft pillows every day and eat grapes in leisure. Success on an individual level is being able to say to yourself every morning, "I can hardly wait to face this day. I'm enthusiastic about what lies ahead of me. I'm learning and growing as a person. I'm facing challenges head-on and winning the daily battles. I fully expect to fall into bed tonight and get a good night's sleep knowing that I've been my best, done my best, and availed myself of the best things possible."

> **Success is embracing life to the fullest, eager for the opportunities and possibilities the day holds.**

So many people are working five to get two. They put in time Monday through Friday so they can call Saturday and Sunday their own. They work during the week and then "have a life" on the weekends.

As far as I'm concerned, these people are losing five-sevenths of their lives. Success is getting up each and every day, regardless of the day of the week, and embracing life to the fullest, eager for the opportunities and possibilities the day holds.

Enjoying what you do, no matter whether it's Tuesday or Saturday—that's success!

Success, greatness, the fulfillment of personal destiny—all of these happen as you live out the life you want to live on a daily basis, enjoying what you do and finding meaning in what you do, feeling satisfaction in how you are living your life in relationship to others, and having a sense that you are in the process of achieving what you are destined to achieve.

There is no ultimate success point for any person in any career. Success is a string of successes—of feeling as if one day has been lived well and to your maximum ability, and then getting up the next day and living well and to your maximum ability, and then getting up the next day and living well, and so forth and so forth and so forth until there's a true pattern of success established in your life. Success involves building the habits of success into your life, no matter what field you have chosen.

One of the finest horse trainers in the world is a man who is past middle age, but he still gets up at 3:30 every morning so that he is the first on the track, and first to greet the horses under his tutelage. Hitting the day early is his habit. He doesn't think much about it. It's what he does day by day to be at the very top of his profession but, more important, to be at the very top of his form. He does what he does because he enjoys what he does, and he has a sense of deep personal fulfillment and accomplishment in what he does and who he is. That's success.

No Shortage of Money

There is no such thing as a money shortage. There is plenty of money in this world. What we have is a motivation, creativity, or idea shortage. Money flows from motivation, creativity, and ideas. If you don't have enough money, you are overspending, or you don't have enough motivation, creativity, or ideas.

Take a look at what you are thinking about, dreaming about, and envisioning. You may need a new or bigger idea! Or you may need a new outlet for your energy and creativity—one better suited to your ultimate purpose in life.

When I was in college, I bought and resold diamonds. I'd buy a diamond from a wholesaler, then resell it, make a little money on the deal, buy another diamond, and so forth. It was a pretty decent little business, especially since so many college students were preparing to get married and needed a good deal on diamonds.

I also found other things that I could purchase cheaply and then sell for a profit. I was always hustling. Buying something and selling it, whatever was available to whomever would buy.

I had been getting more and more into real estate as an investor. All of the ventures were profitable, but they were on a fairly small scale. One investment involved a warehouse for a direct-sales company, and I got involved with this company a little in speaking. I addressed the salespeople several times, and the presentations were taped and the tapes were then distributed by the company. I didn't receive any direct financial benefit from the tapes. At the time, it never occurred to me that the people who were making and distributing the tapes might be selling them. In the end, however, one of the taped sessions provided a big break for me. Lee Braxton had taught me that you never do anything that you don't get paid for someday in some way. He was right!

I've found it to be true through the years that truly productive people always get paid for their effort—through some channel, in some way, by somebody who is eager to pay them. If productivity is high, the money will eventually come, and usually without any scheming, manipulating, or begging.

As the property deal at the lake was ending for Crystal and me, I heard about a brokerage office opportunity. I thought, *I'd like to get on the New York Stock Exchange.* I liked buying and reselling, and I still planned to have my own office and be my own boss. I applied to a couple of places for a brokerage license, but nobody wanted to deal with a guy who was going blind. By that time, I could tell if someone was sitting across the table from me, but I couldn't read or drive. I suspect that nobody who interviewed me thought that I could read the stock exchange postings or keep up with the data involved in investment transactions.

Then one day I got a call from a man who asked, "Do you want to be a broker?"

I said, "I sure do."

He said, "Are you the guy I've been listening to on this tape?" Someone had handed him a copy of a tape from a presentation I'd made to a sales group.

"I sure am."

He said, "You can have an office."

I said, "I've applied everywhere for a license without any success."

He said, "Come see me."

So I flew to his office in a nearby city, sat down with him, and said, "Look, I've got to be honest with you. I know how you run your business and how you expect your people to build their offices, but I'm functionally blind and I want to be up front with you about that."

He said, "Jim, let's not worry about that. I've got guys all over the nation with a bad attitude. That's far more troublesome to me than a guy with bad eyesight."

I studied hard for six months—six to eight hours a day—and passed the New York Stock Exchange Test, one of the toughest exams anybody will ever take. Furthermore, I had to take the test orally, something they told me had rarely been done before. But I ended up with a score in the 98th percentile.

The office they assigned me was in Muskogee, Oklahoma.

Now, the way the firm worked was that a broker received a minimum wage, but then each broker made beyond that on the basis of what was sold. I still had my diamond business and was trading a few other things as I could, so we managed to survive financially during the time I was studying for the exam and training.

Crystal went with me through the training sessions. They trained thirty brokers at a time, so there I was in classes with twenty-nine other would-be brokers, most of whom had gone through business school and many of whom had their MBA degrees. Believe me, Crystal could have passed the test as easily as I passed it, and probably with higher grades than anybody else, because she read and absorbed all the material along the way in the process of reading aloud to me the vast amounts of material they gave us to digest.

They trained us to make a hundred calls a day. I said to Crystal, "We've got a problem we're going to have to overcome. If all those other guys are going to be making a hundred calls a day, we'd better make two hundred." So we opened up our office in Muskogee, connected our computer lines, and started making calls.

We took the directory they gave us, which listed people by name, address, and occupation. We decided that retirees were the people most likely to be at home to receive our calls and that they also probably had the most time to spend listening to us and the most money to invest. So we started making two hundred calls a day to that group of people.

We worked sixteen hours a day. We'd crawl into bed at two o'clock in the morning after doing the paperwork after making two hundred person-to-person phone calls.

A sixth-month report was issued for the thirty of us who had been trained together. I was number one in that class of thirty trainees. During the sixth month alone, I made about $15,000. The number two guy made only $2,100. I phoned the man who trained me, and I said, "This is embarrassing. Not for me, but for these other guys. How can a guy work like we do and make only $2,100 a month?"

He said, "Stovall, you really are stupid. I tell all our trainees to make a hundred calls a day, hoping they'll make ten. And then you go out and make two hundred calls!"

He was right. I was stupid. I didn't know any better than to make all the calls that were humanly possible to make. Stupid—but also vastly more successful in the brokerage business than my peers.

Crystal and I worked hard for about two and a half years in that business, and we were very successful at it. We lived modestly in a little apartment in Muskogee. Other brokers were making less than we made but piling up bills—paying monthly installments for cars and planes and homes and vacation condos in Hawaii. We weren't piling up bills. We were piling up money—doing what we were trained to do and what we advised others to do. We invested wisely!

In the mid-1980s I began to see some handwriting on the wall, and I said to Crystal, "We need to get out of here and out of this. It's not going to be much longer that we'll be able to do what we're doing at this level. Before much longer, somebody somewhere is going to ask, 'How can we let a twenty-five-year-old kid make half a million a year out of one of these offices?' They're going to send in a more 'qualified' person, or they'll ask us to go on salary and move up into the corporate structure. I don't want to be caught up in somebody else's structure." Eventually, that was what happened to the brokerage business as a whole. We opted out just in time.

Spending Is a Matter of Priorities

During those years in Muskogee, Crystal and I continued to drive our aged car, the one we named the Old Green Dog. It was the only car in America that was dented out. I bought the car while I was in college and even at three hundred dollars, I got ripped off. Still, I figured it would give Crystal and me a car for dates, even if she had to do all the driving.

In my third year at Oral Roberts University, the university decided to start a track team. One of the coaches had read that I was once a national weight-lifting champion, so he came over to the dorm, knocked on my door, and said, "Can you throw a shot put or a discus?" I didn't know what either one was. I told him I didn't have the time to go out for sports, that I was working hard to put myself through school, and that I needed to study harder than most of the other students.

He said, "If you can throw this little metal ball, I'll give you a scholarship so you don't have to work to pay for your dorm." He got my attention! So we went down to the track-and-field area. I threw the ball, and he said, "You've got it"—referring both to my ability and to the scholarship.

I thought, *Where have I been? A person can throw this little metal ball across some grassy area, and they will pay part of his college bill? They must be nuts!* But to the coach I said, "Are you telling me that if I throw this metal ball around a bit, you'll pay my room and board bills?"

He said, "Right." I started my track career that very hour.

Crystal would drive me over to practice, and we'd put the shot put in the trunk of the car. Before we realized what was happening, we had dented the car—"out." It rolled around the trunk when we turned corners and dented the car from the inside out.

Even after I was making piles of money in the brokerage business, we drove that old car. Other things were more important to us than investing in a new car.

You see, Crystal and I always had a clear idea that the money we were saving and investing was our way out of the brokerage business into what we really wanted to do with our lives. Neither the money nor the brokerage business was an end in itself.

Being in the brokerage business was something I wanted to do. It was something I trained to do, did, and did very well. But I didn't enjoy it. I recognized that very early on in my work as a broker, but I continued in the brokerage business for the money. I'm not necessarily proud of that fact. I never advise anybody to stay in a position strictly for the money. At the same time, Crystal and I knew that whatever we decided to do next, we'd need money to get it established. That was one of the reasons we were so frugal in saving what we earned in Muskogee. It was our ticket to the next thing in our lives.

When I resigned from the brokerage business, more than one person thought I was crazy. My father couldn't understand how I could leave the kind of money I was earning. Other brokers didn't understand it. Every night each brokerage office receives a night wire. When you arrive in the office in the morning, you'll find that the printer has spewed a pile of paper all over the floor. The night wire gives information about bonds that are for sale, new issues, stock offerings, information about new laws, and so forth. It also lists the top brokers. It's a big ego thing to be listed, and we were often listed there. Brokers considered that a major honor, and most of the brokers who knew us couldn't believe we'd walk away from the kind of business we were doing.

We didn't see ourselves as walking away from a successful moneymaking venture. We saw ourselves as walking into our personal greatness.

Crystal's Vision for Her Success

Crystal agreed to work with me until we were successful enough that I could hire someone else. I wasn't sure what she was dreaming and planning to do once she was no longer working full-time with me, but I knew that she was incredibly smart and had loads of talent and ability. I figured she could do just about anything she set her mind to and accomplish it with ease.

In the meantime, Crystal worked by my side in the brokerage business. She'd go with me when we called on people at their homes. She'd ring the bell, and we'd stand on front porches together. After I'd introduced myself, I'd introduce Crystal, telling the person that we were new in the community and I wanted people to meet my wife so we both could get acquainted with as many people as possible. That was my cover for having her by my side. At that time, I could still see shapes and I could walk, for the most part, without stumbling or running into things. So most of the people we called on never knew that I couldn't see the features on their faces.

As the business developed, Crystal took on the responsibility of reading *The Wall Street Journal* each morning. I never told any of my clients I couldn't see. That was very important to me. So Crystal would read *The Wall Street Journal* and share with me two or three things she thought I should know. We'd put *The Wall Street Journal* on the corner of my desk so when clients were ushered into my office, they'd see it and mention it. The paper was a tool I used for triggering conversation.

While reading *The Wall Street Journal* one morning, Crystal read an article about people who wrote novels at home. She rather casually said to me, "That's what I want to do someday."

I didn't take her seriously. I smiled to myself, and we went about our task that day of making two hundred phone calls and working the brokerage business. Crystal was serious, however. She had found what she perceived to be her destiny. From that point on, working the brokerage business to her was a means of getting to the point where she could spend her days writing novels.

Part of the reason I didn't take Crystal seriously when she first mentioned her dream to me was that I had been told by a so-called expert that Crystal couldn't write well.

ORU had an English proficiency requirement for graduation. The test required the student to write three pages in a blue book that told a story or explained something. Even the athletes who could barely pass a regular college course considered the test pretty much a slam dunk. Virtually everybody passed.

But lo and behold, Crystal received a note in her campus post office box one day that informed her she had failed the English proficiency test! Number one in our class, but she had to take the test again. And to further muddy the waters, she failed the test a second time. She finally passed it on her third try.

I thought to myself, *I'm marrying this girl who is not only the nicest person I know, but she's brilliant, she's gorgeous, she's supportive. So what if they say she can't write? No big deal!*

You can imagine my surprise, given that background, when Crystal said to me one day that after we became financially independent and I was able to hire somebody else to help me full-time, she was ready to begin her career as a writer.

An astronaut, maybe. A nuclear physicist, possibly. A chief justice of the Supreme Court, very likely. But a writer? A novelist? Why did she want to be the one thing I was told she couldn't be?

I've never witnessed anybody work harder at anything in her life than Crystal did at becoming a good writer. She was determined. It was her destiny. She believed for it, envisioned it, focused on it, and poured herself into achieving it. In 1991, she received the Rita Award from the Romance Writers of America, which is the top award the organization gives for a manuscript submitted for review. She has the award sitting on her desk at home, and she recently informed me that it's about a quarter of an inch taller than my Emmy Award. I haven't measured them, but I trust her on that.

Crystal has sold two novels, and she is working on several more. She is on her way. She became competent in what she truly desired to do. Her competency didn't come easy. But it came eventually. And that's really what matters. It doesn't matter how long or how hard you must work to become competent at what you truly desire to be and do. It matters only that you eventually arrive at the level of competency that is necessary for the full achievement of your goals.

The money we made in the brokerage business was a means to Crystal's success—and mine.

Making money in and of itself was not what made us successful. Using that money to pursue our personal dreams helped make us successful.

Opportunity Abounds

All of the good deals aren't over yet. All of the best ideas haven't been thought. All of the greatest companies haven't been founded. All of the new products haven't been invented. All of the money in the world is not in somebody else's bank account.

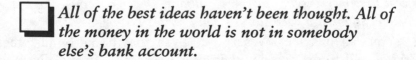 *All of the best ideas haven't been thought. All of the money in the world is not in somebody else's bank account.*

There is still plenty of room for you to make money. And even more so, there is still plenty of opportunity for you to become the person you want to be, to do what you want to do, and to have what you want to achieve.

In spite of the gloom-and-doom purveyors in our culture, the statistics tell us that we live in the richest time and in the richest nation ever to occupy the face of the earth. There were more millionaires created last year than ever before, and there is no reason to think that there won't be more this year, next year, and every year upcoming. Our national output is higher than it has ever been. We may not be growing as fast as we'd like, or as fast as some of our competitors, but we're growing.

Even so, the average American is thirty days from bankruptcy. If you didn't have any income for the next thirty days, what state would you be in?

Consider your current financial situation, including all of your fixed assets (which includes things you own) and all of your liabilities (which includes all the credit card debt you've piled up for yourself). That's a part of being objective and realistic about where you are in your life at any given time.

Rather than ask, however, What am I worth? I recommend that you ask, Why does my financial life fail to reflect what I'm really worth as a person?

> ■ *Don't let your sense of worth be tied to your finances. You are worth vastly more than that.*

Don't let your sense of worth be tied to your finances. You are worth vastly more than that—if you choose to see yourself as a successful person fulfilling your personal destiny.

Your current financial statement tells you about the choices you have been making. A financial statement tells you where you've lost your focus in pursuing your personal destiny. It can reveal ways in which you have been unproductive, even though you've been busy earning a living.

I heartily suspect that your financial situation wasn't created in a day. You didn't earn all your money or acquire all the things you own in a day. You didn't accrue all your debt in a day. You earned and spent and achieved the balance you have today over time. Day by day by day.

Consider any other accomplishment of your life. Your level of schooling. The information you have. The people you know. You didn't acquire any of it instantly.

What you have in terms of money reflects your daily lifestyle, and as such, it reflects something about the direction and commitment you have toward achieving excellence in your life.

Most Americans do not have hefty savings accounts. Rather, they have huge credit card debts.

Most Americans haven't invested heavily in their businesses, their talents and abilities, or their dreams. They've invested in the latest sale at the mall.

Where do we find our greatest financial success stories these days? The stories often seem to involve somebody who has come from a developing nation and is determined to succeed here and does.

Months ago, Michael pointed out to me that a Vietnamese tailor had opened a new shop in a little strip shopping center on a corner we routinely passed on the way to work. We talked casually about the possibility of paying him a visit and perhaps each of us having a suit made.

Several months later, Crystal told me that she saw this tailor on the news. A feature segment described how he had struggled to get to America and learn a new language, how he had saved his money to open his little shop, and how enthusiastic he was about his new business and opportunity.

Well, a few months later, on the opposite corner at the same intersection, Michael noted that a large new building was going up, complete with parking lot. The Vietnamese tailor had become so prosperous that he was building his own shop on a prime piece of property.

I don't know all the details of this man's work and business, but I can guarantee you that he goes about his work day by day by day by day. He does everything he does with excellence and with courtesy to his customers. He's seeking to be a giving member to society. He's not just thinking about success. He's working to have it, fully expecting to have it, and building on it. He has a strong vision of himself as a tailor, an entrepreneur, a successful businessman in America!

And I suspect that this man weighs every expenditure and every investment he makes against his dream of being a quality tailor and businessman. He is not just making money. He is using money to get where he wants to be in life. He's not just building a business; he's building his identity, his life, his reputation, his legacy.

The Means of Doing What You Know Is Right to Do

My grandmother died in 1991. I can't begin to tell you what a special person she was in my life. Shortly after I had lost the remainder of my sight, my grandmother came to visit me in Tulsa.

Grandmother and I always had a very open, honest relationship, but up to the time of that visit, we had never talked about my being blind. After she had been in our home two or three days, she said, "Jim, when you get a chance, I'd like for you to come to my room. We need to talk a minute." I immediately went with her to her room, and she closed the door and said, "Now, don't say anything and don't argue with me. I've already talked to your grandfather about this. This spring, I want to see my flowers one more time, and then I want you to call your doctor on the telephone and tell him to do an operation to take out my eyes and give them to you."

My grandmother didn't know that such an operation wasn't possible for the restoration of my sight, but her saying that to me was just as valuable to me as if I had had such an operation and could see fully today. That's the kind of woman my grandmother was to the day she died—generous and loving and completely supportive.

I don't think I fully understood what having money was for until the day my grandmother called me and said, "Jim, I don't want to die in a nursing home."

Up to that time, money was fun, convenient, at times necessary, and mostly a means of getting us to where we wanted to go in life. But when that call came, I truly understood a greater value in having money—the ability to help someone you love. I said, "Grandma, we'll do whatever we have to do. We'll hire nurses to come to your home and care for you around the clock. We'll bring in a hospital bed. You won't die in a nursing home." And our family did just that.

I visited my grandmother just before she died, and while she was sleeping, the nurse said to me, "Your grandmother is so proud of you and what you do."

I said, "You know, it's rather odd to me that you would say that because I don't even know if my grandmother *knows* what I do." Several years earlier, my grandmother had been astounded that she could sit in my living room next to me and watch me on the TV set at the same time. The technology was something she could hardly grasp.

The nurse said, "Oh, yes, she does know what you do. See that picture of you by her bedside—the one of you holding that Emmy Award? She tells everybody who comes to visit, 'This is my grandson. He does two things in life. He makes it so blind people can see TV, and he travels all over the world and tells people that they can have good things in their lives.'"

Grandmother put into one sentence what I am and do, and she nailed it.

I'm so grateful my grandmother didn't say, "Oh, my grandson is a businessman," or "My grandson makes lots of money." If she had, I would have been the one who was missing the point in my life.

Money allows us to do things for other people. It allows us to find our destiny and pursue the greatness we want for our lives. Money allows us to build things and give things and accomplish things that benefit others. Money can help you do whatever you dream of doing to forge the identity you desire to have.

Use money.

But pursue destiny.

16

SEARCHING
FOR ANSWERS
Be constantly on the alert
for solutions.

I have heard people question about another person, "Does he have what it takes?" Or they say about themselves, "I'm not sure I have what it takes."

The fact of the matter is, very few of us have what it takes to achieve our dreams. But that doesn't mean that you *won't* have what it takes.

I firmly believe that if you can visualize a dream for your life, you will have what it takes to achieve that dream when you need it and in the form you need it. I have strong faith in that concept.

If you buy a puzzle with a thousand pieces in it, and you dump all of the pieces on the table, you have faith that you can find two pieces that go together, and then two more pieces, and ultimately, that all one thousand pieces are going to fit together. Furthermore, you have faith that when you finish working the puzzle, it will match the picture on the cover of the puzzle box. You don't know the person who made that puzzle. You don't know with certainty at the outset of working the puzzle that all the pieces are there or that they will all fit together. But you have faith that they are there and they'll fit.

That's the way a dream is. You must be able to visualize that dream clearly in your mind. It's like looking at the picture on the puzzle box. See clearly what you want to be and do. And then recognize that the picture is a series of pieces that need to come together. All the pieces are there, but you probably will need to work at finding which pieces fit together. It may take a while to find match-ups. Keep looking!

The main reason that people don't achieve their dreams, in my opinion, is that they give up trying to put the pieces of the dream together. They decide way too early in the pursuit of the dream that a puzzle piece is missing or that they'll never be able to figure out how to turn the pieces into a finished dream. Seek what you need until you find it!

And above all, believe that your dream is possible. Believe that all the pieces can come together.

Help Comes in the Form of People

Some of the help that you need will come to you in the form of people. Continually be on the lookout for people who are able, willing, and eager to offer you goods and services that you can use.

Every time you face a change or a major turning point, a person will show up who will be a catalyst for you.

I truly believe that every time you face a change or a major turning point, a person will show up who, for you, is the right person at the right place. That person will be a catalyst for you.

The foremost person in my life in that role has been Kathy Harper, my partner in Narrative Television Network. I may have questioned Kathy's wisdom in leaving her law career to pursue the dream of NTN, but I have never questioned her loyalty. She is the main difference between my speaking and hosting a television show and having a television network, and my sitting in an easy chair in a little room in my house listening to my stereo and radio.

Kathy showed up precisely at the time in my life when I needed someone to help me pursue a dream. She was more than a catalyst.

She became part of the dream itself. NTN may have existed in some form without Kathy, but it wouldn't be the NTN we have today.

I don't know what you are dreaming of being and doing, but I believe this: Somebody will come alongside you to help you, and in the process, that person will be fulfilling the destiny for his life, too!

Watch for that person. Welcome what she has to offer.

For Every Lock, There's a Key

Not too long ago, my friend Spencer called me. He called at an interesting time. I was in a hotel room in New York trying to figure out how to put on a tuxedo so I could pick up my Emmy. I don't know who designed tuxedos, but let me assure you, they didn't have blind people in mind! A tuxedo is a pretty amazing contraption to wear even under the best of circumstances.

I was trying to get dressed, and Spencer called with a problem. He had heard about a scope that would revolutionize the detection of child abuse and, thus, the prosecution of child abusers. He had figured out how to put the device in various places and had gained the cooperation of a team of knowledgeable people at a university to analyze the readings, but he didn't know how to transmit the readings from the scope to the university.

Many children who are abused are only toddlers—three or four years old—and I could understand the wisdom of being able to send a video image of a scope test to medical experts for diagnosis rather than force little children to travel for a day or more to be examined and treated at the same center. Furthermore, I knew from my work with Spencer that very often the best time to get evidence of abuse is before a child has been cleaned up or the wounds treated. And furthermore, I knew that timely action was necessary in abuse cases. The quicker a diagnosis can be made and the abuse documented medically, the quicker an abuser can be found and arrested. The timing is often vital since some abusers aren't related to the children they abuse and they often flee the scene if a child is hospitalized or if they think they may be implicated in the abuse.

I had no doubt that this means of scoping patients and sending the video results to a university medical center was a critical move toward helping abused children. It was definitely a lock worthy of a key!

My first response was to say, "The only way I know off the top of my head is to use a satellite."

No sooner were the words out of my mouth than I started to think like an expert. *A satellite?* That would cost thousands of dollars an hour. Spencer probably couldn't get satellite time and certainly not around-the-clock time. The idea wouldn't work.

I caught myself just in time. *Stovall,* I said to myself, *you're starting to sound like one of those experts.* There was no way I was going to tell Spencer how long I'd been in the television business or how sure I was his idea wouldn't work. So I said to Spencer, "Let me think about it and I'll call you tomorrow. I don't know what we'll do, but this is not a problem."

Spencer replied, "Do you know how many times you say that—'I don't know, but this is not a problem'?" I had never really stopped to think about it before, but as I reflected about it, I realized that I probably do make the statement often, and that I am pretty glad I have that approach to life and to challenges.

> *Have faith that every problem can be solved in some way, at some time, by somebody.*

Being optimistic about a solution doesn't mean that you are blind to the problem. It means that you have faith that every problem can be solved in some way, at some time, by somebody.

When I say that I don't know how something is going to get done or be resolved, I am *not* saying that I believe it can't be done or resolved. I'm saying that I don't know at the time what the solution will be, but that I expect a solution to be discovered.

After I talked to Spencer, I finished dressing, and then I made my way down to the ballroom where the Emmy Awards ceremony was being held. As much public speaking as I've done during the last few years, I'm still not comfortable in crowds, attempting to meet and greet people and find my way around. At the same time, I'm determined to meet and have a meaningful encounter with at least one person whenever I venture into a room filled with people.

So, I went into the ballroom and found my table and chair. I sat down and sensed there was a man sitting on my left. Before I asked him to pass the butter, I decided that he was the guy I was going to meet at this event. I turned to him, stuck out my hand, and said, "Hi, my name is Jim Stovall."

He said, "Yes, I know. I've read all about you. I think it's fabulous that you're receiving an Emmy for developing technology that has expanded the scope of television."

I thanked him and then asked, "What are you here for?"

He said, "Well, I'm receiving an Emmy Award as well."

I thought, *That's amazing. There are only a handful of us in this big room who are receiving awards, and one of them is sitting next to me. That's pretty neat.* I asked, "What are you receiving your award for?"

He said, "I developed and patented a way to send a video image through a telephone line."

I gulped.

You can call it an accident. A serendipity. A destiny moment. Whatever you call it, you need to recognize such moments when they come.

I said, "Do you mean to tell me that I could take a scope and examine a small child who has been abused in Chicago, for example, and send that image on a telephone line halfway across the nation to a university where the image could be analyzed by a team of knowledgeable people and have no more expense than the long-distance phone call?"

He said, "I think you could."

He immediately huddled with his colleagues there at the table with us. They were members of the pocket-calculator, slide-rule crowd. They started talking about this possibility and that possibility, and all through the awards ceremony, these guys with their calculators were trying to figure out how to make such a transmission work. After the first of the awards was presented, the man next to me leaned over and said, "Jim, we've talked about it, and this is not a problem!"

Not a problem!

I could hardly wait to call Spencer the next morning.

I don't know what the *how* solutions will be for you to solve the problems you encounter as you pursue the *what* of your goal, but I do know this: You need to approach the problems with an attitude of "I don't have the answer right now, but I will have the answer!"

And then keep your inner ears and eyes open for what you might hear and see. Stay sensitive to the people who come your way and the knowledge they might have. Be open to suggestions and receptive to innovative, creative ideas. The *how* will eventually reveal itself.

17

STAYING CLOSE
TO WHAT KEEPS YOU
BRIGHT-EYED AND SMILING

Don't lose contact

with what motivates you.

Motivation to take action is usually prompted by one of two things: pain or pleasure.

In many ways, those of us in the United States are at something of a disadvantage when it comes to strong motivation because we have very little pain and a great deal of opportunity for pleasure in our society, at least by comparison to people in other nations. Even if you do virtually nothing with your life, you're still going to live better than 90 percent of the people in the world when it comes to material possessions and access to education, health care, and spiritual nourishment.

My secret wish for many of the people I meet is that things will get a lot better for them or that things will get a little worse. Why a little worse? That sounds coldhearted and cruel. But I suspect that if things got a little worse for some people, they'd hit bottom and be forced to face their lives squarely, and in doing so, they'd likely make some changes that would ultimately make things a lot better.

You are going to have to look within—more than at outward circumstances in most cases—for your motivation. What is the inner pain you no longer want to endure? What is the inner pleasure that you can hardly wait to experience?

■ The strongly motivated person knows that trying is more important than winning.

In my opinion, the person who has a strong inner drive, an intense inner motivation, is more fearful of *not* trying than he or she is fearful of failure.

The strongly motivated person knows that

- trying is more important than winning.
- being faithful to oneself is more important than scoring.
- following one's deep inner convictions is more important than being rewarded for having the convictions.
- pursuing one's sense of personal destiny is the very quest of living and that without that pursuit, life has less meaning, less fulfillment, less joy.

You don't have to say to a strongly motivated person, "Get up in the morning and psych yourself to do a good job today." A strongly motivated person is already geared to do that.

You don't have to say to a strongly motivated person, "Here's what you need to do to get excited about life." The strongly motivated person is already excited.

You don't have to say to a strongly motivated person, "Get a reason to live." The strongly motivated person has one.

You don't have to say to a strongly motivated person, "Work hard so you can have fun." The strongly motivated person works hard and sees the work as being fun.

If you don't have a well-defined direction for your life—a dream, a goal, a destiny, a purpose for being, a personal agenda, whatever name you may call your personal aspirations—there is really nothing I or anyone else can say to you to motivate you. Motivational phrases and stories are going to seem like just so much hype to you.

I have a friend who knows a young man who sincerely believes that he is going to be president of the United States someday. My friend has conveyed to me how this young man lives and how he makes choices. I don't know whether he will be president one day or not, but I do know that he is living his life today as if he will be. He is careful about his activities so that there will be no skeletons in his closet and no behaviors that he may have to live down someday if he subjects his life to the very close scrutiny politicians receive. He is careful about his associations, choosing very wisely his mentors and advisers. He enters into relationships with others with an eye toward having these people as colleagues and friends for the rest of his life. He weighs his words before speaking, and he studies issues and comes to well-researched and well-reasoned opinions before he voices his ideas. He is avid about pursuing a healthful lifestyle and about being physically fit and well-groomed at all times when he is in public.

I've never met this guy but I can tell you this about him: Even if he isn't the president of the United States of America in the future, he is going to be at the top of his field in something. He has already envisioned himself there, and he is living the way he will live once he reaches the pinnacle of his destiny. There is going to be a seamless quality about his life—that he has always lived as if he were president.

The truly motivated person has a dream for her life that is compelling, challenging, motivating. The dream drives the motivation.

This is the exact opposite of the way some people think about motivation. They think they need to get motivated and then go out and apply that motivation to a task. They get themselves revved up every morning and then spin their wheels all day, or they get themselves all psyched up and then run around all day like chickens without heads. Oh, they have energy. Yes, they have enthusiasm. But at the day's end, they often have a headache and they collapse into exhaustion, feeling worn out because they didn't achieve anything during the day.

If You Aren't Motivated, Get a New Dream

To get motivated and then look for something to which to apply that motivation is to put the cart in front of the horse. The dream comes first. The stronger the dream, the more motivating it will be. The dream carries with it a power and a life surge. The more vivid and more focused the image you have for what you want to be, do, and have in your life, the stronger your drive is going to be to achieve that dream. The more important your dream is to you, the more you are going to go after it with all your being.

□ *To get motivated and then look for something to which to apply that motivation is to put the cart in front of the horse. The dream comes first.*

If you aren't motivated, you probably need to get a new dream. The dream comes from your choices, and your choices are based on your desires and your personal hopes for what your life might be like and might be worth.

Start at the right point. Start with what you want in life, out of life, and to give to life. Start with your dreams and goals. Make choices until you are focused on the one, two, or three things that are most important to you to be, do, and have. Stay focused. Stay focused. Stay focused. The dream—if you hold it strongly enough and tightly enough and long enough—will compel you to take action. It will brew inside you until you must do something to make your dream a reality.

Being selected as one of the Ten Outstanding Young Americans by the Jaycees was a high moment for me. The first awards of this type were given by the Jaycees in 1930. The people chosen have been in their twenties or thirties, so they aren't really famous yet. Among the people receiving TOYA Awards have been Charles Lindbergh, Walt Disney, John F. Kennedy—the list goes on.

One thing that's amazing to me is that the Jaycees have selected these people while they were still so young and only at the beginning of their success in their chosen fields. I went to the awards ceremony as curious to meet the other nine recipients as I'm sure they were to meet me.

I wasn't disappointed, let me assure you.

Perhaps because I had also played football, and perhaps because we both experienced serious physical adversity in our lives, I was especially eager to meet Dennis Byrd. Dennis had played football for the University of Tulsa before he was drafted to play in the National

Football League. In a freak accident he broke his neck and was paralyzed from the neck down; he was told he would never walk again. Many people have watched Dennis as a sports commentator, so Dennis and I also had a TV interest in common.

At that time, although Dennis had made miraculous progress, he was still far from being fully recovered. In addition, the week of the awards ceremony, he had the flu, and it had weakened him. He was scheduled to take the stage right after I spoke. Dennis had given instructions to the people with him that they weren't to help him stand until it was the exact moment for him to go out on the stage. He was very weak from battling this virus, and he had been using a wheelchair for several days. Some of those with him, as well as others connected with the awards ceremony, had doubts about whether he would be able to walk out on the stage.

I'd read Dennis's book, *Rise and Walk*, before the event and had sat backstage talking with him for about an hour. He knew my story. I knew his. There was a lot we didn't need to say to each other because we both automatically knew certain things about each other given what we've both experienced. An almost immediate bond developed between us.

> **Stay focused. Stay focused. Stay focused. The dream will compel you to take action.**

Right before I was to walk out on the stage, I was doing my utmost to concentrate on walking to the podium. It takes energy and concentration for me to do what I do when I speak. As I was pulling myself together to go out in front of the audience, a couple of stagehands near me were talking into their headsets to the point of distraction. A bit irritated, I finally asked one of them, "Is there a problem?"

He said, "We don't think Dennis is going to make it. He's never going to get off that couch they have him lying on, and we're trying to figure out an alternative. Perhaps we can show his video, or we can bring him out in the wheelchair—"

I interrupted him. I had talked with Dennis for only about an hour, but I knew the man. I said, "If you guys will be quiet and leave me alone in silence here, I promise you that Dennis Byrd will get off that sofa and make it across the stage. I know him like I know myself. And I know he'd rather die than go out there in a wheelchair to accept an award for overcoming his accident. Trust me. He'll get up and walk out there just like I'm about to."

I walked across the stage, got my award, said my speech, walked back into the green room, and said to Dennis, "Time to go, buddy." He never complained, never said anything. He got up and walked out and received his award, just like everybody else that night. It cost him mentally and physically more than most people will ever know. And the way he felt afterward was probably a deeper feeling than most people will have about anything they do in life!

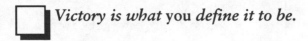 *Victory is what* you *define it to be.*

Walking across that stage that night was as big a deal to Dennis Byrd as any victory he ever had on the football field. I know that. He knows that I know that, even though we've never talked about it.

The point is, victory is what *you* define it to be. Nobody else.

Walking across the stage at the Performing Arts Center that night was important to me. I had practiced the steps to the podium and then the steps off stage much of the afternoon. If I had walked up to a group after the event and had said, "Hey, guys, want to hear something exciting? I walked across that stage without a hitch!" they probably would have looked at me a little cross-eyed. But it was a big deal to me. I had hit the mark.

When I do a television show, people will often tell me afterward that it was a great interview, but I alone know whether I nailed the show. I have to memorize the eye coordinates for the location of camera one, camera two, camera three. I need to know where my chair is, where the person being interviewed is. And then I need to know exactly where I am in time. If I have three and a half minutes for a segment, I need to stay within and completely fill that precise time frame without the benefit of a timer or a TelePrompTer. I have to set all the timers and compasses inside myself and keep track of them even while I'm talking, listening, and thinking about the task at hand. And I know when I hit the mark.

I know how much it takes for me just to get into the game. I've already got a big victory going to be there on the set in front of the camera. And if I didn't know within myself that I'm doing a fantastic job, I'd be sorely disappointed much of my life because others don't truly know the victories that I have or the wins that I score because they don't have to do what I do.

My success is *my* success. It's what I define it to be.

In the final analysis, your success will probably relate directly to how inner-motivated you become. Your motivation must—repeat *must*—flow from the inside out. Any other form of motivation will quickly fade or die.

In nearly all cases, virtually everybody else on the planet is going to think your idea is stupid. A few close friends or family members may embrace your idea, but they may embrace it only because it is important to you and not because they think that your idea or your dream is the greatest idea or dream they have ever encountered.

Furthermore, the more time you spend developing your idea, the less your family members and close friends are likely to embrace your idea because they will think the time you spend developing your dream is time you could better spend with them!

Prepare yourself to face the hard, cold reality that nobody is going to be a continual source of motivation. You are going to have to become your own source of motivation.

Candidly Evaluate Why You Do What You Do

Ask yourself, Why do I do what I do? Are you doing what you do because you want to do it? Or are you doing it because that's the only door that seemed to open when you went on a job search? Or is it because of what others have told you that you ought to be doing or that you need to be doing (perhaps for *their* sake)?

If you can't look yourself in the mirror and say with all honesty, "I do what I do with my time, my energy, my talents, and my money because I am 100 percent convinced in my heart that this is what I want to be, do, and have," something is seriously wrong.

I met a woman who gave me a fairly general line about why she was starting her new business, and I could tell she was just saying words. She wasn't telling me the real reason. I let her ramble on for a few minutes, and then I said, "Listen, I have only ten more minutes to spend with you. Why are you in this business?"

She started crying as she said, "My daughter is twenty-four years old. When she was seven years old, the dentist told me she needed braces. We didn't have the money for them, and we never did figure out how to afford them for her. All during her teenage years, I knew her self-esteem was low in part because of the work she needed on her teeth. I finally decided that more than anything else in the world, I wanted to be able to buy braces for my daughter. So I called the dentist and found out how much it was going to cost for me to do that, and I started this business with that purpose in mind."

You may say, "Well, is this woman doing what she's doing for her daughter or for herself?" She's doing it primarily for herself. This is something that this mother wants to do. I don't know whether the daughter knows what is going on, but I suspect from what that mother told me, the daughter will be delighted with her mother's gift.

You can have another person involved in your reason for doing what you do, but you need to make sure that you are doing what you want to do without any manipulation or pressure from another person. You may very well want to talk your decisions over with someone else. Lots of people I know choose to talk over their decisions with God. That's fine. I encourage you to do that. But in the end, given whatever input you have sought out, the decision to act must be yours and yours alone.

You may very well say, "After listening to my financial advisers, attorneys, and spouse, I've decided . . . ," or "After praying about this a while, I've decided . . . ," or "After thoroughly researching this to the best of my ability, I've decided . . . ," or "After taking this series of aptitude tests, I've decided . . ." But the key words need to be *I've decided*.

Own your decision. Do what *you* want to do.

Your Reason Needs to Be Big Enough to Motivate Only You

What motivates one person may seem like a small reason to another person. So be it. Each of us is motivated by something different.

I met a woman who decided to enter a sales business on a commission basis for what may seem to you to be a rather small goal. I met this woman with her husband during a meeting at which I spoke. The couple was quite poor, and both of them were pretty emotional after the presentation. I shared with them my concept that success in life is like choosing from a menu—there is no right or wrong choice. We choose what is right for us and what we desire to have, and then we work to achieve that.

I asked this woman's husband what he wanted out of life, and he gave me a pretty routine litany of car, house, boat, and other material possessions. He was focused on what he wanted to have, rather than what he wanted to be or do.

Then I asked the woman, "What do you want?"

She said, "I have two little girls I love more than my own life. Every day I send them off to school knowing they are the two worst-dressed little girls in that school. Next year on picture day, I want to be able to send both of my girls to school in brand-new dresses—not dresses we've picked up at a secondhand store. I want them to have photos in which they look their absolute best."

Wow! There was a goal I could work with. There was a woman who really wanted what she wanted. And I knew that if I could get her started in the right direction toward accomplishing that goal, she had all the motivation needed to achieve it.

To others, that goal might have seemed very small, but it was a giant goal to that woman.

The size of your goal is never what matters most. What matters most is having a goal, one that you really, *really*, REALLY want to accomplish.

That woman called me one day a little more than a year later and said, "I won't embarrass myself or you by sending you a copy of the pictures, but I want you to know that my girls did go to school for picture day wearing new dresses."

She made my day. But even more important, she reached her goal.

Your Motivation May Be People Who Are Counting on You

Have you ever had someone say to you, "I'm counting on you"? What often goes unsaid in a statement like that is this: "I'm counting on you to do this so I'll look good" as your parent or boss or friend or whatever. That's a lousy motivation.

On the other hand, you may find it motivating to pursue an area of interest and a level of personal success because you want others to be able to count on you and because you delight in having them count on you.

Good parents know that feeling when it comes to their children. Parents want to do things right and do the right things simultaneously so as to be role models, examples, and inspirations to their children. Parents know intuitively that if they quit or fail or aren't available at the necessary times, they will have let down their children. Children are perhaps the best motivators of parents.

Even if you don't have biological children, you very likely have people who look up to you or who seek to follow in your example. Teachers feel a responsibility to their students. Pastors and counselors also seem to recognize that they are being watched by people they help. The fact is, however, that most people in a position of authority, influence, or leadership are being watched virtually all the time by others and are being emulated to some degree by those who seek to be like them.

If you have any leadership role whatsoever, take heed. You are being watched, and what you do will influence others. You owe the people who are watching you your best effort—to be, do, and have the very highest quality in your life. This is true if you are a committee chairperson of a club or its president, if you are a Scout leader or a coach, if you are a first-line supervisor or an executive in an organization, if you are a political representative or a person with a high recognition factor in the media. This is especially true if you are an aunt or uncle, a grandparent, a godparent, a day-care worker, or a regular baby-sitter for a family.

You may say, "But I thought I was supposed to be motivated by what I want to be and do rather than by what others expect."

You are. But you need to be aware that others are being influenced by you whether you like it or not. It's one thing to do things because others demand them of you or expect them of you. It's quite another to make certain choices in your life because you recognize that you are influencing other people and you accept the responsibility for doing so.

I don't know a successful person who doesn't in some way, and most of the time, take into consideration that he or she has a certain reputation to uphold as an example to people who are important to him or her. That's the way life works. Successful people aren't slaves to their fans or to their loved ones, but they are mindful that what they do influences people watching their lives.

Even if you go out of your way not to wear your success on your sleeve—or not to accumulate certain outward tangible goods that indicate material success—if you are striving with focused and diligent effort to reach a particular goal, others are going to take note of that. They will see you becoming what you want to be. They will see the change in you, and if that change is positive in your life—which in virtually all cases it will be—they are going to be attracted to it in a way they can't describe.

Don't try to run away from your responsibility as a role model. Embrace it. Accept it as part of your destiny. And allow it to be motivating to you that others are watching and taking cues from your example.

Whenever I go out into society, I make an effort to dress well. I'd just as soon people see me not as a blind person but as a person. Obviously, sooner or later they are going to come to the realization that I'm blind, but I'd much rather that be later than sooner. I'd rather that they notice other things about me first.

This is only a small example of a much larger principle. You will have the challenge of wearing your success well. In whatever area you choose to pursue a personal destiny, live in the fullness of that identity before others. Be a light on their path.

Your Motivation May Be People You Don't Know

As strange as this may sound to you, the closer you come to achieving your vision of personal greatness, your motivation may very well become people you haven't met yet.

Successful people tend to lend their energies to a charitable cause. Something is built into human nature that causes us to want to leave behind a legacy of doing good for others. Find a cause you can give to—not only your money, but also your time, interest, talent, concern, presence, influence, abilities. In so doing, you'll be helping people you may not know.

As I have alluded to in previous chapters, one of my main concerns is helping children who have been abused. From the minute I heard about the organization with which I am involved, I knew that I wanted to have a part in helping the children it helped. I've met very few of these children through the years, but I "see" them clearly in my mind's eye. I have visualized them before, during, and after the help they receive from this organization. I have a clear understanding of their lives. I have a love for them. And I'm motivated by them.

Another group of people that I help are college students at my alma mater, Oral Roberts University. While I was a student living in the dormitory at ORU, six of us became very close friends. We often stayed up late at night talking or studying together. We dreamed about our future lives after graduation. None of us had any money at the time, but we decided that if we ever did succeed in reaching our goals and if we ever did have money, we would help other students who were struggling as we once had.

Several years after we were out of school, we found ourselves together again as a group. We were attending the wedding of Dave Crowell, one of our group. We recalled those late-night dormitory conversations, and we started a scholarship fund. To date, we've helped more than one hundred students with scholarships or with other forms of assistance.

Who needs *you*?

Focus on one particular person or type of person. There are so many needs in the world, you won't have to go far to get ideas. You may be drawn to people who are homeless, abused, sick with a particular disease, poor, illiterate or uneducated, dying alone, terminally ill, disenfranchised, mentally ill, or orphaned.

The need may or may not be linked to your experience. I don't feel particularly drawn to help blind people, although that might be the logical assumption many would make about me. I certainly wasn't abused as a child. But I feel drawn to help abused children in a way I can't explain, and that is where I put my efforts.

The more you get involved in helping real people with real needs, the more motivating the people will be to you. Not only will you want to be a good role model for them in the way you live, but you will want to achieve certain levels of influence or reward so that you can help them even more. You'll want to do even more with your life so that they can do more with theirs. You'll want to be more, so they can be more. You'll want to have more, so they can have more.

Helping others is a way in which to become a person who gives generously, and the person who is a generous giver is a successful person in virtually everybody's eyes!

Your Motivation May Lie in Redeeming Your Past

Many people have found deep personal motivation in attempting to right a wrong, redeem a past failure or mistake, or overcome a disaster. That was true for one man I met after a speaking engagement.

My college degree is in psychology and sociology. Whenever I'm around academic people, at least one of them will chide me in some way about having sold out to become a businessman rather than pursue one of these professions and help people as a counselor, caseworker, or licensed psychologist. My response is this: I deal with more people in a one-on-one environment than most of the counselors I know.

As I shared in a previous chapter, my way of dealing with crowds after a speaking event is to have people talk with me on a one-to-one basis for no more than fifteen minutes a person. I talk to literally hundreds of people a year in a personal way. Some amazing things have happened during the fifteen-minute meetings. People have shared tough choices, marriage problems, and personal difficulties with candor and emotion.

One gentleman came with his wife to the event where I was speaking, and I could tell immediately that he hadn't wanted to attend. He came only because his wife insisted. When I asked them about their personal dreams, she shared with me a couple of dreams. I quickly realized she was doing all the talking, so I asked him, "What are your thoughts about this?"

He belligerently replied, "It's none of your business."

I said, "That's fine. No skin off my nose. I've got fifteen minutes to give to you, and then I'm going to turn to the next guy who is waiting. If there's something we need to deal with, let's deal with it. But let's not leave it like this. If you've got a problem with me or what

I've said, let's deal with it."

He became angry. "Okay, hot shot," he said, "you think you're so good. I'm going to tell you something I've never told anybody during the past twenty years except my wife. See what you can do with this.

"I was in Vietnam with my best friend—a guy I grew up with. I got to be a helicopter pilot, and he was sitting in the second seat next to me. We were in a gunship flying behind enemy lines. Our job was to seek out and destroy sniper teams, and the enemy had really come to hate us because we killed a lot of snipers. That meant that if one of our helicopters was shot down, the enemy didn't make it the least bit pleasant for any POWs. My buddy and I agreed that if we were shot down, we were going to kill ourselves rather than be taken prisoner. We carried sidearms for that purpose. We also made a pact that if we couldn't shoot ourselves for some reason, but we could see that we were going to be taken prisoner, we would shoot each other before we would allow ourselves to be taken prisoner and tortured and killed by the enemy.

"Well, one day, we took a round through the side of the helicopter, and I looked over at my friend. He was bleeding profusely, and it looked like half his head was gone. The helicopter was going down, spinning out of control, and I couldn't hold it steady. My friend looked at me and said, 'I don't want to die like this, being tortured as a wounded prisoner.' I knew our pact, and he knew our pact. So I took the revolver off my hip, and I shot him right between the eyes. He died immediately.

"Then a big gust of wind came up, and somehow the chopper righted itself. We cleared the trees by just a few feet and were able to fly back out to the ocean and crash-land on the deck of a ship. The guys on the ship rushed to pull us out of the wreckage, and I heard one of the flight surgeons say as he reached my best friend, 'What a shame! We could have fixed this wound on the head, but he's been shot between the eyes.'"

We had only fifteen minutes, and somehow, we talked through all that during that time. We talked about how he had lived the last twenty years of his life and how the only legacy he had given his best friend was twenty years of bitterness and anger and devastating hurt. I asked him what he would have wanted his best friend to have done for him if the roles had been reversed. He said, "I would hope that he would have loved me enough to do what we had agreed to do."

I said, "Well, you loved him enough to do that. You can't belittle the love he had for you or the trust he had for you. You can't discount the love that motivated you to do what you did. The only thing you can do now is live your life in a way that is going to be a suitable legacy for that friend. I'm going to leave this auditorium in a couple of hours and I'll probably never see you again, but you will know and you will know that I know that whatever you do with your life from this day forward is going to be in honor of your friend."

I received a letter about two months later from that man's wife. She described for me the dramatic change in her husband and how he had acquired an incredible passion and zest for living, how he was accomplishing some of his goals, and how he seemed to have found new peace and joy.

That man traded in his misery for motivation. He turned his bitterness into energy to succeed.

I refuse to pass judgment on what he did, or what he hadn't done for twenty years. I applaud in his life the fact that he is now pursuing a dream of his choosing, and he is self-motivated to achieve that dream for reasons that are purely his own.

Acknowledge the source of your motivation, and use it to propel you toward your personal destiny.

Whatever motivates you is what motivates you. It may be something in your past. It may be related to a person. It may not be either. Whatever it is, acknowledge that as the source of your motivation, and use it to propel you toward your personal destiny.

Your Motivation May Be to Honor Someone in Your Past

One day I asked Lee Braxton if there was anything I could do for him. He was approaching the end of his life, and we both knew it. I said, "Mr. Braxton, you've given me everything you've known to give. What can I give to you?"

He said, "Jim, there's not a thing you could ever do for me or give to me that's of a tangible or material nature. I've been blessed in having everything I could ever want and more. The only thing you can do for me is to someday, somewhere, pass on to someone the information I've given you. Pass on the truth of what I've shared with you. That's the only way you can ever repay me for these hours we've spent together."

At some point in your life, you're going to have an opportunity to give to people not only what you have but also what you know. Don't limit your involvement with a cause or benevolent organization to money or tangible giving. Give of yourself. Give your skills and abilities and time and influence. And then beyond that, teach somebody what you know to be true. Every good parent does that, of course, but I'm talking about moving beyond your immediate family to find someone—perhaps only one person or one small group of people—who wants to know what you know and who is willing to learn what you have to teach. Share what you know to be true and valuable with that person. Give your knowledge freely.

Lee Braxton isn't the only person who motivates me today to do my best and to give to others what he so generously gave to me. Another man in my past has greatly influenced my desire to give. I feel a special motivation in relationship to him each Christmas.

When I was about six years old—just old enough to start giving some thought to buying Christmas presents with a little bit of help—I made the decision to buy my mother a football. I really wanted to have a football, and I couldn't imagine everybody else around me not wanting a football as much as I did. Since I couldn't think of anything else to give my mother, I bought her a football. She was very gracious about receiving it and said that she thought we could share the football, which we did, much to my delight.

By the time the next year came around, I was seven and much wiser. I realized by then that I hadn't purchased the most appropriate gift in the world for my mother the previous Christmas, and I wanted to make up for it. I wanted to find a very special gift for her.

Close to our home was a store that had lots of nice things in it, and I rode my bicycle there to see what it might have for my mother. My mother loves daisies, and this store had a large framed picture of daisies. It must have been four feet square. I decided that was the perfect gift. After I discovered it, I rode my bicycle to that store every day to look at it and to confirm that it was definitely what I wanted to give my mother for Christmas.

The only problem was that the picture cost $58 and I had only $14. I may be a dreamer, but I'm also a realist. Even at age seven, I knew that I couldn't buy a $58 framed picture with $14, no matter how much I wanted it. So I looked for other things in the store, but I just couldn't find anything that was as right for my mom as that framed picture of daisies.

Two or three days before Christmas, the store manager—who had greeted me every day when I came in—said, "Do you really want that picture?"

I said, "I sure do. I want to give it to my mother for Christmas, but I have only $14."

He put his arm around me and said, "Well, we're having a special Christmas sale, today only, and that picture has been reduced to $14."

I couldn't believe my ears! I was so excited. I said, "I'll buy it!"

It wasn't until I was leaving the store that it dawned on me that there was no special Christmas sale going on, and that the picture really hadn't been reduced to $14. I went back in and said, "Sir, what can I do? This isn't a good deal for you. It's not right, your giving me this $58 picture for only $14. Is there some way I can pay you that doesn't cost money right now?" I even offered, "I can tell my mother that this is from both of us."

He said, "No, you tell her this is from you. But there is something you can do. Every year, at Christmastime, you do something special for someone, but never tell the person that you did it. If you do that, we'll be even on this picture."

Well, I gave that picture to my mother, and it's still hanging on the wall in her office. I'm sure it will always hang there.

And every Christmas, I have the opportunity to do something nice for someone who will never know that I was the one who did it.

Am I repaying this man? Not really. He gave me a far greater gift than the $44 discount on my mother's picture. He gave me the gift of an opportunity to give. One of the best gifts I've ever given became one of the best gifts I've ever received!

Your Motivation May Lie in a Relationship
That Matters Greatly to You

I'm not at all embarrassed to say that much of why I do what I do is related to my wife, Crystal. She very likely is the strongest motivating force in my life to be all I can be and do all I can do.

Do you recall the story of the Wizard of Oz? The Wizard doesn't give Dorothy anything magical or mystical that changes her world. He reminds her of something wonderful that she already has. I am reminded daily of what a wonderful gift Crystal is to me.

At one point when we were dating, I found that I loved Crystal so much that I didn't want her to be married to a blind person. I thought that would be a terrible drag on her life. I wanted her to find somebody else to marry.

But Crystal wouldn't leave. And in a profound way, that was the greatest evidence she could ever have given me that she truly believed in me. I know that if I went home today and told her we were giving up the television network and everything else we're doing, and we were going to move to a farm and raise chickens, she'd start loading the car. In every person's life there are times when you have to circle the wagons and see what you've got, and sometimes you find yourself in a pretty small circle. But Crystal has always been there. She has never failed me.

I worked the entire time I was in college. I started my own business before I graduated so I could have a little money saved prior to our marriage. We married the month after we both graduated.

During our college days, Crystal and I were poor. We didn't think we were poor. From our perspective, we just didn't have any money. Other couples would go out to dinner and to the movies on dates, but we'd walk over to the library building and sit in one of the empty classrooms. I'd stand at the chalkboard and draw out for her in detail what we were going to do and have as a couple together. When I look back on that now, it seems totally absurd to me that I would do that, but it seems even more absurd to me that she'd sit there and believe every word! Crystal was the only person back then who believed everything I told her we were going to do.

Crystal was a wonderful example to me in that. I doubt that people can become successful or achieve what they desire to achieve unless somebody believes in them and believes that they are going to do what they have planned and purposed to do.

One thing that is so motivating to me about Crystal is that she and I have agreed to be positive people and to be positive toward each other.

We have several ground rules for our relationship. They may not work for other people, but they've served us well. Our number one rule is, "Every day is separate." If I do anything to Crystal today that hurts her, she has until the time we go to bed to tell me about it. We discuss the situation and work through it. But if she chooses not to bring up the hurt, tomorrow is a new day. The same goes for me. If something is bothering me, I've got until bedtime to bring it up. Hurts in the past are out of bounds. We don't hang on to them or bring them up.

This one rule has had a powerful impact on each of us. We don't carry around any emotional hurts or emotional baggage that can turn into bitterness. This rule has forced us to confront issues and to talk candidly. As a result, we know pretty much what hurts the other and, therefore, how to avoid it. It has also forced each of us to learn to let go of hurts. We bring up a hurt or let go of it. Either way, it's out of us, and we don't let it fester, brew, or erupt later.

Crystal and I have also agreed not to tell anybody outside our relationship about any of our problems. There have been times in the past when we had no money. We were so broke we were sleeping on the floor or in our car. As I've stated, I wouldn't exactly call us poor during those periods because poor people can't pile up the kind of debt we had. But we didn't talk about our money problem with other people. We figured that nobody wants to do business with or associate with somebody who is always talking about problems or about how rough things are going. Furthermore, most people to whom you'd tell your problems can't help you anyway.

I've never heard Crystal say anything negative about me to anyone, nor have I said anything negative about her. If I have anything to say to her, I go to her. And she comes to me.

Would I purposefully make choices in my life that would destroy my relationship with Crystal or denigrate her in any way? Would I choose to pursue a vision for my life that discounted Crystal or caused her to become disillusioned with me? Hardly.

I'm motivated by the love that my wife shows to me. So be it. I only hope you have so great a motivation.

Motivational Materials Can Keep Your Motivation High

I seriously doubt whether motivational materials of any kind can create a personal drive to succeed. Their value lies, rather, in helping you keep your motivational level high. They can remind you of the many reasons to achieve your goals and become all you envision you can be.

A study was done a few years ago of our nation's business leaders. A major business magazine surveyed the chief executive officers of the top five hundred largest companies in the United States in an attempt to discover what the leaders had in common. Did they all go to church, work out, have spouses, do something in common, share a similar value? The number one characteristic in common among the five hundred leaders was this: They all read or listened to motivational material on a daily basis.

I don't know about where you live, but where I live, folks will routinely tell you—no matter the subject or idea—that your idea won't work. People are constantly down on this or that, continually criticize whatever there is to criticize. No matter what you tell them, they've got a negative response. I especially listen for their line, "I knew a guy once who tried that." Invariably, the guy failed.

The only way I know to counterbalance that ongoing daily bombardment of negativism is with powerful, positive messages. Period. I don't care in what form you find your positive message— books, tapes, videos, live events—make sure you feed your mind something positive to think about.

You'd be hard-pressed to find somebody who owns more motivational cassette tapes than I do. In addition to the many books on tape that I own, I buy tape courses. Many of them are inspirational in nature. I listen to them mostly while I'm in the limo or while I'm on my treadmill, but the point is, I listen daily to someone, on some subject, from some angle. These speakers and authors give me a positive boost and help me withstand the onslaught of negative talk that a person can't help hearing in our world.

I also have my "Dear Jim" file. It contains letters from people who have written to me through the years. The vast majority of them are variations on this theme: "Dear Jim, hearing you changed my life."

Some of the letters are letters of congratulation—from the president of the United States, personal friends, celebrities, and corporate colleagues.

Whenever I'm having a bad day, we get out some of the letters, and if I'm having a seriously bad day, we get out a serious pile of letters, and we read through them.

They motivate me to continue to do what I do and to be who I am.

The Ultimate Motivator

No other person is going to be as motivating to you as you are going to be to yourself, however. The number one motivational voice to which you will respond is your voice.

> *The number one motivational voice to which you will respond is your voice.*

As I mentioned earlier, every night, just before I go to bed, I review the day. I justify to myself what I've done and said. To some people, *to justify* means "to make excuses." That's not the meaning of the word I'm using here. *To justify* primarily means "to prove right or true."

I go over what I've done and said during a day with the thought that I need to prove to myself what is good, right, true, and noble about the day I've just lived. As I review in my mind various conversations, appointments, and decisions, I ask myself, Did I do the right thing? Was I true to myself? Did I make the noble and good choice?

Doing this on a daily basis keeps me honest with myself. It also means that I don't need to go off someplace every few months and ask, Where am I, and what am I doing with my life? I engage in self-appraisal on a daily basis.

If I'm not satisfied with a decision or choice I've made, I get up the next morning determined to make a better decision or choice, and then I make it.

I've accepted the responsibility for being my best motivator.

Have you accepted that responsibility about yourself and for yourself?

18

GAINING AN
UNOBSTRUCTED VIEW

*Pull it all together
to be your BEST.*

Throughout this book, I've had one supreme goal in mind: to share with you
how you can be your best, go for your best, and achieve your best in
life. My desire is to see you become the person you were destined to
be, with maximum success and a powerful sense of personal fulfillment. There is no substitute for excellence in whatever avenue of life
you choose to walk.

When I speak, I often give the acronym BEST to the audience as
a means of remembering the core of my message. It stands for
something, of course:

> B = Balance
> E = Enthusiasm
> S = Single-mindedness
> T = Tenacity

Let me discuss each of these vital concepts with you briefly as a
means of pulling together all of the other ideas we've covered.

Balance

After you have envisioned a central goal or dream for your life, you are going to find yourself in a juggling act of sorts. You are going to have to develop balance in your life that allows you to move toward a greater goal and, at the same time, to lead a quality life. It's a little like juggling several balls in the air and walking twenty yards toward a specific object.

The tendency is to try to juggle too many things at any given time. Then you wonder why you don't seem to be making any progress or why certain areas of your life seem to be falling apart. The likelihood is that you are trying to do too much at the same time. If you want to stay balanced, pare your life down to what you truly want most, and limit yourself to that.

It's on the dreams that you really want most that you will devote the bulk of your homework, build solid and lasting and mutually beneficial relationships, and spend the majority of your time and energy.

■ *To achieve balance means to raise every element of your life to excellence.*

To achieve balance doesn't mean to bring every element of your life to a level of mediocrity. It means to raise every element to excellence. Balancing isn't a lowering process; it's a raising process of bringing things to a new level in every area.

I don't believe it's possible to be truly successful as a person if you are successful in only one area of your life. If your career is skyrocketing but your home life is rotten, you may be considered successful as an executive, salesperson, performer, lawyer, or manager but not as a person. To be a successful person means that you have all your life in balance. There's a sense of wholeness about you.

Your narrowly defined dreams about what you want to be, do, and have are going to be kept in balance only with practice.

Consider how a juggler works. He must be able to touch—even if briefly—each object he is juggling frequently and regularly. The same is true for every relationship and project you have that is connected to your central goal and dream. You can't have a good marriage if you don't see your spouse and spend quality time with your spouse. You can't have a successful career if you don't spend time on the job. You can't be a good member of any group if you never show up at the group's meetings.

If your central dream is to be a family person with a successful job, make your family and your job your focus. Only take on memberships, engagements, and events that build up your family and your career in balance.

If your central dream is to excel in a particular profession, keep that profession always at the center of your mind. Only take on obligations and associations and activities that will take you closer to the goal you have in mind for your life.

Recognize that you will need to spend concerted and frequent time and energy on any goal to reach it.

Be Able to Laugh at Yourself (and Others)

You can do several things to enhance a sense of balance in your life. One is to maintain a sense of humor about yourself—and about human foibles in general. I'm not advocating laughing *at* a particular person, of course. But there is plenty about human nature in general that can evoke an abundance of smiles. We all make mistakes, and if we can laugh at them even as we learn from them, we stay healthier psychologically.

I often use humor in addressing audiences. I usually begin a presentation by warning the people in the first three rows that I wander around while I talk and they need to stay alert because if I fall, I can wipe out at least three rows of people on a bad day!

Humor is important to me when I speak because it seems to defuse anxiety and pent-up emotion—not in me, but in my audience. People often don't know how to relate to a blind person. When they realize they can share a joke with someone who is visually impaired, the tension lowers significantly.

I love to tell about a time Kathy and I were in Hawaii. I was scheduled to speak at a convention, and she was leading me around through the airport. From what she could see, no driver was waiting to pick us up.

We found a phone and paged the limo service, neither of us realizing that our intended driver was standing about twenty feet away from us. To answer the page, he had to go all the way down a long hall and upstairs to the house phone, only to discover that we had been standing in eye range all the time.

How had he expected to find us? Well, he had been standing there holding up a card with my name on it. Holding a card to greet a blind passenger? I wonder how he had thought we would connect!

Once while I was in Las Vegas, I saw a show featuring Don Rickles. A good portion of his humor is embedded in stereotypes, but one thing I wasn't prepared to hear was his emotion-filled conclusion to his act. He said, in essence, "Look, folks, I remember when we couldn't laugh about our differences as people, and it was a terrible world. Now we're getting to the point where we can laugh about the fact that we're different, and in that, I see hope for a better tomorrow."

Keeping a sense of humor can keep you balanced.

There are times when I have to laugh at the fact that I'm blind. Some of what I do as a blind person is funny. I'm not always suave and debonair. I don't know any fully sighted people who are always suave and debonair. We all have our clumsy, awkward moments. And we might as well enjoy the joke that we are at times.

Keeping a sense of humor can keep you balanced.

Choose to Stay Realistic

Another thing that can help you stay balanced is to choose to remain realistic about your condition.

For a long time I was in a bit of denial about my eyesight. I didn't really want to be in denial—being in denial sounded like being a coward and I wasn't that—but I also didn't want to admit to anyone that I had a problem. That sounded too weak, which was also something I wasn't. So I just didn't tell anybody about my failing eyesight.

If people didn't need to know for some reason, why tell them? That was my approach, even after I had lost all my vision.

When Cheryl, my first mobility teacher, began working with me, I didn't want to use a cane. But then I discovered that a cane might be a useful thing.

For one exercise, she took me to the mall in the middle of the day. I said to her, "Why can't they make these canes in a less-conspicuous color?" She ignored me and led me out among the masses in the mall and gave me the challenge of getting from one place to the next.

If you've ever been in a crowded mall, you know that navigating is no picnic. People bump and jostle you continually. And without my cane, they bumped and jostled me, too. But when I pulled out my white cane, I felt like Moses parting the sea. People had been body-to-body, but suddenly, there was lots of room. It also got really quiet around me. Occasionally, I'd hear a mother tell her child, "Well, he's blind and that's why he's got that cane," but most of the time I heard nothing. It was a surreal feeling.

Someplace along the way between having poor vision and being completely blind, I had to admit to myself, *I can't see. I am not and will not be a sighted person.*

That's not being negative. That's facing reality.

And reality is essential if you are going to set goals for yourself that are achievable.

Stay rooted in reality. If you have good mentors and referees in your life, they'll help you stay rooted there.

Choose to Be a Positive Person

Being positive or negative in your attitude is a choice you make, subconsciously or consciously. Nobody is born with a good attitude or a bad attitude. You allow yourself to respond to life's circumstances in particular ways. You can choose to be a positive person even if everything confronting you is negative.

> *Stay positive. Even if you fail, look for the lesson learned and apply it to your life.*

John Wooden, the very successful former basketball coach at UCLA—whom I had the privilege of being on a show with recently—said, "Things turn out best for those that make the best of the way things turn out."

Stay positive. See the best in every result you encounter and in every person you meet. Look for the one thing that can propel you forward. Even if you fail, look for the lesson learned and apply it to your life. See the experience as a positive one toward reaching your eventual goal.

Choose to Enjoy Some of Life's Rewards Along the Way

After I had become totally blind and had managed to make it to the park on my own the first time, I found it easier and easier to make return visits. Some days I'd take my guitar with me and sit and play whatever songs came to mind. Some days I'd just sit quietly on a bench, enjoying the sounds, smells, and other sensations of being outdoors.

One day at the park I encountered a guy who was working with a young bird dog. He was teaching the dog to retrieve objects that he threw. His five-year-old son was with him.

The only trouble was that the pup didn't want to retrieve objects that were thrown into the distance. He wanted to play with the object and with his owners. Once the dog had the object in his mouth, he ran all over the park with it—having fun, splashing through the creek, taking full advantage of the eighty acres at his disposal. Meanwhile, the guy trying to train the dog was yelling and screaming after him—which caused the dog to run faster and farther. The pup didn't have any idea he was supposed to be learning something. He thought he was playing a game of keep-away.

Finally, the dog returned to the man and his son, and the man took a rolled-up newspaper and beat the dog. His son started to cry. The man became more exasperated and said, "You've got to understand. We're teaching the dog a lesson. Now think for a minute. What lesson are we teaching this dog?"

The little boy was silent for a few moments, and then he said, "I guess we're teaching him that when he pays attention to you and finally does what you say, he is going to get a beating."

I thought about what that little boy said for quite a while that day. I tried to imagine what might be going through the mind of that young pup. If I had been that dog, I would have been thinking, *I'm not sure what I'm going to do next time the guy throws that thing away, but I'm sure not going to come back to him with it in my mouth because look what happens to me!*

I don't know how to train bird dogs, but I suspect that a reward system should be employed. Most creatures respond to reward. It seems to me that if the man had rewarded the dog immediately upon his return with the thrown object, the dog would have been a lot more eager the next time to return to his owner.

Rewards are important to each of us. And we need to take time to reward ourselves periodically as we climb the staircase to our destiny. Don't wait for all of your rewards to come in a heap at the end of your journey or at the end of your life. Some of the rewards are meant to be savored along the way.

A balanced person learns to play as well as to work, to enjoy as well as to achieve, to smell the roses as well as to grow them.

Never Look at the Daily Take

In recent years, I've visited with numerous people in the entertainment business, most of whom have been performers. I've noted that top performers rarely read the reviews of their performances. They don't depend on the so-called critics or experts to tell them whether they've done a good job.

Genuine stars learn early on that the critics are sometimes wrong, the fans are sometimes fickle, and the tides of fame can turn quickly in either direction. Genuine stars continue acting. They take it as a career, a job, a craft. They do what they do, to the best of their ability, and as often as possible, in the highest quality project they can garner, and then they let stardom fall where it may.

As you look at your efforts from day to day, keep your eyes focused on the work you have done. Stay task oriented. Stay people focused. Don't let your mind dwell on the reviews that you have received from others—whether supervisor, peer, or supervised employee—and don't let your attention become focused on the rewards you may have picked up during the day.

The salesman who says, "I talked to forty customers today," should focus on the fact that he talked to forty customers. If he gets his mind on the fact that he made a $10,000 sale and that his commission is going to be $1,500, he is likely to take tomorrow off and go fishing. In so doing, he has allowed himself to become sidetracked from the big goal of his life, which is not one $10,000 sale but a string of sales that will add up to a massively successful sales career.

If he didn't make any sales for his forty calls, he needs to avoid dwelling on that fact, also. If he thinks too long about his lack of sales, he is likely to become discouraged and want to hide his head in the pillows the next morning.

The golfer who is more concerned about her scorecard than her next stroke is going to have a lousy round. The pianist who concentrates on the missed note in the previous movement is not going to be ready to hit all the right notes in the finale.

Stay balanced. Don't let one mistake or one success define your day. Define your day by the effort you expend toward reaching your goals and dreams. Take the glitches and the glory as they come and then move on, always looking to what you can control more than to what you cannot control.

You can't make a person buy what you sell. You aren't going to score a perfect golf game every time you hit the course or hit all the notes in every symphony you play. Mistakes happen. You can't control these things. What you can control is this: Find your stride, and then walk out your dream, day in, day out.

A positive, realistic, dream-filled person with a good sense of humor, a person capable of enjoying life's pleasurable moments along the way, a person who has a daily life focused toward a goal and who refuses to be ruffled by one off day—now that's a well-balanced person in my opinion. Such a person is already well along the path toward personal fulfillment and the joy of personal success.

Enthusiasm

When your life is in balance and you are actively pursuing a goal, you can't help having more enthusiasm. Enthusiasm is not only a by-product of a balanced, fulfilled life, however. It's also an ingredient in creating such a life.

Go about your homework or research with enthusiasm. Be an eager learner. Chances are, as you learn new things and come across new information, you'll be automatically more enthusiastic about the possibilities that you see. Approach the new area of possibility with enthusiasm and you'll likely attract enthusiastic people who will be eager to pursue the possibility with you. Enthusiasm breeds enthusiasm.

Don't let your enthusiasm get out of bounds, however. Keep it channeled. Or, in other words, maintain your intensity.

People can feel intensity. They very often feel as if they can see it, smell it, taste it—when they are more likely only hearing it in your voice. And people will follow it. Show me a person with passion and I'll show you a person with followers.

William Wallace, the man credited for rallying the Scottish people to demand their independence from England at the end of the thirteenth century, was not a man who was highly educated or who had a long and distinguished military career. Much of what he accomplished was against great odds and with a motley band of soldiers. What Wallace had was an "I don't care if I die trying this because if I don't try, I surely will die" attitude. And that's the attitude of passion and intensity that compels other people to follow. Stop and think about his situation for a moment. He was trying to free his people. He was calling his people to give their lives—on a battlefield most of the time—and if not to give their lives, certainly to risk giving their lives or being seriously wounded. That's not exactly the most exciting prospect to most people. But because William Wallace was willing to lead the way toward the cause he was pursuing with all his heart, mind, and soul, others followed, and gladly so!

If you want to die happy, find a course and a cause for your life in which you believe with all your heart. If you die in the pursuit of that course and cause, you indeed will die happy.

I remember watching Reggie Jackson late in his career, dueling with a pitcher. In the minds of many of the fans who were watching him that day, Reggie Jackson was over the hill. Lots of people had said that they thought he should have retired rather than play the season. And there he stood, facing a young relief pitcher, a kid who was throwing smoke. He was squeezing his pitches in on Reggie, and the old guy just couldn't get around on the ball. He couldn't seem to do any better than to foul the ball away.

And then Reggie Jackson stepped back out of the batter's box and looked down at the dirt for a minute. At precisely that moment the center-field camera zoomed in and got a close-up shot of his face. I could still see at that time, and the look that I saw on Reggie Jackson's face is a look that I like to remember every once in a while because I draw strength from it. Reggie Jackson had a look on his face that said, "I'm taking this next pitch downtown. I'm not taking this anymore. You're making me look bad, kid, and I'm fed up with it." *That's* an I'm-not-taking-this-anymore attitude.

As his next pitch, the kid hung a slider out on the outside edge of the plate, and Reggie hit it over the wall.

I met Reggie Jackson one day. We were at a cable television convention, standing in our respective booths and greeting people and signing pictures. Reggie was one of the few players who ever hit five hundred home runs in the big leagues. I found him to be a wonderful gentleman who is very easy to talk to.

I asked him, "Reggie, on what days did you feel most like a champion—that you were really operating at your highest level as a major league player?"

He said, "Jim, somehow deep down inside me, I developed such a will to win that the times I felt the best were when I was up against the best pitcher that the opposing team had, and he threw his fastest pitch at me—one I could never have hit on my best day as a hitter—and he knocked me down into the dirt and I came up out of that dirt with a smile on my face and said to the other team's catcher, 'You'd better tell your man that if that's the best he can throw, he's going to have a long day out there.' I felt like a champion in those times because I know that a champion never lets the other guy get to him."

Don't let anybody water down your intensity. Keep moving at full strength!

Determination

Determination and intensity are closely related. One is almost a synonym for the other in my opinion. The degree to which you are determined to succeed is the degree of intensity you have.

Now that I'm blind, I often remember inspirational things that I have seen. I find pleasure in calling them up on the inner screen of my mind. I often do this right before I speak or before I tape a television show. I like to remember something that was, and is, very positive and very challenging.

I especially like to recall the determined expressions that I have seen on people's faces—a certain look that says, "This belongs to me, this is part of me, and nobody can take it from me."

Someone who has that look in competition is Jack Nicklaus. One of the last things I remember seeing with my physical eyes was Jack Nicklaus winning the Masters when he was forty-six years old. As he walked down the eighteenth fairway, he had that certain look on his face. All the commentators were talking about what an amazing feat it was for the old guy to make the cut and be in the tournament, much less be near the top of the scoreboard.

Nicklaus had already won five Masters Tournaments, more than any other person. He had won his first Masters in 1963. Nobody expected him to win in 1986. Except Jack.

Nicklaus needed to birdie the eighteenth hole to win the tournament. He had a great first shot, and then a super second shot, which landed him about eight feet from the pin. It was a difficult putt, but as he was lining it up, he happened to look for just a second or two right into a television camera across the green. In his eyes was a look of incredible intensity, a look that said nothing in the world at that point mattered besides him and the eight feet of green between his ball and the eighteenth hole. I really didn't have to watch the shot. I knew he was going to hit his mark. There was no other conceivable possibility. And make that putt he did! He became the oldest man to win the Masters, and that, for a record sixth time.

Jack Nicklaus is no longer in the prime of his game. He has lost a lot of his depth perception, and he relies on his son to be his caddy and to tell him how to read greens. He can't hit the ball with the power he once did, and he can't extend his limbs like he once did. But none of the other players I watched that day had the look in his eyes that Jack Nicklaus had.

I've seen that look in the eyes of other athletes. I recall seeing tapes of Cassius Clay fight Sonny Liston—before Cassius Clay became Muhammad Ali. If you saw Clay before that fight, you wouldn't have had any idea that he was a three-to-one underdog. Cassius Clay wouldn't have had a shot at the heavyweight championship if Angelo Dundee hadn't set up the fight. But if you caught a look at Clay's eyes before the fight, there was no doubt in your mind that he was already wearing that heavyweight champion's belt around his waist. He was just waiting to go through what he had to go through to put it on so everybody else would know what he already knew: He was the champ.

A few years ago while doing a cable show in California, I met Joe Frazier. Joe often speaks of one of his fights with Muhammad Ali. Joe felt he was winning, and he knew he had hurt Ali badly. He said, "I thought I had a good chance to win, but then he came out and he gave me that look. And I found myself looking into the face of the guy who was the greatest fighter of all time, and I knew I couldn't beat him." Frazier had thought he had a chance. Ali didn't think anything. He had already made up his mind. He had already won the fight in his mind.

That's the look I like to recall before I go out to do something I consider to be important. That's the look I feel in my eyes, even if I can't see through them.

What in your life is so important to you that you know it belongs to you and that it is your destiny? If you don't have that intensity about what you are pursuing in life, why not? Perhaps it's because what you are pursuing isn't really your destiny.

■ You were put on this earth to do something unique.

You weren't put on this earth to have a safety net under you and a glass ceiling over you. You were put on this earth to do something unique. You are to be the champion of the course in life that has been set before you, and that is totally in line with who you are and what you are capable of being.

Discover that course. And then pursue it with intensity.

Your "Hot Button"

Enthusiasm also refers to your "hot button." What issue really starts you talking with conviction, maybe even heat? What concern do you have that really gets your adrenaline going? What interest truly excites passion when you talk about it to others? Zero in on that thing.

In the last few years, I've interviewed some of the most famous and prominent actors, politicians, athletes, and other public figures of our time. I've discovered that regardless of their chosen fields, they have all been people of incredible passion. They love what they do. They care about what they do. They can't imagine living without doing what they do!

I have routinely asked movie stars, "What do you think you would have done had you not gone into acting?"

Several of them named other professions. In some cases, they considered or even started to pursue other professions before they realized that their real destiny was to be in the performing arts. But I'll never forget the response from the late Helen Hayes, who was called the first lady of the American theater for years. She said, "Why, it never occurred to me not to be an actress. I was born to be an actress. If I couldn't have made a living as an actress, I suppose I would have had to find some way to sustain myself while I continued this life. But being an actress is me. It's what I do. There is nothing beyond that."

That's intensity. That's enthusiasm. That's passion.

My wife, Crystal, goes to writing conferences. She usually brings back tapes of the speakers with whom she is most impressed, and I've listened to many of them. One of the speakers I've heard on tape is Janet Dailey. As part of her presentation, she asked a room of several hundred writers a question that I initially thought was pretty odd. She said, "How many of you are writers?" Every hand in the room went up. Naturally. It was a conference for writers.

But then she said, "The next question I want to ask is this: How many of you have written today?"

Only about 10 percent of the hands went up.

She said, "I want everybody to look at the writers. *These* are the writers in the room. The rest of you used to be writers, or you were writers yesterday or last week or last month. Some of you want to be writers. But these people who wrote *today*—*these* are the writers in this room."

Your "hot button" is what you would choose to do, even if you didn't have to do it. It excites you, compels you, and intrigues you. It's your cause. It's what you feel you have to do every day to be alive.

Some of the greatest people I've met in the business world have made a million dollars and then lost it. Why are they great? Because they have a drive to get back what they've lost. They know what they're missing, and they have an inner drive to achieve that level of success again.

The same goes for actors I've met who have given remarkable performances but then have gone for a few years without a good role. They want success again with all their hearts because they know what it is to be great artistically.

Most people, however, haven't achieved such successes so they don't know they can do it or they don't believe they can do it. Therefore, they have little drive to try to do it. The result, of course, is that with no trying, and no drive to try, they never reach the top of what they might be!

The number one way you know that you have locked onto the right dream for your life is that you have tremendous enthusiasm for the pursuit of that dream. If you aren't enthusiastic about what you perceive to be your destiny, I contend that it isn't truly your destiny. It's a destiny you think you *should* have rather than a destiny you truly desire to have.

When you find the one, two, or three things in your life that you can truly be enthusiastic about, that's the direction in which you should move!

Single-Mindedness

None of us—sighted or visually impaired—is able to hold more than one dominant thought at a time. We don't have two-track minds, although we might claim to have them. We think only one thought at a time.

Staying single-minded means holding a dominant thought. That dominant thought might be your concept of yourself as wealthy, healthy, happy, fulfilled, at peace—whatever the thought, hold that concept of yourself. Keep it at the forefront of your identity. And then stay focused.

The real key to staying single-minded is having a strong visualization of your ultimate goal or dream. People with a clear, well-defined image of what they want to be or do in life are going to stay single-minded, often without even having to think about it. They are willing to put up with all kinds of inconveniences along the way. They are going to keep working, keep calling, keep trying, keep at it until they get to the place they want to be.

Back to the example of a juggler for a moment. A juggler who is moving toward an object keeps her eyes on the object, not on the items she is juggling. The juggling happens with peripheral vision, or with a sense of objects moving almost as if they are parts of a whole. Staying single-minded doesn't mean that you need to be rude to people or that you have license to ignore certain basic responsibilities to yourself and others. It does mean that you have an ability to move toward your goal and still keep everything else moving as part of your whole. The whole of you is moving toward a goal.

If you have a family, you aren't the only person moving toward a goal. Your entire family is moving toward that goal. Your identity isn't just your identity. It's the identity of your entire family. And the more you create that identity for your family and point out the validity of your goal to your spouse and children, the more likely you are to move as a unit toward that desired state.

Not too long ago, I was in a high-rise office. I had full confidence as I sat in that office that I could get up and walk out the door and to the elevator. I had noted where the elevator was located, how many steps I had taken to the office door, and so forth. But to get back to that elevator required me to be single-minded about my task. I couldn't try to carry on a conversation, think about what I might order for dinner that night at a restaurant, or wonder whether the Cowboys might win their game next week. Getting to the elevator required my sole concentration.

Getting around my house requires me to be single-minded, but because I'm familiar with my house and I've walked its paths so many times, I can juggle more things in my mind as I walk. I still need to be more alert than perhaps a sighted person might need to be to get to a goal without banging into something, but I can think about other things as I walk.

The more experience you have with certain routines in your life, the more you may be able to juggle various ideas and concerns even as you stay aimed toward a singular goal. But you can never take the things you are juggling for granted, and you can never lose sight of the fact that they are a part of you as you move.

I've seen this happen to many people. They are so intent on career success that they forget a spouse, and pretty soon, that spouse walks away from the relationship. Then they are so intent on reestablishing the relationship with a spouse that they no longer are in pursuit of the big dream or central goal for their lives.

Being single-minded doesn't mean that you have tunnel vision. You always must be aware of people around you, of new information, of the totality of your life. That's how being single-minded relates to balance.

Being single-minded doesn't mean that you are so intent on getting to your goal that you run over other people or ignore all warning signs around you. It doesn't mean that you operate at breakneck speed and lose your health and your family or friendships in the process.

We all know the fable of the tortoise and the hare. The hare sped from place to place and then stopped to nap, while the tortoise continued to plod a steady course and eventually bypassed the sleeping hare and won the race. That story is often used to illustrate consistency, diligence, and persistence.

I think it also illustrates focus. Successful people aren't necessarily in the fast lane when it comes to the speed of their decisions or the rapidity with which they move through a day. But successful people stay in the lane they've chosen for their lives. They keep moving within the boundaries of their dream. And to that extent, they plot a course and then plod the course—with fast or slow steps—until they arrive at their goal.

As a blind person, I have to stay single-minded and tightly focused in my work on camera. If I'm going to hold all the information in my mind that I am processing at any one time and use it—stay on track in a conversation or interview, keep my eyes on the camera lens, stay on my feet even—I've got to be able to focus on one thing, one person, one activity, one project at a time. I can't allow myself to become sidetracked or to be distracted. If I do, I become disoriented.

If you allow yourself to become sidetracked by a new idea or this exciting new opportunity or that interesting new project, you are likely to spin your wheels when it comes to your primary goal or dream. The person who is continually sidetracked wanders in circles—sometimes very fast-spinning circles, but circles nonetheless. Such a person expends a great deal of energy but has little forward motion.

Focus is different from concentration.

You can concentrate on many things—tying your shoelaces, chopping up lettuce for a salad, watching an episode of *Oprah*, thinking about a novel you are reading. Concentration simply means to turn your attention to a thing and to do so without diverting your attention away from it.

Focus is more than concentration. Focus has to do with direction.

Focus means that you have your eyes on a goal, and you do only the things that get you from where you are to the point where you want to be.

Having a goal is central to focus. If you don't have a goal, or if your goal isn't big enough or important enough, it won't serve you well when it comes to focusing. For example, I've heard of people who can photographically remember the pages of a phone book. As far as I'm concerned, that's a ridiculous waste of concentration power when phone books are readily accessible, change often, and you can look up what you need when you need it. If your goal is to be able to memorize a phone book, it's probably not a big enough goal.

Reminding yourself often of your goal is also integral to focus. Remember who you are. Remember what you want to be. Remember the identity you have forged for yourself in the secret chambers of your imagination. Be that person. Live out of that dream and that goal. Remind yourself continually that as that person, you do certain things and don't do other things; you make certain choices and don't make other choices; you live as if you are already the person you want to be. And don't allow yourself to become easily dissuaded or detoured.

When you have your inner vision focused on a goal, you keep moving toward that goal, and you deal with other things in your life in a more peripheral way. You let some things go. You give less notice to some things. You don't allow yourself to stop to concentrate, at least for very long, on things that are extraneous to your goal. And always, *always*, ALWAYS you are looking to see how other things fit into your goal or dream. You are continually asking such questions as these:

- How does this help me reach my goal?
- How does this benefit the cause that I'm really about?
- How might this blend in with my goal or dream?
- How does this relate to my true and genuine purpose for being?

Again, don't assume that a goal is something material, financial, or tangible. The foremost goal you may have for your life is to have a successful relationship with your spouse and children. That's a worthy goal. If that's your primary identity in life, you are likely to see your job, your activities, your hobbies, and your affiliations in a different light. You will continually be asking,

- How does this relate to my spouse and children?
- How can this benefit me and my family?
- How can I use this to bring greater joy and purpose to my family life?
- How does this affect my identity as a good spouse and parent?

Focus. You won't reach your goal without it!

Your Dream Is Your Baby

There were two warring tribes in the Andes, one that lived in the lowlands and the other high in the mountains. The mountain people invaded the lowlanders one day, and as part of their plundering of the people, they kidnapped a baby of one of the lowlander families and took the infant with them back up into the mountains. The lowlanders didn't know how to climb the mountain. They didn't know any of the trails that the mountain people used, and they didn't know where to find the mountain people or how to track them in the steep terrain. Even so, they sent out their best party of fighting men to climb the mountain and bring the baby home.

The men tried first one method of climbing and then another. They tried one trail and then another. After several days of effort, however, they had climbed only several hundred feet. Feeling hopeless and helpless, the lowlander men decided that the cause was lost, and they prepared to return to their village below.

As they were packing their gear for the descent, they saw the baby's mother walking toward them. They realized that she was coming down the mountain that they hadn't figured out how to climb. And then they saw that she had her baby strapped to her back. *How could that be?* One man greeted her and said, "We couldn't climb this mountain. How did you do this when we, the strongest and most able men in the village, couldn't do it?"

She shrugged her shoulders and said, "It wasn't your baby."

Your goal, your dream, your sense of personal destiny, is your baby. Nobody will care for it, rescue it, or work for it like you will. Don't expect it of others. Do expect that kind of care and hard work on your part. And do expect that you will need to pursue your dream with that kind of single-minded focus.

Tenacity

Tenacity means sticking with your dream or goal, staying single-minded and balanced, and doing the work that you need to do until you are, do, and have what you want to be, do, and have.

Tenacity means hanging on when everybody else lets go. Tenacity means sticking with your plan and goals even in the face of adversity. Tenacity is perhaps another word for commitment.

Tenacity keeps you locked into the day-to-day effort that will bring you ever closer to seeing your dreams realized.

When you have tenacity coupled with a high level of intensity, it's almost as if things happen by the sheer force of your will. Link an "I'll never give up" tenacity with an "I'll win or die trying" intensity, and you'll get where you want to go in life. I don't have a doubt about it.

Tenacity Carries You Through Adversity

I have a friend who owns a private plane and enjoys flying as a hobby. I used to fly with him a lot. We'd take off and just fly around.

I discovered that an airport can close during bad weather, and a pilot can't take off or land his craft there if he doesn't file a flight plan. The reasoning seems to be that if you file a flight plan and have a destination in mind, the airport knows that you'll rise above the turbulence as quickly as possible and be out of the stormy weather in a matter of minutes. But if you're just planning to go up and fly around a while, the chances are much greater that you'll get into trouble and possibly crash.

Part of the difference no doubt has to do with whether you are planning to fly in a straight line toward a destination or whether you are going to be cruising around in circles. It's as planes turn in bad weather, or as their wings become uneven in flight, that crashes so easily occur. Those who can hold a straight line in flight, and can hold a straight horizontal position of the plane's wings to the ground, are the ones much more likely to make it through a storm.

All of us have to deal with adversity. It goes with the territory of living. But if we have a goal in mind, it's like filing a flight plan and traveling in a straight, steady line. Our tenacity in holding an even keel can help us get where we're going. We head toward our destination, and even if turbulence hits, we rise above it or fly through it.

If you know where you're going and you have a strong motivation to get there, you're much more likely to persevere and to deal with details and problems that would otherwise ground you or cause you to stall. Equally so, if you're tenacious, you're going to hang on to your goal and stay motivated regardless of the problems that arise. Tenacity and motivation go together.

There are going to be days when you don't feel like working, don't feel like trying anymore, don't feel like giving your best effort. At that point tenacity needs to kick in. At that time your goal needs to loom up and say to you, "I'm still worth achieving. Keep trying." Always believe, *it's too soon to quit!*

Tenacity Builds Habits

You'll discover that tenacity builds habits. There are certain things you need to do every day, every week, or every month to keep you on track toward achieving your destiny. These things need to become habitual.

In building a habit, give yourself an initial goal of twenty-one days. A number of studies indicate that it takes three weeks to develop a new habit. If you do something for twenty-one days, the chances are that you will continue to do it. It doesn't matter if you're talking about going on a diet, stopping smoking or drinking, or getting exercise. Do what you envision as being a good habit for twenty-one days. Discipline yourself for that three-week time frame, and then take stock of your situation. In all likelihood, you are going to want to recommit for another three-week period.

If I get on my treadmill and walk for twenty-one consecutive days, but then I don't walk on the twenty-second day, something doesn't feel right. I miss walking. I may not enjoy walking on the twenty-first day more than I enjoy it the first day. It may seem like just as much work to me. I may perspire just as much. But the habit has become ingrained, and I sense something to be wrong if I don't walk.

The point is, there may be lots of tasks and chores and jobs associated with your pursuit of the life you want to live that may not be fun. You may not enjoy every minute of your quest. There may be times when you need to take out the trash or scrub a floor or untangle a knot. These times aren't fun. But there's a sense about doing a task repeatedly and wholeheartedly that sets your mind into a habit of work, a habit of doing the things that you know will eventually lead to the fulfillment of your dreams and goals.

Tenacity Is Your Work Ethic

Tenacity and work go together like hand and glove. Your degree of tenacity as you pursue your dream *is* your work ethic. It's the force that keeps you humming even when the tasks at hand seem tedious or unimportant.

When we first started to seek advertisers for our network programs, I had a special need to stay focused. My goal was to sell advertising. I knew that to sell advertising, I needed to call and then call and then call again. My experience as a stockbroker taught me that.

I made a promise to myself that I was going to call until I succeeded. I did my homework. I decided that the best people for me to call would be the top one hundred advertisers in America. I figure if you're going to try to sell commercial time to somebody, you may as well sell to somebody who spends a lot of money on commercials! I got the list, and then with all the enthusiasm I could muster, I began to call. I set my focus—set my mind, set my direction, set my will—to call each of these advertisers until I got a firm yes or no out of each one of them, and from somebody who had full authority to make that final decision. And I decided to take even a "no" answer as meaning "no, not at this time."

> Tenacity and work go together like hand and glove. Your degree of tenacity as you pursue your dream is your work ethic.

I started with the letter A and called all one hundred advertisers—every day. Most of the time, I'd get a person who would say, "Well, Mr. So-and-So buys all our commercials, and he won't talk to you."

I'd say, "Fine. Take my name and number. I'll call him back

tomorrow, and perhaps tomorrow he'll talk to me." And then I'd call back the next day.

A guy at one of the largest corporations in America finally came on the line one day and said to me, "Mr. Stovall, I don't know who you are, but do you realize you've called my office fifty-seven days in a row?"

I said, "Yes, my records also indicate fifty-seven times. And if you don't talk to me today, tomorrow will be the fifty-eighth time. And when you retire, tell the guy that takes your job that I'll be calling him every day until I get a firm yes or no from your company. You can buy a commercial or you can choose not to buy a commercial, but I think that what I have is worthy of your attention and at least a 'yes' or 'no' decision. I'll keep calling until you at least hear what I have to offer you."

He finally heard me out. He didn't buy a commercial. But by the time he heard me out, I didn't really have a slot to sell him! Kmart bought many of our first commercial slots, and other advertisers filled in what that company didn't buy. My job was not to sell a commercial to each of the top one hundred advertisers in America but to sell commercials to the top one hundred advertisers until all of my commercial time was sold. And that's what I did.

I always approach selling as a task. It's my job to perform that task. I can't quit until the task is performed. The numbers will fall where they fall.

Every salesperson knows that the exact people who purchase from you will vary in any given day, and the people who end up buying may not be at all the ones you expected they would be. If you set a goal and continue to go after it, day after day after day, you're going to reach people who will like what you're doing and buy what you're selling. If that's only one in a hundred people and you need to sell five a day of whatever you are selling to make a profit, you are going to need to make five hundred calls. If you need only one in twenty people to buy what you sell in order to make the profit you want, you need to make twenty calls. But you aren't going to know how many calls you need to make until after you've made several hundred calls and can figure out your percentage of successful contacts. Therefore, start by deciding that you are going to have to make a lot of calls, and I mean a *lot* of calls. Set yourself single-mindedly to the task, and don't allow yourself to be moved away from it.

The calls you don't make today are not going to wait for you tomorrow. Tomorrow's calls are tomorrow's calls. The calls you don't make today are calls you have missed, and they reflect a certain number of missed sales.

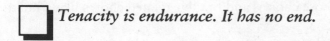 *Tenacity is endurance. It has no end.*

If I had taken the stance that selling commercial time doing the fairly routine and sometimes tedious work of making a hundred calls a day to would-be advertisers—wasn't nearly as important as interviewing a movie star, I wouldn't have a network today. The tedious work made the fun work possible, and both were required for a program to be completed.

None of us has control over all aspects of any task. I don't care what that task may be. If it involves anything that is living, you can't have total control over it. You can't control your own body completely. You can't control your family by yourself. You can't control your company. You can do only what you know to do, and do it to the very best of your ability and to the maximum of your energy, and then let the results come as they may.

I can't have a goal for tomorrow to have a temperature of 80 degrees with no wind and low humidity. That's not something within my control. But I do have control over the thermostat I set in my office space.

I have no control over whether anyone buys a commercial from us, but I do have control over whether I will eventually get a "yes" or "no" decision from a person with authority to make that decision on behalf of the organization. I do have control over how many times I will choose to call a company. I do have control over what I say to the decision maker once he or she receives my call.

I have to do what I can do—and then not beat up myself mentally about things beyond my control.

At the time I was seeking advertisers, I didn't know that people usually hire agencies to do that work for them. Today, I might not call advertisers directly. I might choose to pay somebody else to make the calls. But that's still a choice I have to make. (If I choose to have someone else make the calls, I have to pay that person, which means I'd better be choosing to do something even more valuable with my time or I'm operating at a loss!)

We all have choices. Make ones that work BEST for you, that allow you to stay single-minded on your general goal or dream, and then cling to those choices and to their related chores like a bulldog with a juicy bone.

Someone asked me, "How long do you hold on to your goal if you just don't seem to be able to make any progress?"

I replied, "If a car just flipped over on your child, how long would you try to get that car off your child?" You'd keep trying until the car was off your child. And that's how long you keep trying. Until you reach your goal.

Tenacity is endurance. It has no end.

No Substitute for Excellence

There is no substitute for your being your BEST:

- *Balanced* as a person and in your relationship to others
- *Enthusiastic* and intense in your quest for greatness
- *Single-minded* and focused in your pursuit of your own personal destiny
- *Tenacious* in your commitment to your goals and dreams

Can a person with that profile fail to succeed? I don't believe it is possible. If you are going for your highest and most noble dream in life with all of your energy and passion, and you refuse to be dissuaded or discouraged, you will arrive at your destination point.

You may encounter difficulties. But you'll overcome them.

You may have to try a dozen methods before you lock on to the one that works for you. But you'll find that method.

You may make some mistakes or experience a failure or two. But you'll rebound from them.

You may not convince everyone around you about the worthiness of your cause or the validity of the purpose you feel in your heart. But you'll convince enough people that you'll have not only their respect but also their help.

You may not get to your ultimate dream. But you'll get a lot closer to it than you are today, and in some cases, you'll pass it by and find yourself dreaming an even bigger dream, one that far surpasses anything you might be able to imagine right now.

Is success attainable?

Yes.

Can you have it?

Yes.

Is it worth going for?

Yes.

Must it be a success and a destiny of your own vision?

Yes.

My goodness, yes. You don't have to be blind to see that it's so!

19

STEPPING INTO THE SPOTLIGHT

You may be closer to achieving
your personal success than you think.

After the Emmy Awards banquet, I returned to my hotel room, and I happened to turn on Larry King's show. He was interviewing an entertainer from New York. I began musing about what a magical moment it was to be able to link up Spencer with the solution to his problem. Suddenly, Larry King began talking about a blind man who developed a narrative technique to help visually impaired people enjoy television and movies, and how he had received an Emmy Award that very night.

I sat there stunned. He was talking about *me*!

There I was, sitting in a hotel room in New York City, having just been given the highest award you can ever receive if you're in the television business, and I was being discussed on a nationwide broadcast. A few years earlier, I had been sitting in my room, thinking that I'd never leave it again.

A few years before that, I had been upset because I couldn't shovel concrete for a living any longer.

Do you think that you're in a dead-end situation and that there is no way anything wonderful can happen in your life? Do you think that the good days are all in the past? Do you expect your next good day to happen a decade or two from now?

Take heart.

Your success may happen a lot sooner than you think. You may be far closer to personal greatness than you presently can imagine.

My grandfather is one of the wisest people I've ever met. He was born in 1903, but at the time I'm writing this book, he still lives in his own home, drives a car, works in his yard, and has an active mind. My grandfather has only an eighth-grade education, but he is one of the smartest men I know. When I think of stability and integrity, I think of my father, but when I think of the *ultimate* in stability and integrity, I think of my grandfather.

As we were talking one day, I told him how ironic I thought it was that I was working with and traveling with a person who was legally blind. It seemed that the blind really were leading the blind in our company, and yet it seemed to work for us.

> ■ *It's a whole lot more important to know what to look at than how well you see it.*

My grandfather began, "I don't know much about it . . . [which is the way my grandfather always introduces profound ideas] but it seems to me that it's a whole lot more important to know what to look at than how well you see it."

How true!

How utterly, vastly true!

Your journey to your ultimate destiny and personal greatness will begin when you see who you are created to be, and when you begin to envision what you have been designed and equipped to do and to have.

> ■ *If you're ever going to open your eyes to your future, open them today.*

If you're ever going to open your eyes to your future, open them today.

And if you're ever going to make a run for your destiny and your dreams, do it now.

■ *Nothing is more powerful than making a beginning, making a decision, starting a course.*

If you aren't going to do it now, you're never going to do it at all. Nothing is more powerful than making a beginning, making a decision, starting a course. If you don't make a beginning, you'll never advance.

An old expression that everybody knows is this: "There's nothing more powerful than an idea whose time has come." There's another expression that I believe to be equally true:

**Nothing is more powerful than a
person
who knows his or her destiny
and has chosen
NOW
as the time to pursue it.**

As far as I'm concerned, the almighty God, who created the heavens and the earth and everything we have and know, would not have given you the hope or dream or ambition or idea that you hold in your heart if it wasn't time for you to act on it *right now*.

Today's the day!